FROM THE AUTHORS OF MAPWISE

Think it–Map it!

HOW SCHOOLS USE MAPPING TO TRANSFORM TEACHING & LEARNING

IAN HARRIS & OLIVER CAVIGLIOLI

Published by Network Educational Press Ltd
PO Box 635
Stafford
ST16 1BF
t: 01785 225515
f: 01785 228566
e: enquiries@networkpress.co.uk

Editor: Carol Thompson
Page layout: Neil Hawkins
Design and illustrations: Oliver Caviglioli
Printed in Great Britain by MPG Books, Bodmin, Cornwall

contents

Acknowledgements

The authors would like to thank and acknowledge all the schools and authorities that have become MapWise over the past three years by inviting us in to work with them on INSET closure days. It is the work we have done with teachers that has resulted in the work that they have done with pupils that has resulted in *Think it – Map it*! Many MapWise individuals and schools have made specific contributions to this book.

So if you are a MapWise school or teacher or a pupil who has made a contribution to the book, we'd like to say a big 'thankyou'! It will become obvious to the reader that *Think it – Map it!* could not have been written without you!

We would particularly like to thank the teachers who took the time to write detailed case studies of their work. You are named within the book.

We would like to single out Jo Grail's work with her Year 6 pupils. Jo is now a headteacher in Cornwall. Working with her Year 6 pupils, she adapted the model mapping format to suit the different text genres. Through the use of model mapping she transformed her pupils' attitudes towards literacy generally and writing in particular. We think she has made a very significant contribution to literacy development and we are excited that her work will be made available to all her teaching colleagues around the country in the form of text genre mapping posters. Her work is proof that if we focus on dispositions towards and the processes of learning the results take care of themselves.

Finally, we need to apologize for 'mixing up' some of the maps. As a result we have not always been able to attribute maps to specific schools or pupils. At this stage we can only offer our apologies and promise to label maps for future books with a more permanent method than Post-it notes. If you do see your (or your pupils') work and want it acknowledged in future editions please send details to theoffice@modellearning.com stating the page number, map title, name of school and the relevant year group and, of course, the name of the map's author. So, we are sorry and it won't happen again!

We would also like to thank our editor Carol Thompson and Neil Hawkins who laid out the book, for their support, advice and flexibility under pressure. We hope you would be as happy to work with us again as we would be to work with you!

Foreword

by John MacBeath

Have you ever stopped someone in the street and asked for directions? Have you then got hopelessly lost? This experience is familiar to most people and parallels an all too common classroom experience of listening to a teacher and struggling to find a way through a verbal welter of information. From the teachers' side their greatest source of frustration is that children never follow directions, no matter how many times you tell them.

Well, perhaps the problem is in the telling. Perhaps there is some deep-lying fault line in the process of giving information. Something elusive seems to happen between the giver and receiver with the result that information loses its way. This must be what David Hargreaves means about knowledge being 'sticky', not in the sense of 'sticking' in your head, but sticking somewhere *en route* to your head. Would-be learners who say they simply can't 'take it in' have identified the most significant problem with knowledge, that it can't come in until it has found a place to enter.

In response to this age old dilemma there is a fairly simple explanation. The simple explanation is that we cannot navigate physically or intellectually without a map. Before maps were invented people didn't travel too far for fear of falling off the end of the world. Before we discovered the cognitive map the favourite metaphor for teaching and learning was the bucket or the sponge. We have now replaced that superstitious notion with one informed by research and cutting-edge classroom practice. We now understand something about the cognitive map – that wonderful intricate set of pathways in our brains that help us to make sense of the world and to know where and how to travel confidently.

The map, as this book explains so well, is a powerful metaphor and a highly practical tool. Maps, of course, come in myriad forms and are not always helpful. There are maps with too much detail and maps with not enough. There are linear maps, like the route maps you get from the AA or multimap.com that are fine as long as you stay on the advised route. Then there are maps that give you the whole picture so that you can always find your way back to where you were before you went astray. It is this kind of map that is of most use to the learner and to the teacher. As Ausubel, quoted on page 79, contends, the single most important factor in learning is what the learner already knows. 'Ascertain this and teach him accordingly.'

So the learner needs a map that always lets him or her find their way to what they already know and enables them to navigate from there to their desired destination. Teachers who have used mapping techniques recommended in this book testify almost evangelically to the profound difference it can make to classroom learning.

This book is not, however, simply about useful tricks as magic techniques. It is fundamentally about how learning works and how teaching can be transformed when it grasps and respects some cardinal principles – about facts and knowledge, about memory and retrieval, about language and thinking, about individual and social learning.

This book sheds new light on some deep truths about peer learning, about talking your way to meaning, about learning as liberation from a ruthlessly lockstep progression through the curriculum. It is a salutary reminder in an age of attainments targets, SATS, key stages and value added that learning is what schools are for and it is what makes teachers want to teach. This book is a real treasure trove of good ideas and sound pedagogic principles.

Professor John MacBeath is Chair of Educational Leadership, University of Cambridge

introduction

Why this book is important

Have you ever wondered what was going on in your pupils' heads? How often have you wondered what they were thinking? Do you ever wonder if what you are saying is making sense to your pupils? Have you ever said to yourself (or others) 'I need to get my thoughts together' or 'my thoughts are all over the place today'? Do you try and interpret or 'read' the look on pupils' faces in an effort to work out if what you are saying is going in? How often are you surprised by what has (or hasn't) gone in at the end of the lesson? Would you accept that, for the most part, we haven't got a clue what is going on over there, in their heads? Have you ever understood something but been unable to turn that understanding into effective linear speech or writing? Do you think it's possible that pupils may have this experience sometimes?

What would happen if you could see what was going on in pupils' heads, if you could see the sense that they have made of what you were saying? What would happen if we transformed the act of thinking from something that was previously fleeting, invisible and private into something that was concrete, visible and public? This is what model mapping does. This is what *Think it – Map it!* is about.

When you introduce model mapping into classrooms, nice things happen. It affects areas such as literacy, thinking skills, study skills, boys' writing, inclusion and G&T extension in a very positive way. It can transform levels of communication and collaboration in the classroom. How can it do this? Essentially, because model mapping provides us with a model for understanding *how we understand*. Underneath all the many ways that we are different, and underneath all the many ways that we can set up the environment and manage the process of learning, lies the one thing we all have in common: a built-in need and desire to create meaning from our experiences. We all want to understand. This book is important because it enables us to understand understanding.

The content

The three most common questions that we are asked on INSET days regarding model mapping are:

1 Why do we need to know this?

2 When do we do it?

3 How do we do it?

Think it – Map it! addresses these questions directly and is organized into three sections accordingly.

By reading and using this book it will soon become clear why model mapping is an essential teaching and learning tool for anyone involved in education. Its application is not – as some believe – limited to areas such as SEN, revision or planning; nor is its usefulness limited to only particular 'types' of learner. Such beliefs are based on an inadequate understanding of what model mapping is and how it can be used within schools. This book will leave you in no doubt as to the relevance and usefulness of this powerful learning tool within every classroom and with every pupil and member of staff.

Overview of the three sections: Why, When and How

Claire Hunking, a Year 3 teacher from Plymouth, along with Megan Howe, one of her pupils and the Big Friendly Giant (BFG) are going to help us to introduce you to the world of class maps.

In a letter to the authors Claire wrote:

'Please find enclosed a linear example of the BFG character. This work was the result of reading the text with my Year 3 children and picking out relevant describing words. This was then "dumped" on their own whiteboards. We discussed what we had found out and created a model map together. Using the model map they wrote their own descriptions of the BFG.'

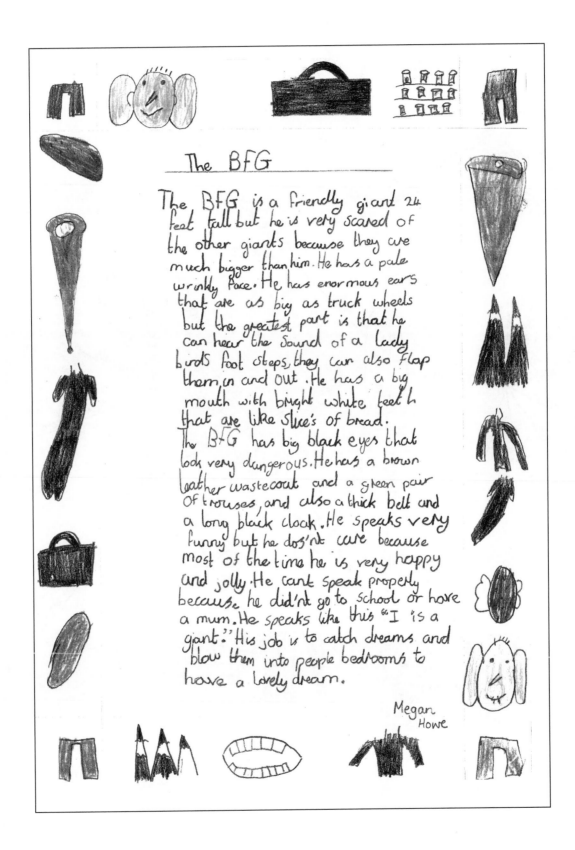

The BFG

The BFG is a friendly giant 24 feet tall but he is very scared of the other giants because they are much bigger than him. He has a pale wrinkly face. He has enormous ears that are as big as truck wheels but the greatest part is that he can hear the sound of a lady birds foot steps, they can also flap them in and out. He has a big mouth with bright white teeth that are like slice's of bread.

The BFG has big black eyes that look very dangerous. He has a brown leather wastecoat and a green pair of trouses, and also a thick belt and a long black cloak. He speaks very funny but he dos'nt care because most of the time he is very happy and jolly. He cant speak properly because he did'nt go to school or have a mum. He speaks like this "I 'is a giant." His job is to catch dreams and blow them into people bedrooms to have a lovely dream.

Megan Howe

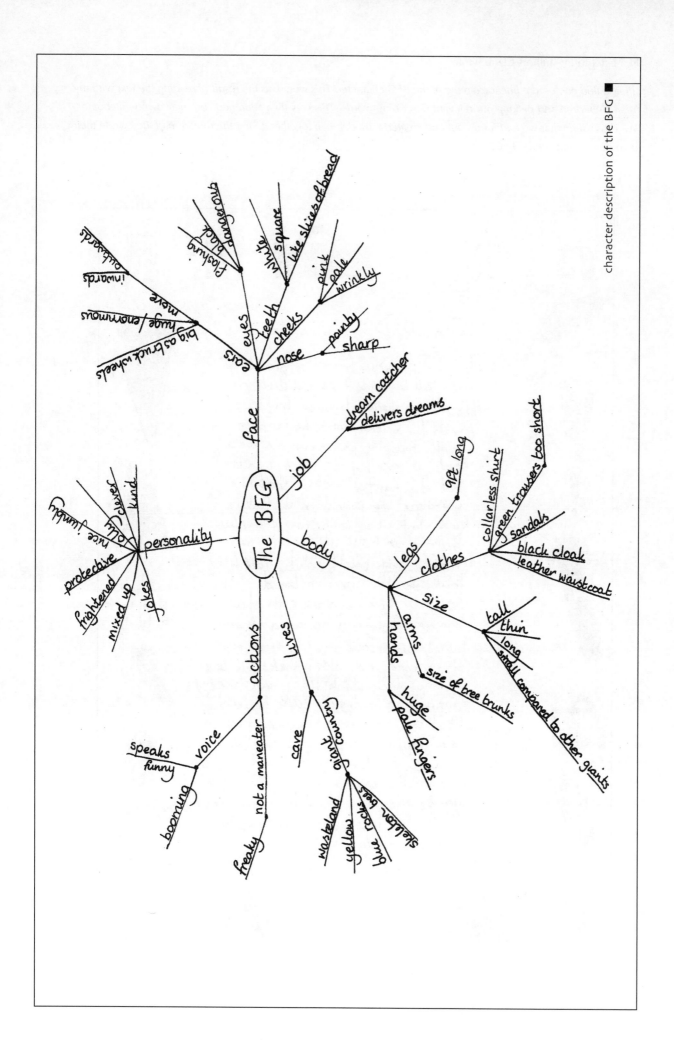

Why model map?

Megan and Claire know why model maps are significant. They know that the mapping process provides teachers and pupils with the tools they need to make learning a social process during which they collaboratively build their models of understanding. (See chapter 1.1, Models of Learning.) They understand that learning is about forming, developing and constantly modifying these models of understanding, that psychologists call schemas, and that this is far more likely to happen when the process is made visible through the use of model maps. (See 1.2, Schemas.) This process, as the two illustrations in the introduction show, involves two acts of transformation: Act 1 – when we listen or read we turn linear language into holographic (non-linear) schemas; and Act 2 – when we write or speak we turn these holographic schemas back into linear speech or text. As Megan's work shows, transformation is easy when the schemas are built up in front of you. (See 1.3, Holographic–Linear.) If you look carefully at the branches on the BFG model map you may see that there is a hierarchical structure that permeates the whole map. You may realize that it is not the words themselves that convey most meaning. Rather it is the spatial (almost triangular) relationships between them that carry a deeper more significant level of meaning. Claire's class know that beneath the linear layout of language on the page lies a deeper semantic structure. (See 1.4, Language Triangles.) Because all her pupils

a) understand how they process information,

b) know that this works best when done socially,

c) know that models of understanding are called schemas,

d) realize the benefits of making schemas visible, and

e) have explored and understand the structure of language,

they understand that underneath the many ways we are different there is a single common denominator. We are all meaning makers. (See 1.5, Thinking Styles.) We are all trying to understand. While the ways we like to do it may differ, the fact that we all do it is unquestionable. And model mapping makes this process explicit. It enables teachers to model the process for pupils and it shows pupils how to build their own models. This model building/modification is what we do when we think. You could say it is what thinking is. (See 1.6, Thinking Skills.)

When do we do it?

Take another look at the BFG model map. In your mind replace the letters BFG with the title of a current topic you are teaching at school. Now, imagine yourself talking pupils through an overview of the forthcoming topic or lesson or scheme of work. You are giving them the Big Picture. (See 2.1, Big Picture First.)

This could equally be you at the start of a staff or management meeting providing an overview of what is to be discussed or provided. (See 2.9, Meetings.) Or it could be you browsing over the School Improvement Plan for the year or term. (See 2.7, Development Planning.)

Now imagine yourself going into the lesson and creating a map showing what the students already know about a topic before you start. Imagine yourself or the pupils recording new insights or ideas onto an existing map. (See 2.2, Simply Connect.) At the start of a topic or lesson you ask the pupils to map out what they already know. You ask them to add to the same map at the end of the lesson or topic. You can see what they have learned. (See 2.6, Formative Assessment.) Imagine the pupils mapping out what they know individually and then moving them into pairs or threes and then into fours. (See 2.3, Collaborative Group Work.) Imagine a display in your classroom or in the corridor growing as pupils add new connections and ideas as you proceed through the topic. (See 2.8, Displays.) Imagine your pupils working alone, in groups or as a class to produce revision maps that then go on display during the course of the year and then again in the period leading up to the tests. Imagine their explaining these maps to each other and yourself, referring to them little and often in the period leading up to the exam. (See 2.4, Total Recall.) Imagine yourself helping a pupil make new connections, or helping to organize his thoughts in a way that enables him to communicate his understanding to you. You have a tool to help pupils with Special Needs. (See 2.10, SEN.)

Now take yourself back to the stage where you had sat down and planned a whole term's work on one page. (See 2.5, Teacher Planning.) Finally, return to the BFG map and notice how Megan has transformed the map into linear text. How much easier might writing be in your subject if pupils knew what planning for writing looked like? (See 2.11, Planning for Writing.)

How do we do it?

In the How section we set out exercises designed to teach the essential skills that you will need to be able to map. You will see how, in order to create meaning out of our experiences, to make sense of our world, we have to be able to categorize. Categorization is the most important and fundamental thinking skill. If you look at the BFG model map you will see that Claire has worked with her class to identify the categories that they will use to describe the subject. Off these main categories are sub-categories. Imagine these same words on the page randomly spaced. You will realize that, without the act of categorization, the BFG map would largely be meaningless. (See 3.1, Categorization.)

The chapters entitled The Geometry of Understanding (3.2) and Different Approaches (3.3) further develop the essential skill of categorization and take you through exercises designed to ensure that you are able to map sucessfully. In response to teachers' requests we have included a chapter on developing your mapping skills and on taking notes. Section 3 aims to provide all you need to know to be able to teach pupils to map.

The structure

Each of the three sections consists of short, accessible chapters. In the Why and When sections these chapters are preceded by a model map to give you an overview of what is to follow. Preview and review questions help you reflect and consolidate your learning. Each chapter is illustrated with maps – mostly produced by children – that are relevant to, but not always directly linked to, the content of the chapter. These enable you to get a real sense of what the book is about, simply by looking at them and reading the short captions that accompany them.

Enjoy learning.

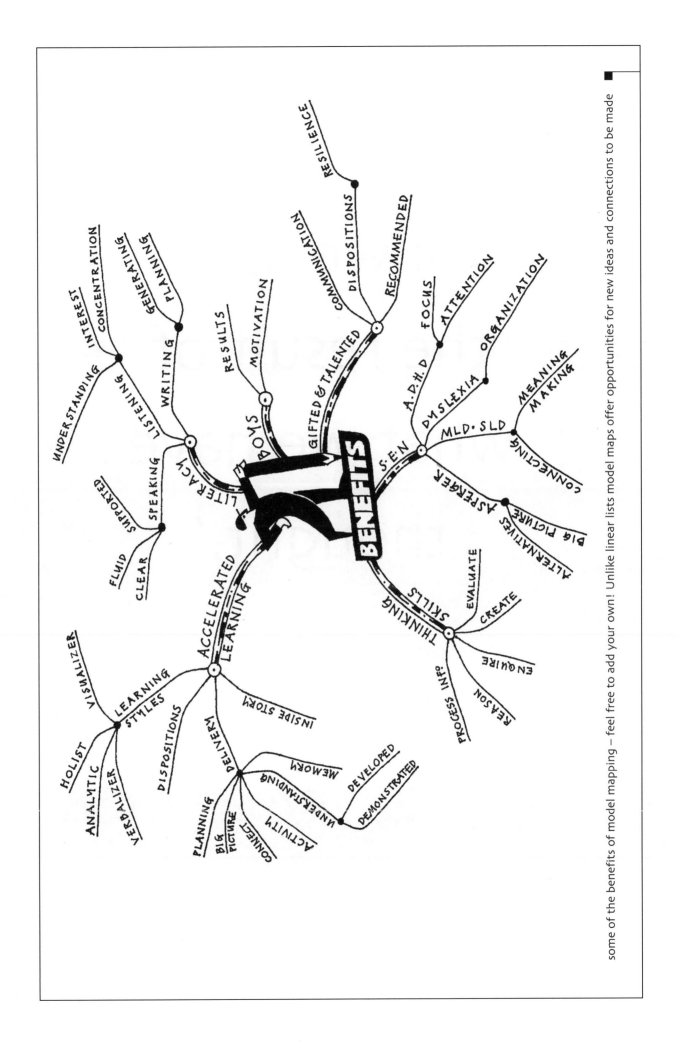

'All we are is
the result of
what we have
thought.'

Buddha

W H Y

I

- Do I have a theory of learning? If so what is it?
- What are models of learning and why are they important?
- How does model mapping relate to models of learning?
- How can model mapping support my pupils?

models of learning

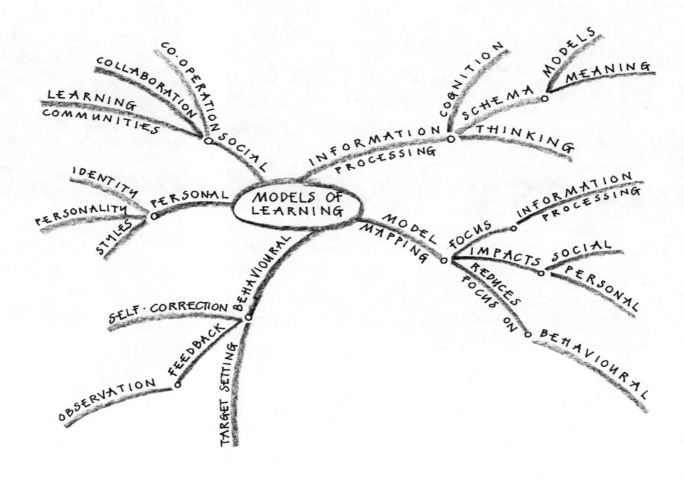

Professional
from models

> 'Through the selection of appropriate models, content can become conceptual rather than peculiar; process can become constructive rather than passive reception; and social climate can become expansive not restrictive'
>
> *B. Joyce, E. Calhoun and D. Hopkins (2000)*

What are models of learning?

Models of learning provide us with ways of reflecting, examining and understanding the learning process. Like all models, they are not real and they are not to be followed slavishly, but they do provide frameworks for understanding what is going on in classrooms.

In their fabulous book *Models of Learning – Tools for Teaching*, (2000), Joyce, Calhoun and Hopkins pool 25 years of research to identify four families of learning models which they call:

1 the information processing models

2 the social models

3 the personal models

4 the behavioural systems models.

Each provides us with a means of studying how learners learn and in doing so they promote reflective classroom practice.

1 The information processing models are concerned with the processes that learners use to create models of meaning (schemas) from the stimulus provided to them by teachers. (See next chapter, Schemas.)

2 The social models examine the importance of co-operation and collaboration in the classroom and explain why we learn best when learning communities are encouraged and developed.

3 The personal models are concerned with the importance of personal identity and personality. These models attempt to shape education so that learners come to better understand themselves.

4 The behavioural models are based on our capacity as human beings to self-correct as a result of feedback. These models concentrate on observable behaviour, communicating progress and on setting clearly defined tasks.

Why are these models important?

The first two models of learning briefly outlined above have been shown to dramatically accelerate rates of learning by helping learners understand their own cognitive processes and preferred modes of enquiry in a way that traditional 'chalk and talk' teaching simply cannot do. By providing learners with the appropriate model of learning, passive reception of information can be transformed into constructive enquiry; instead of content being particular it can become conceptual and the learning environment can become one that is expansive, not restrictive.

Models of learning are important because they provide a basis on which to examine current practice, to reflect, and therefore to change. It may be that simply by reading the very brief definitions of the four model families above you have realized that your teaching method best supports one particular model of learning. But now you know there are other models, you have other approaches available to you.

work
of learning

Unless we place the art of teaching inside models of learning we run the risk of becoming a promiscuous profession running from one 'quick fix' strategy to the next.

It is beyond the scope of this book to go into detail or advocate any one model above the others. If you are serious about being serious about teaching and learning then *Models for Learning – Tools for Teaching* is, in the authors', opinion, a 'must have it' book.

What do models of learning have to do with model mapping and why is all this relevant to me and my classroom?

Model mapping powerfully supports the personal, the social and the information processing models of learning. We would add that all of these models can be held inside of a theory of learning called constructivism. Constructivists, such as the child psychologists Vygotsky and Piaget, see the learners as active builders of their models of understanding – their schemas.

 'We lack sophisticated theories and models of knowledge creation in Education simply because such activity has not been seen as a key to educational improvement'

D. H. Hargreaves (1999)

Understanding how we form and modify our schemas, not only about our work but also about others and ourselves, can have a profound effect on how we view ourselves. Not insignificant is the fact that, when we make our schemas of ourselves visible through mapping, it makes it easier for us to question them and share them with others. Similarly, with people's schemas 'on view', levels of communication, collaboration and co-operation in social learning practices such as paired and group work are transformed.

In short, by revealing to learners how they process information, we can significantly and positively impact on their view of themselves. The learners then have the tools they need to collaborate and co-operate. You may well see unwelcome behaviours disappear.

 'Research on learning has demonstrated that students understand best, remember ideas most effectively and think most intuitively when they feel personally responsible for getting meaning out of what they are learning instead of waiting for a teacher to shovel it into them.'

Jane M. Healy (1999)

Can you say a bit more about how model mapping supports teachers and learners?

The cognitive processes required to produce a map encourage and reflect the cognitive processes set out in the information processing models of learning described on the previous page.

The thinking processes of induction and deduction can be made explicit and completely accessible to learners by utilizing mapping in the classroom. Model mapping is concerned with information processing and making this process explicit and available to learners. When people understand how to process information so that they can understand, they take real responsibility for how they learn.

Classrooms become far more social places to be when teachers and learners are mappers. You can ask children to share their maps with each other or get them to map out their understanding in pairs and in groups of three or four. Enjoy the two-way communication that results between you the teacher, and the learner, when there is a map between you to focus attention and support questioning. Notice the difference that speaking and listening makes to your pupils' ability to write linear text. It's all connected.

The two tables that follow set out feedback from two role-play exercises. The feedback is from teachers attending one of our MapWise courses. In the first exercise teachers are asked to talk about and describe something to a partner. The speaker is playing the role of the teacher. The listening partner can speak to them and ask questions but is not allowed to see what the explainer is talking about. The listener is playing the role of the teacher. Look at the comments in table 1 below and then compare them to those in table 2 over the page. What, you may ask, has happened? The experiences of the teacher and the learner have been completely transformed. How did this transformation take place? Easy, in the second roleplay the listener could *see* what the explainer was talking about as the explainer had a model map in front of her. The listener now has access, not just to the product of the teacher's thinking, but also to the schema from which she is talking.

explaining	listening
■ hard	■ hard to concentrate
■ frustrating	■ didn't get clear understanding
■ all over the place	■ drifted
■ didn't know how to explain	■ stressed
■ stumbled with words	■ struggled to keep up
■ didn't get a sense of partner	■ easily confused
■ made assumptions	■ felt tense and anxious
■ difficult	■ felt 'done to'
■ lonely	■ it was like a test
■ not fluent	■ didn't remember much
■ couldn't get point across	■ got lost early on
■ didn't sense partner's grasp	■ content seemed remote
■ waffled	■ couldn't 'place' the content
■ dull	■ confused
■ no structured order to content	■ scared
■ struggled	■ wanted to get it right

Table 1

explaining	listening
■ clarified own understanding	■ was interested
■ easier to present	■ felt involved
■ more organized	■ got overview of topic
■ possibilities of flexibility	■ remained focused
■ forced you to define ideas	■ could look ahead to next bit
■ timing was aided	■ questions just popped up
■ made no assumptions	■ understood
■ made explicit connections	■ easy to remember
■ saw gaps in my explanation	■ relaxing
■ stayed focused	■ engaged
■ non-repetitive	■ felt a partnership with talker
■ captured detail	■ content more relevant
■ gave comprehensive overview	■ able to internalize
■ enjoyable	■ anticipated the sequence
■ made me more confident	■ wanted to ask questions
■ memory jogger	■ kept on task
■ extended my original thinking	■ didn't have to hold info in head
■ fluent	■ felt an active listener
■ good pace	■ multisensory experience
■ no 'waffle'	■ felt an ownership
■ sequence was obvious	■ learned a great deal quickly
■ elaborated original thinking	■ had a deeper understanding
■ logical process	■ sustained my concentration
■ clarity of presentation	■ could 'see' the point
■ animated	■ structured for understanding

Table 2

case study

What question or task can model mapping be used for?

At Mount Pleasant Primary School in Dudley, model mapping is used extensively by all staff and pupils:

■ Foundation Stage

Used to plan afternoon activities with younger pupils. Pupils are shown the range of activities and discuss them together so that the teacher can check how well the pupils understand what is expected of them. The teacher also uses model mapping to help retell a story and a group will construct a model map together with their teacher or helper to enable them to recall facts about the story.

■ Key Stage One

Model mapping is used in literacy to plan ideas before writing, with particular emphasis on vocabulary and descriptions. Model mapping is also used to introduce a lesson, particularly in humanities subjects, where the topic is introduced to all pupils at the beginning of the half term prior to delivery. The same model is then used to revise how much of the project has been covered and remembered. Model mapping has also been used in Circle Time where staff help the pupils to construct a model map of their feelings. Children are welcome to come to the model map and insert their own ideas. Children then retell their ideas as they explain their part of the model map to others. This has been a good way to get children to talk more clearly about their views and feelings.

Model mapping is used by staff to introduce sections of learning that will take place over the next week, term, and so on. (sharing the schema). It is then referred to again at the end of delivery to check that all areas have been covered and to see how well children can recall the areas of learning. Children also use model mapping more independently as an assessment tool, that is, to see how much the child has remembered. (Below is an example of model mapping in Year 6 where the children were asked to construct a map of their understanding to date on forces. This was initially completed in pencil. The teacher then planned what needed to be taught to the class or groups. Following the delivery of the plan, the children went back to their original model map and added their new learning in pen. It was easy to see the impact of the new learning and again the teacher could identify any pupils who had not grasped basic concepts and who required further teaching in this area.) Model mapping is also used for display where, at a glance, pupils and teachers can be prompted. Displays of model maps in Year 5 have at their centre 'A story has…' and the pupils and teacher have added all the characters of story writing. Model mapping has also been extended in Year 6 to 'mini-model mapping'. 'Mini maps' are brief model maps about smaller units of learning and are used for pupils to complete quickly during registration time. At the centre there may be 'equilateral triangles' for example; the pupils would be expected to add to the model map all the characteristics of equilateral triangles. This would then form the basis for the start of the numeracy lesson on triangles.

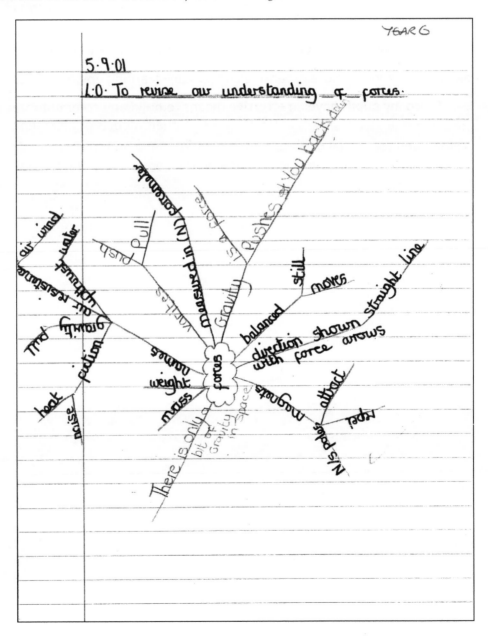

■ Staff use

Staff are still generally in the habit of using bullet point lists for note taking during meetings, but a small group of staff are using model mapping for this purpose. There has been much discussion around changing the way in which we plan to incorporate model mapping into this process.

What difference did mapping make?

Staff feel that pupils are encouraged to look at and recall visually the contents of the model maps. Model mapping and mini-model mapping was used to a large extent for Year 6 revision prior to SATs. We know that many children learned model maps off by heart and could recall much if not all of their content even under pressure of time. We are working towards creating a more consistent approach to using model mapping throughout the school. We feel that such an approach would benefit the development of model mapping for everyone.

Mount Pleasant Primary School, Dudley, West Midlands

review

What models of learning are in operation in my classroom? ■

Can I make my classroom a more expansive and sociable learning environment? ■

Do my pupils have an effective means to build and communicate ■
their models of meaning?

How can I use model maps to improve my teaching and fulfil the basic ■
principles underlying the core models of learning?

■

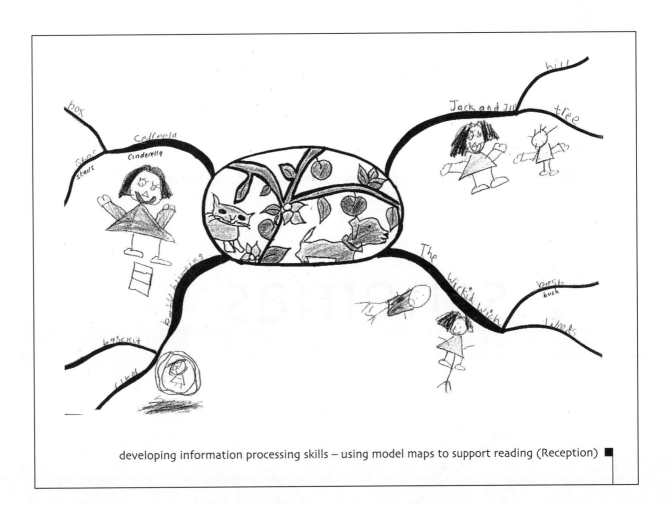

developing information processing skills – using model maps to support reading (Reception) ■

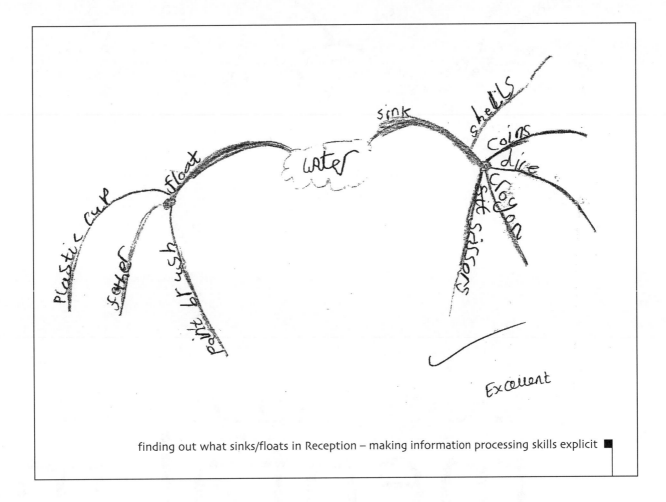

finding out what sinks/floats in Reception – making information processing skills explicit ■

■ What are schemas?

■ How are schemas important to my teaching?

■ How do schemas relate to model mapping?

■ How can schema theory be of use to me and my pupils in my classroom?

schemas

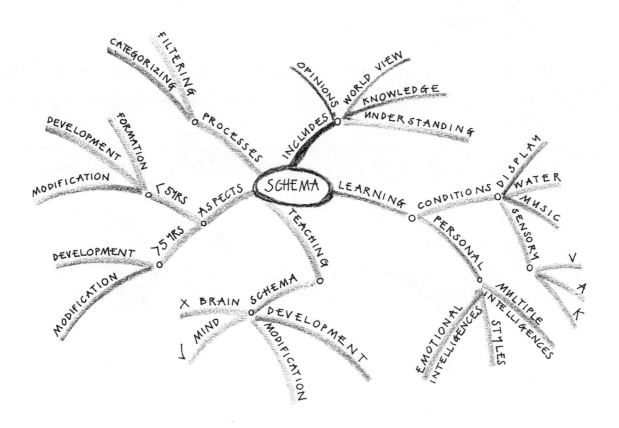

Model maps are yo
mental mo

What are schemas?

Schemas are our mental models of our world. Our mental models incorporate our views, opinions, attitudes, knowledge and understanding of the world. So if someone asks you a question, your schemas are where you go to for an answer.

We can say that schemas represent our world view. But we need to know they are not the world – but our own, unique, mental models of it. Woody Allen, the world famous comic actor, says that the only map or model he has ever found useful is one drawn on a scale of 1:1 and was laid out in front of him. How many times have you noticed that your view, or schema, on someone or something was different from that of someone else?

Our schemas are personal to each of us and we can share many elements of them with others. We as individuals are responsible for forming and modifying our schemas. They are the framework and structures through which we are able to think and understand.

How do they work?

We form and modify our schemas by filtering and categorizing experiences and stimuli. We don't notice all stimulus made available to us. We notice what we believe to be of relevance and importance to us at any one particular moment. This is called filtering. We then categorize our experiences to help them fit into existing schemas. This process is so automatic we don't know that we do it.

It is useful to realize that we all have schemas about absolutely everything.

Can you give me some examples?

Imagine yourself about to meet someone you have not seen or spoken to for 25 years. You will have a memory of their appearance and personality as they used to be. You may also think of certain places and activities that you associate with them. You are accessing your schema of this person. Alongside this schema you will have another schema called 'how people age'. You (and your schemas) meet the person and your schema of the person adapts to a new 'reality' as you get to know each other again.

Imagine that you take your partner along to meet this person. Unlike you, they have never met this person before. They only have what you have told them on which to base their own schema. After the meeting your partner lets you know that they do not like your old friend and that, while they agree that he has aged well, they found him confrontational and aggressive. You argue that he is simply confident and assertive.

ur
dels mapped out

> 'The limits of my language are the limits of my mind. All I know is what I have words for.'
>
> *L. Wittgenstein*

Your partner arrived and left with a different schema, as did you. You both met the same man, heard him say the same things and yet you have different schemas about him.

Think of a time when you were surprised or even shocked by something. Perhaps you went into a shop where the shop assistant at the till sang to you! You were surprised because it was unexpected, not normal – because it did not fit your schema of how shop assistants behave.

The next time someone asks your opinion about something, notice yourself automatically accessing your schema to answer. If you cannot answer the question, it is either because you do not know the answer (it is not contained within your schema) or because you cannot access it – you have not unlocked the door to your schema.

When we change our opinion about someone or something we are adapting or modifying our schema. When we learn something or have that wonderful 'ah ha' moment of understanding we are again adapting or modifying our schema.

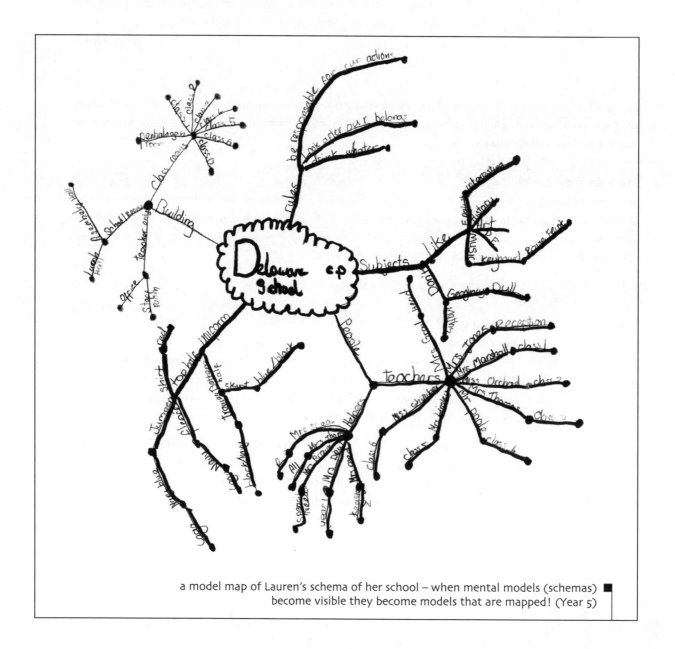

a model map of Lauren's schema of her school – when mental models (schemas) become visible they become models that are mapped! (Year 5)

What have schemas got to do with teaching and learning?

Absolutely everything. All that we do in schools is related to schemas. Pupils and staff arrive with schemas in place about themselves, others, the school and the curriculum. They leave at the end of the day with these schemas having been adapted or reinforced in some way.

When you explain something to a child or a class, you are sharing your schema. At the same time your pupils are trying to deduce what you are talking about and build or modify their own schema. When you set up explorations or investigations in class, pupils are engaging in inductive thinking and are trying to construct and develop schemas. This is what Vygotsky and Piaget, great child psychologists who have shaped our own schemas of how children learn, have called Constructivism.

 'When educators realise that each one of us has our own "model of the world", and this model is the reality as each of us perceives it, what a difference in education there will be...increased rapport and subsequent effective communication would be natural outcomes. Schooling itself would change.'

C. Van Nagel, M. Reese and R. Siudzinski (1985)

When pupils listen or read, they are developing and modifying schemas. When pupils write or speak, they are speaking from their schemas. Given the centrality of what we are describing we find it totally unbelievable that over 90 per cent of the newly qualified teachers we work with do not hear the word 'schema' throughout teacher training. Did you?

Why do teachers need to know about them?

We believe that understanding how the mind works is more relevant than knowing how the physical parts of the brain operate. A biologist knows how, in detail, the body tastes food and digests it. A cook doesn't necessarily need to know this to be a great cook. A neuroscientist knows a great deal about the brain but, judging by our experience of their presentations, knows very little about how to teach. Likewise, teachers who find out about how the brain works do not necessarily know how to teach. Teaching is based, not on neuroscience and the brain, but on a knowledge of the mind – a field called cognitive psychology.

'To the extent that the world around us seems coherent and organised and systematic, so the content of the brain must be coherent and organised and systematic. In my view the brain must contain nothing less than a working model of the world.'

F. Smith (1990)

Where does model mapping fit into all this?

As we have said in our previous book, *MapWise* (part of the Network Educational Press 'Accelerated Learning' series), model mapping gives us access to the 'inside story' of how learning happens. The vast majority of accelerated learning techniques may make schema formation more likely but they do not make it explicit. At the epicentre of teaching is the development and expansion of children's schemas. Learning is about expanding and interconnecting parts of your own schemas.

How can I use this knowledge?

The When and How sections of this book deal extensively with this question. Essentially, model mapping can help you become really clear about your own schemas on subject material. Modelling your schemas into maps can make them visible. How can you expect pupils to be clear if you are not? Maps also support your pupils in showing you what they know and how they know it. If you are explaining something, maps will help pupils deduce what you are talking about. If you are setting up explorations or investigations, maps support pupils in thinking inductively.

When you understand about schemas and how model mapping reflects and supports schema building, you can no longer see model mapping as just another 'add on' or 'quick fix' tip to be picked up for a while and then forgotten. Schemas – and therefore model mapping – are at the epicentre of how we learn.

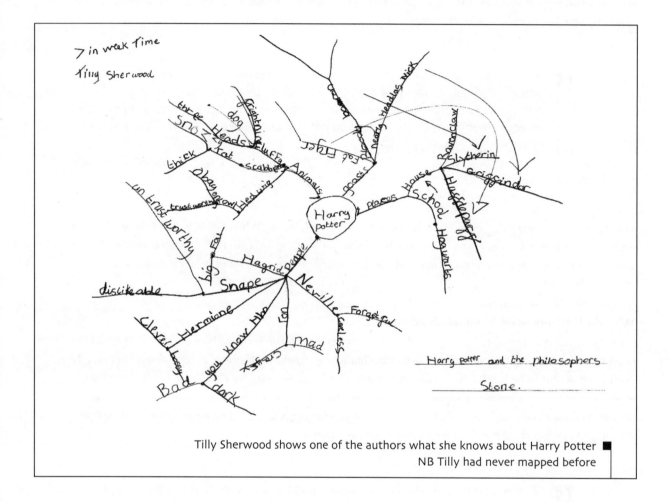

Tilly Sherwood shows one of the authors what she knows about Harry Potter ■
NB Tilly had never mapped before

review

Am I clear about how we learn and build understanding? ■

Do I communicate my schemas clearly to pupils? ■

Does my teaching enable pupils to expand their own schemas? ■

How can I use model maps to make information processing, meaning making and understanding more explicit? ■

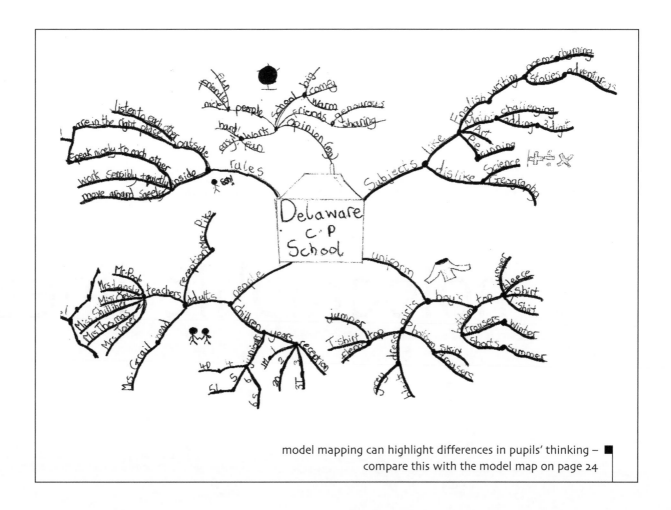

model mapping can highlight differences in pupils' thinking – ■
compare this with the model map on page 24

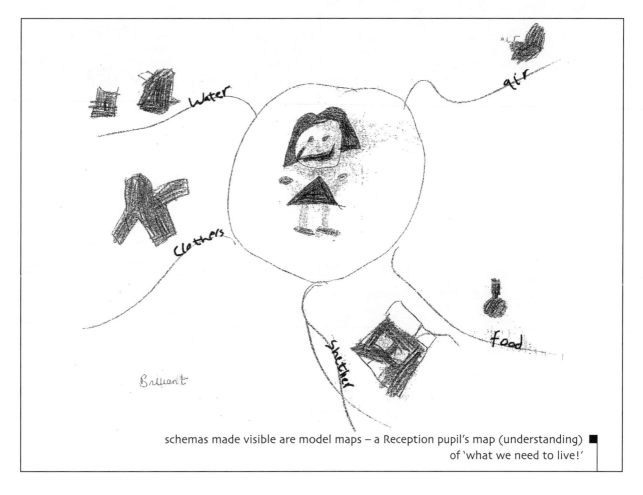

schemas made visible are model maps – a Reception pupil's map (understanding) ■
of 'what we need to live!'

- What is meant by the term holographic–linear?
- How does this idea link with schemas?
- Where can I see holographic–linear processes in action in my classroom?
- Why is the holographic–linear process so crucial to learning?

holographic–linear

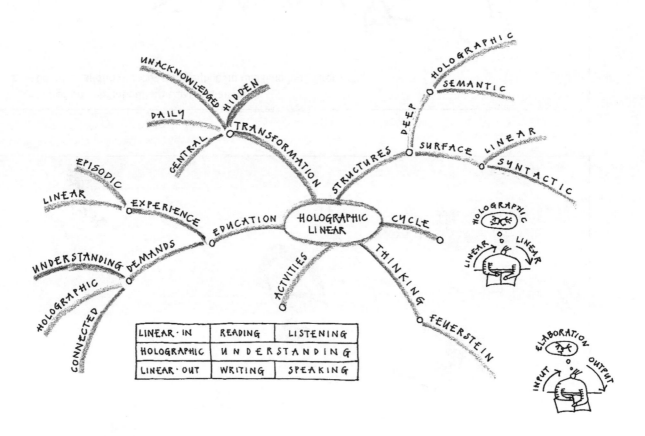

LINEAR · IN	READING	LISTENING
HOLOGRAPHIC	UNDERSTANDING	
LINEAR · OUT	WRITING	SPEAKING

The linear word rev
no obvious CO

'Before the invention of the printing press…learning was a holographic, gestalt, concrete affair.'

D. Meier (2000)

What does holographic–linear mean?

Holographic–linear is a term we use on our courses to help explain how we all think and learn. We say that learners do not receive and represent their understanding in the same way that they form it. The word 'linear' is used because we receive information, via our senses, in a linear fashion – one word at a time, attending to things one a time. When we demonstrate our understanding through speech or written text we also do this one word at a time. In between listening, looking and reading, and speaking and writing, something else is happening: we are processing information – and we do not do this in the same way. This process is holographic, or non-linear. If it were linear we would not be able to make much sense of our world.

Can you give me some examples?

When you watch a soap opera the scenes cut from one story to another every few minutes or seconds. Your experience is linear in that the scenes come up one at a time. Without knowing it, when a new scene comes up on screen you automatically make connections to the last time you saw that character or story. Cleverly, you are also making connections across storylines. If you weren't doing this, why would you watch the soap?

When you read a book you read it one word, one page, one chapter at a time. Even if you skim read, your direct experience is a linear one. But when you get to page 145 of a book are you *only* linking it to page 144? No, you are linking it to lots of other pages of the book. The more you do this the more you get out of the book!

 'When we generate written or spoken sentences, we must transform information from a hierarchical to a linear structure. Conversely, when we read or hear messages, we must transform linear sequences into a hierarchical structure in order to assimilate them into our minds.'

J. D. Novak and D. B. Gowin (1984)

In both scenarios you are automatically categorizing the stimulus into different groups and simultaneously making connections between them. This process involves the whole – it is holographic in nature.

Has this got anything to do with schemas?

Well yes! 'Schema' is the technical word for what we have called the holographic stage of the non-linear world of our mind. Reuven Feuerstein, an eminent Israeli psychologist and 'father' of the thinking skills movement, calls this the 'elaboration' stage in his three-stage input–elaboration–output model. In the last chapter we learned that our schemas are our personal understanding. By understanding the holographic–linear distinction we can see that our schemas are interdependent, interconnected and interrelated.

eals
nnections

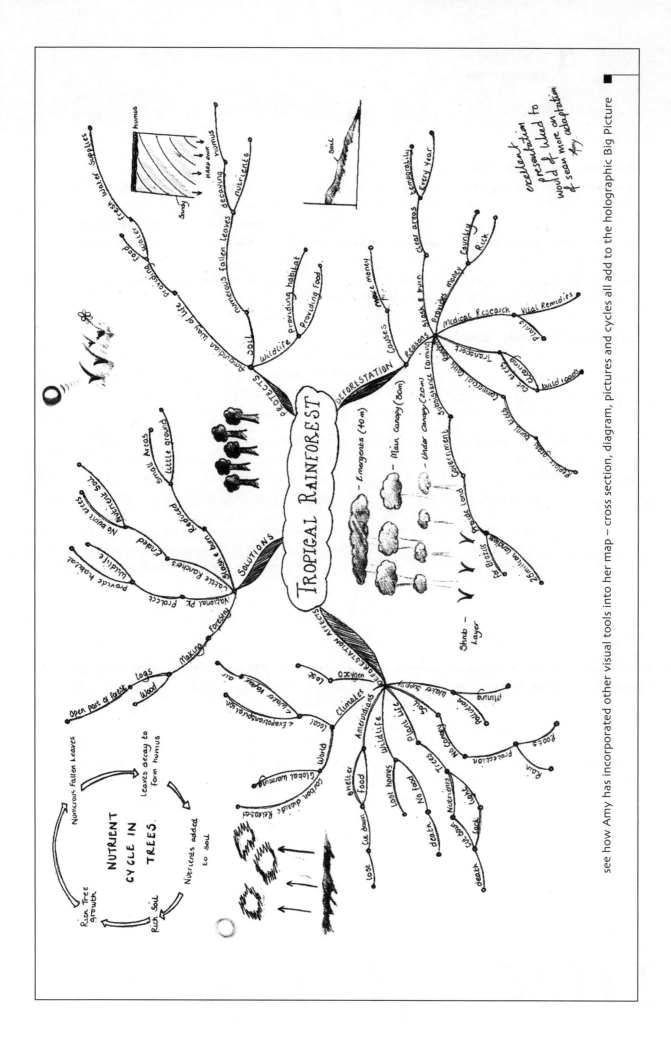

see how Amy has incorporated other visual tools into her map – cross section, diagram, pictures and cycles all add to the holographic Big Picture

What has this got to do with me?

We believe the most important and crucial distinction in the whole learning process is the one of seeing and making explicit the holographic and linear process. In fact it is vital in order for human beings to communicate with one another. Once you understand and fully realize the significance of this, nothing will be the same again! You will see holographic–linear processing going on every time you see two people talking and every time you teach. The next time a stranger asks you for directions, you will most probably give them linear verbal instructions. In doing this you are accessing your holographic understanding of your town. You select the linear sequence of words that will best describe the way to go. When a pupil listens to you in class or asks you a question, you go to the holographic understanding (your schema) that best helps you talk or explain. The problem in both cases is this: the stranger and the learner cannot see your maps! How much easier would explanation be if these maps were made available to us.

What has this got to do with understanding and results?

Everything! Success in schools, irrespective of how we measure it, is determined by how successful your learners are at completing the holographic–linear cycle. We ask learners to transform linear input into holographic models in their heads. This is what listening and reading is. We then ask them to turn these holographic models back into linear output via the spoken word and linear text. This is what writing and speaking is. You cannot separate literacy and thinking skills from the curriculum or from each other; they are both part of the same holographic–linear cycle. The curriculum merely provides the materials to play with.

But what about those learners that have difficulty with listening and reading, speaking and writing?

Have you ever understood something but been unable to turn that understanding into words? How do you feel when that happens? Imagine spending most of your life hanging around with people who relate to you as if you don't understand. How would you feel about them and about yourself? Maybe the truth is that often we do understand but we have no idea how to turn our mental models into linear words or text! For how long would you sit still if you were listening to someone talking and didn't have a clue 'where they were coming from' (or more accurately, you couldn't see the schema from which they are speaking)?

 'language is hierarchically organised...the brain must activate whole clusters of words (or of potential words) at a time, organise them into groups that are appropriate, and then line them up so that they come out one at a time and in the right order.'

F. Smith (1990)

So is holograhic–linear a real mental process?

It depends what you understand by the term 'real'. It is real in the sense that we all do it; we have to so that we can make sense of our world. Looking at it another way however, we would have to say no, holographic–linear is a schema that we have made up to describe a mental process. Ultimately it is a model, and models are not reality but they can help us to understand ourselves and others.

Are you saying all learners do this?

Yes. Underneath all the differences we have as human beings lies a fundamental desire to create meaning. Underneath all the emotional intelligence, learner preferences and multiple intelligence ideas, this is what we all try to do: make sense of our world. It's a continuum. At one end we have individuals who are highly proficient (intelligent?) at making sense of things, interweaving connections and demonstrating understanding effectively. Teachers are at, or towards, the top end of this continuum. At the other end we have a small percentage of

1. **Jesus – the evidence**
   a) Did Jesus exist?
   b) Jesus in Christian writings
   c) The Synoptic Problem
   d) Jesus as seen by the Gospel writers

2. **Suffering – is there an answer?**
   a) Moral and natural evil
   b) Why people do wrong
   c) Jesus the rescuer
   d) Jesus the ransom and the substitute

3. **Guidance for Muslims**
   a) The life of Muhammad
   b) Why Muhammad was popular
   c) The Qur'an and Hadith

4. **The mosque**
   a) The building
   b) Islamic art

5. **The Five Pillars**
   a) Prayer – roots and shoots
   b) The benefits of fasting
   c) Id-ul-Fitr and Zakah
   d) Why go on pilgrimage – Hajj

6. **The Church**
   a) The Roman Catholic Church
   b) The Eastern Orthodox Church
   c) Protestant churches
   d) Quaker and Pentecostal worship

7. **The Church in Brazil**
   f) Imagine being poor
   g) Christianity, Brazil and slavery
   h) Life in Nova Iguacu
   i) Liberation theology

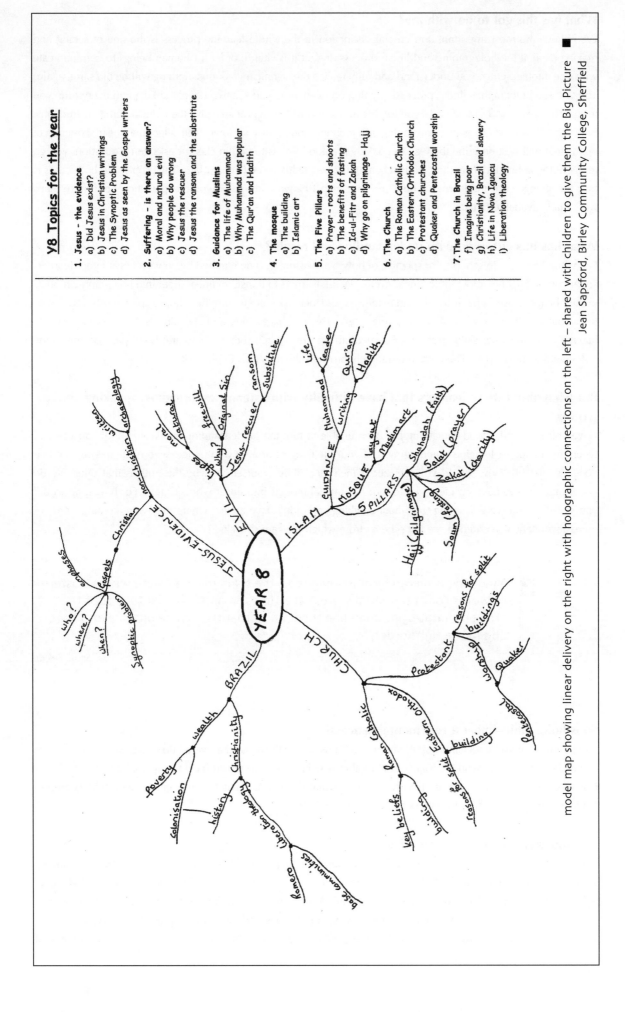

model map showing linear delivery on the left – shared with children to give them the Big Picture with holographic connections on the right

Jean Sapsford, Birley Community College, Sheffield

individuals – people with Autism – who have what Feuerstein calls an 'episodic grasp of reality'. These individuals can have profound difficulty in categorizing their experiences and can be left with the perception that things are always new to them. Most of us live somewhere between the two extremes and spend our lives trying to improve on something of which we are totally unaware.

How can I use this knowledge?

Read the rest of this book, use the strategies outlined in the How section and copy the work of the teachers in the When section!

review

Can I describe the holographic–linear processes to someone else, with examples? ■

Do I understand its relevance to teaching and learning? ■

Can I think of times when pupils would benefit from being given access to the holographic as well as the linear? ■

How can I use model mapping to aid the holographic–linear cycle and so help understanding? ■

- What are language triangles and why are they significant?
- How does knowing about language triangles help me and my teaching?
- What is the practical relevance of this theory?
- How do language triangles relate to model mapping?

language triangles

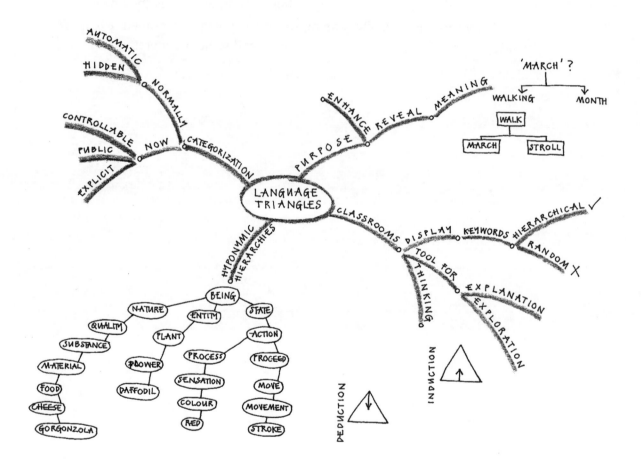

Language triangles vocabulary

What are language triangles?

Language triangles are the deep structures that give vocabulary meaning. For example, let's look at the word 'march'. Within the following sentence it has a particular meaning: 'I saw the man march quickly down the road.' To understand the meaning of the word 'march' in this sentence the learner has to access a level of meaning deeper than the sentence's linear surface structure. As the diagram below shows, to understand 'march' the learner needed to know its relationship to the words 'walk', above and 'stroll', which is parallel to it. All language exists in these hierarchies or what we have called language triangles.

Some words are more important than others in the sense that they capture and organize other words in their orbit. 'Trainers', 'slippers' and 'boots' for example can be captured by the word 'footwear'. 'Boots' however can capture words like 'wellingtons' and 'football'. As you get more familiar with visualizing this a strange realization can take place. All language fits this structure. You will begin to see that one word above is able to capture and hold many words beneath it. A triangle starts to form with broad, concrete words at the bottom being marshalled by the singular, more abstract word at the top that does the organizing. The word 'marshalled' is used because this word governs the meaning of the words beneath it.

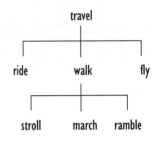

How are language triangles formed?

Language triangles are formed through the categorization of language. Categorization is the most fundamental thinking skill. Categorizing includes the skills of attention and labelling, and identifying similarities and differences. It is by labelling differences or similarities that we create language triangles. The moment you create a label it becomes the word at the top of a new triangle.

change mere
into meaning

The toys were spread out on the floor.

By exploring similarities and differences we were able to identify different categories of toy.

The children put the toys into the four categories that they had identified deciding as they did this that the bear was more cuddly than he was noisy!

We explored different ways of grouping them; with me using language triangles on the flip chart to show what the children were doing with the toy on the floor.
The children illustrated the resultant maps for review.

J. Tindall – Early Years Teacher (retired)

using real objects in early years to reveal the hierarchical nature of language

'The mind automatically sorts information into distinctive pyramidal groupings in order to comprehend it.

- Any groupings of ideas is easier to comprehend if it arrives pre-sorted into pyramids

- This suggests that every written document should be deliberately structured to form pyramids of ideas'

Barbara Minto (1995)

Can you give me some examples?

Look at the following words: 'London', 'New York', 'Paris'. What label comes to mind? Is it 'cities' or 'capital cities'? Take the words 'fly', 'wasp', 'ant' and 'beetle' and you may come up with the label 'insect'. Take the words 'insect', 'animal', 'fish' and 'bird', and you may come up with the label/category 'living things'. Take any group of words and write them randomly on a sheet of paper. Try not to write down words that can be categorized. As soon as you get to five words you will start to categorize them anyway, maybe even before then. By the time you have seven words you will have formed at least one, and possibly several, categories.

So what?

When we are speaking or writing we are constantly moving up and down these language triangles, explaining an abstract word by going to more concrete words below it, extending understanding by grouping concrete words and creating new categories for the listener. When we listen or read we are continuously accessing our existing triangles to make sense of, or categorize, what we are reading. Language triangles work alongside holographic–linear processing to help us make sense of our world.

'It is the hierarchical relationships between word meanings that has most evidently far reaching influence upon our thinking.'

J. Britton (1993)

Does it really happen like this?

We are not saying that you have language triangles inside your head! We are saying that language triangles seem to explain how we create meaning from words and experiences. Our minds are not just full of vocabulary lists which, if we were able to extract them, would come out in a long sequence in the order in which they went in. James Britton wrote about the structure of language over 30 years ago in a book called *Language and Learning* (originally published in 1970). He called these word groupings 'language hierarchies'.

So how is this relevant to classrooms?

Classrooms are full of language triangles. In fact, take them away and there is very little left. The curriculum has them but generally keeps them hidden. Each subject has its key vocabulary that organizes and marshalls the other vocabulary beneath it. At their most obvious these language triangles appear as: 'science', marshalling 'biology', 'physics' and 'chemistry'; as 'geography', marshalling 'human', 'physical' and 'social'; as 'history', marshalling different periods such as Tudor, Georgian and Victorian, and these in turn marshalling 'social', 'economic' and 'political'. The language triangles are endless. We display key words in class and we spend time explaining them to learners. The point is that when learners really understand the deeper meaning of a word they are able to locate it within recognized triangular relationships and can create new relationships of their own. When they have not understood or have merely been engaged in rote learning, these relationships are not understood.

For example let's take the sentence 'The boy ran quickly to the shop.' For the reader to understand this sentence she would need to understand the hierarchies shown on the right.

Unless learners understand this obvious but hidden spatial triangular arrangement of vocabulary, they have not truly understood the meaning of the words. Model maps make these relationships explicit.

Write down a sentence that includes key words from your subject area. What language triangles are implicit in what you have written? What assumptions do we make about pupils' understanding when we speak to them using key subject vocabulary or ask them to read from a subject textbook?

We help learners by displaying key vocabulary. We can help them more by displaying the key vocabulary within its hierarchical context. For example, look at the key words displayed in the diagram below. What meaning do you make from the words? Now look at the language triangle on the opposite page. The point we are making is this: it is the spatial relationships between words that carry most meaning. These hierarchical relationships are buried both within the text (as in this example) and beyond the text (as in the example of the boy running to the shop). Model mapping can make both of these relationships visible and therefore accessible to pupils.

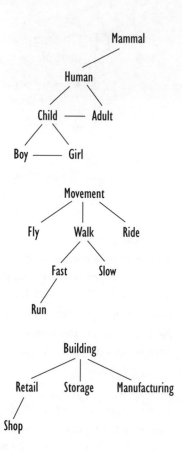

---

mapwise the inside story of learning
RANDOM KEY WORDS

drinking   countryside

shopping   clothes

friends   party

New Year

CDs

eating

dancing

walking

cycling

model learning

© Model Learning

The teacher does not just say one word after another randomly labelling them. She is constantly trying to make connections by linking them with other words – sometimes others that are higher up in the language hierarchy. Have you ever had the thought that learners were not following what you were saying? Maybe it's because, as you speak, they access their own language hierarchies. If theirs are not the same as yours, the learners will begin to misunderstand and misinterpret what you are saying. This book is about making these language triangles visible in classrooms – using model mapping.

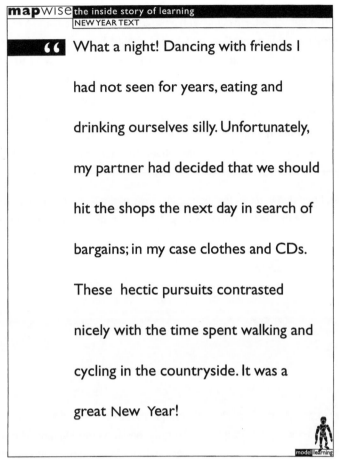

© Model Learning

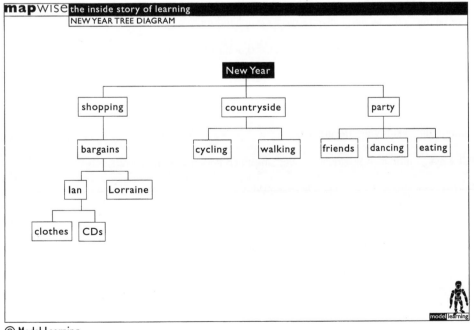

© Model Learning

case study

Impact on literacy

Model mapping is now a way of life for me and for a growing band of students in the school where I work. Here is how I came to introduce this critical thinking tool into my own educational setting.

A new headteacher arrived at our school. He came with a progressive reputation, and a colleague who had known him previously advised me that, when meeting with him, I should be concise and clear, and that unplanned meetings should last no more than 15 minutes. Thus, when I met with the new head I had all my key points mapped out in my planner. As time went by and I progressed to using mapping software, I would leave the headteacher a copy of the points we had considered in the course of a meeting. One day I visited him less prepared than usual (a PC glitch had meant that I didn't have my pre-prepared map). I apologized for this and at the end of our meeting our headteacher presented me with the course details for a 'MapWise' seminar to be held in Stirling. Quite frankly, the day spent with Ian and Oliver changed my life. I couldn't believe that I hadn't considered the educational potential of this system myself.

On my return to the class, I decided to teach the technique to my entire teaching group. This amounted to around a hundred 12–17-year-old students. Each group was taught the technique with a very specific purpose in mind:

- paragraphing

- essay writing

- note taking

- revision

- talk delivery.

I also decided I would try to analyse the impact the technique made on my students. This in itself was quite a task and in genuine research terms, the work I completed was quite basic. As most teachers know, it is difficult enough to make teaching ends meet, without embarking on personal whole-teaching-group comparative studies in the effectiveness of different teaching and learning approaches. However, on the strength of various attitudinal surveys and shared observation of work samples, a picture began to emerge.

- Note taking and planning activities were completed more easily and to a higher standard.

- Essays produced were more clearly organized and more detailed.

- Summarizing skills were developed.

- Revision activities were more structured.

- Paragraphing skills were developed.

- Talk organization/planning/delivery was simplified and grades improved.

- Students developed independent learning skills.

- Pupils perceived mapping to be a useful learning tool (see chart 1 opposite).

- Writing assessment grades improved (see chart 2 opposite).

Chart 1. STUDENT SURVEY: HOW USEFUL IS MODEL MAPPING?
Survey of 100 students (S1–S5 ... 12–17 year olds) Dingwall Academy, April 2000

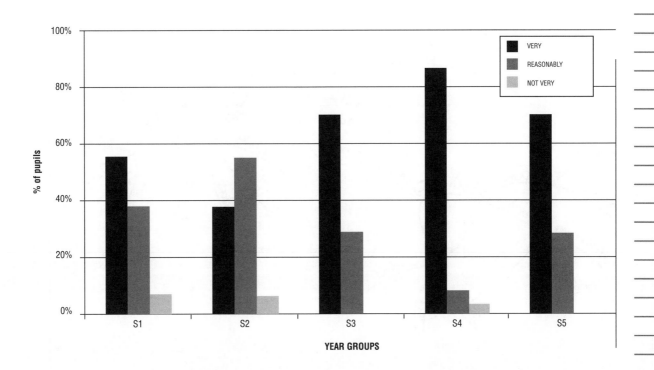

Chart 2. EFFECT OF MODEL MAPPING ON WRITING LEVELS
Study based on S2 (least able) English 5–14 assessments Dingwall Academy, Feb–Apr 2000

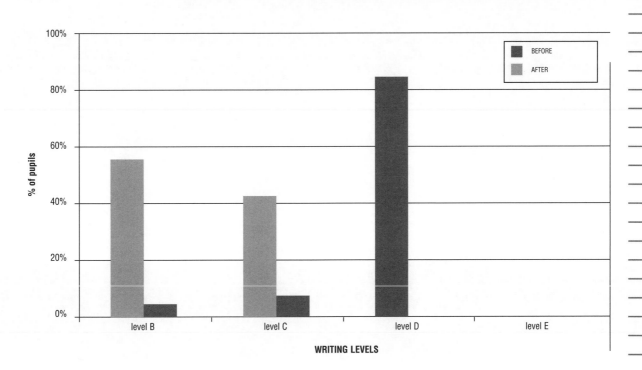

Note: Level D is a higher grade than level B in Scotland.

Gerry Dolan, Dingwall Academy, Scotland

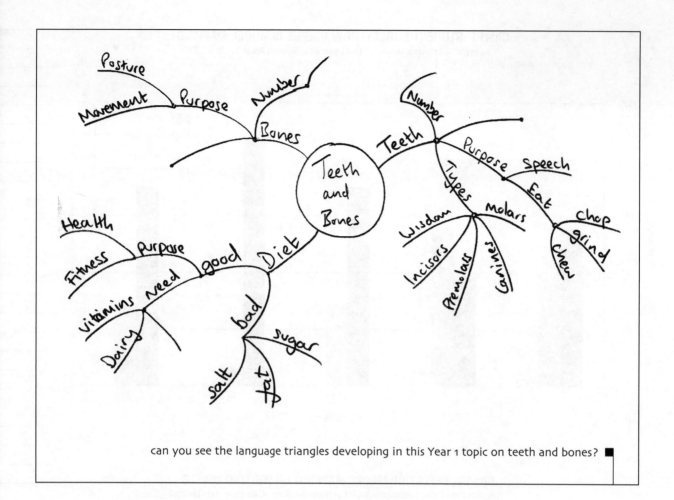

can you see the language triangles developing in this Year 1 topic on teeth and bones? ■

review

Do I understand what language triangles are? ■

Is it clear what part language triangles play in understanding? ■

Do I give enough emphasis to key vocabulary in my lessons? ■

How can I use model mapping to make language triangles
more explicit and therefore aid learning? ■

■

■ What beliefs about learning styles do I have?

■ Do I understand how humans cognate, or think?

■ How can model mapping work as a tool to aid pupils of all learning styles?

■ Why is this so important for my classroom?

thinking styles

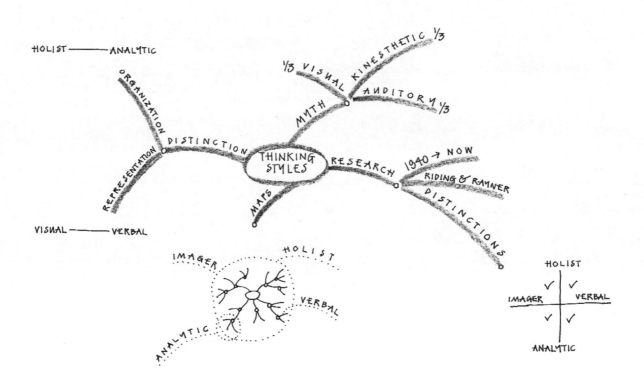

Beneath all our diff

common

> ❝ 'They [maps] stimulate active thinking, develop cognitive skills of analysis, categorisation and synthesis, and provide a visual means of communication and evaluation… Model Mapping can help information flow to and from students and teachers…They provide a whole language framework in all the areas of language skill – speaking, listening, reading and writing.'
>
> *R. Fisher (1995)*

How can you say model mapping is for all learners – surely it is suitable for only visual learners?

This question is one that the authors have been addressing during training days in schools and colleges. The question itself reveals a lack of understanding about the link between learning styles and cognition. This chapter addresses this and explains why and how model mapping can support all learners irrespective of their learning style preferences.

> ❝ 'Many of the calls for visual learning in schools are based on the idea that school learning is primarily verbal while most children just entering school have been operating in a predominantly visual environment.'
>
> *D. M. Moore and F. M. Dwyer (1994)*

But surely there are lots of learning style models – we can't all be the same can we?

No, of course not – and we are not saying that recognizing learning style differences isn't useful. Teaching to a variety of learning styles is important in that it ensures we cater for the wide range of ways in which people like to approach learning, but it does not explain what learning actually *is*. Once you get beneath the differences of how we prefer to 'approach' or 'stylize' our learning, we do get to a level of commonality – we all form schemas, or mental models (see chapter 1.2, Schemas).

Can you say a bit more about this?

We believe that most of the work around 'learning how to learn' is very superficial. Finding out that you learn best when you are relaxed, hydrated and stimulated in the way that you like best (VAK) has been useful in that it has caused us all to reflect and consider, even question, the processes of, and conditions for, learning. But when we look closely at all of this, it is really about 'making learning more likely'; it does not explain what learning *is*. For that we need to understand how we think, or cognate, to create schemas. When you access this deeper level of understanding you can then see how and why model mapping supports all learners, irrespective of the profiles they may have discovered.

Fortunately, a lot of our work on this subject has been done for us. Richard Riding and Stephen Rayner (1998) from Birmingham University looked at all the learning style models from the 1940s to the present day. Their research revealed that underneath all the candyfloss there are two distinctions that all the models have in

erences lies our
need for meaning

common. One distinction relates to how we all organize information, the other relates to how we represent it. We argue that our schemas provide the domain in which this representation and organization – the understanding – can take place. Mapping provides us with a way of making this process visible.

Can you explain the two distinctions in more detail?

As the diagram below shows, both the organizational and representational distinctions are a continuum. The organizational continuum relates to whole–parts relationships or how we work out how things fit together. Some of us like to start with the whole and then break things down into their constituent parts. Others like to build up from the parts to the whole. As you will see in the next chapter, Thinking Skills, whole-to-parts thinkers are engaging in deductive thinking, whereas parts-to-whole thinkers are engaging in inductive thinking. At the extremes of the continuum a whole-to-parts thinker may be someone who is great at getting the idea, the Big Picture, the 'possibility' of something, but who struggles massively to break this down into step-by-step procedures. At the opposite end of this continuum you have those of us who get so bogged down in the detail that we find it hard to get the bigger picture – 'to see the wood for the trees'.

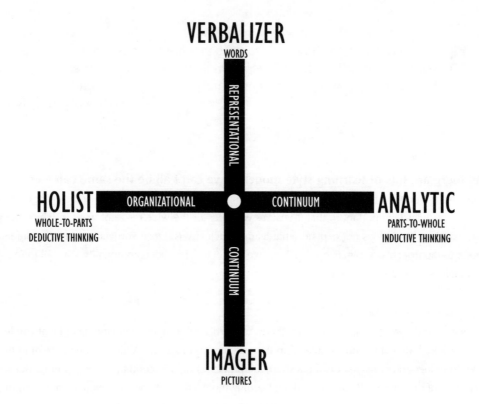

What about the representational continuum?

Riding and Rayner (1998) argue that we represent our information internally on a verbal–visual continuum. Put simply, we could say that some of us are happier remembering pictures than words and vice versa. At a deeper level, however, the reality is that you cannot separate words from pictures. Look at a picture, any picture – what do you think about it? How do you express those thoughts? Through words? Some of you may say 'What about feelings?' Well, how do you express feelings? With words! As you have seen in the chapter on Language Triangles, it is the spatial relationships of words that convey deeper levels of meaning. That spatial relationship is a visual one! You cannot separate the visual and verbal relationship.

What has this got to do with model mapping?

We call model maps by this name because they are models of the maps (schemas) that we have in our heads. The business world calls schemas 'mental models'. We say that when our models stop being mental they become 'models' that can then be mapped. The organizational and representational distinctions are all present on a map. The learner can see the whole and how the constituent parts make up the whole. The map is a visual representation of understanding. This visual representation is also verbal since key words are present and, most important, it is the visual–spatial relationships of these key words (their location on the map) that conveys the meaning.

'It is the spatial relationships between the words that carries deeper levels of meaning. These relationships are buried beneath the surface of linear text. Model mapping brings these spatial relationships to the surface and makes them explicit. Because the relationships between the words is a spatial one, it is also very much a visual one. The gap between visual and verbal processing is bridged... in fact you can't separate them.'

Ian Harris

What has this got to do with classrooms?

As we have already set out, the simple message of this book is that model mapping provides us all with a way of making our thinking visible and therefore accessible. When we do that, benefits relating to literacy, thinking, teaching and learning occur.

'Even left-brained verbal thought can be enhanced with right-brain visual structure. Even right-brained art can be enhanced by strong verbal description.'

D. M. Moore and F. M. Dwyer (1994)

We have all, I suspect, tried at some time in our lives to describe something to someone and wished we had the actual object we are describing there with us to show them. Few could disagree that showing things to pupils helps them to ask questions and focuses attention. It also helps to stimulate conversation and encourages learners to think more widely about the object in question.

In classrooms, learners are constantly being asked to identify whole–part relationships and then find some way of representing this understanding – in fact this is what we are all doing all of the time!

Irrespective of where your pupils are on the visual–verbal, holistic–analytic continuums, model mapping supports their thinking. All the processes involved in thinking, teaching, learning, knowing and understanding can be transformed from being something that is private, hidden and implicit into something that is public, shared and explicit. As you saw in chapter 1.1, Models of Learning, model mapping provides a very powerful way of making classrooms language-rich, collaborative places to work. Finally, as you will see in chapter 1.8, Memory and Mapping, mapping supports short- and long-term memory.

In short... your learners are different from one another. Underneath these differences lie some commonalities. We argue that catering for these commonalities is a more realistic option than just focusing on their differences. Not only is it realistic, but it is also inclusive.

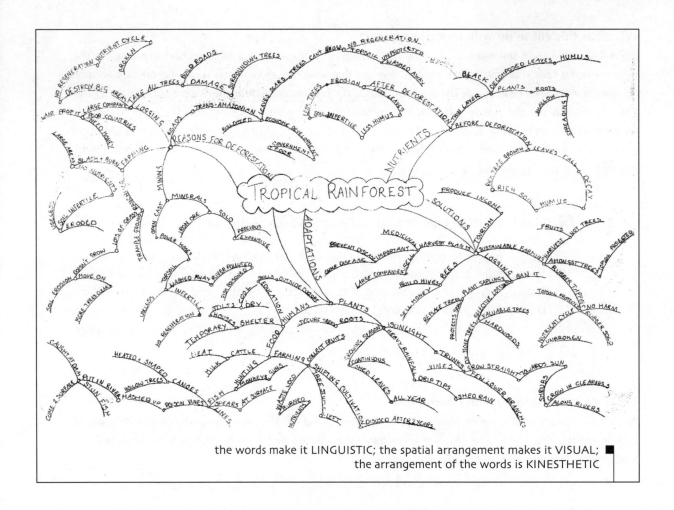

the words make it LINGUISTIC; the spatial arrangement makes it VISUAL;
the arrangement of the words is KINESTHETIC

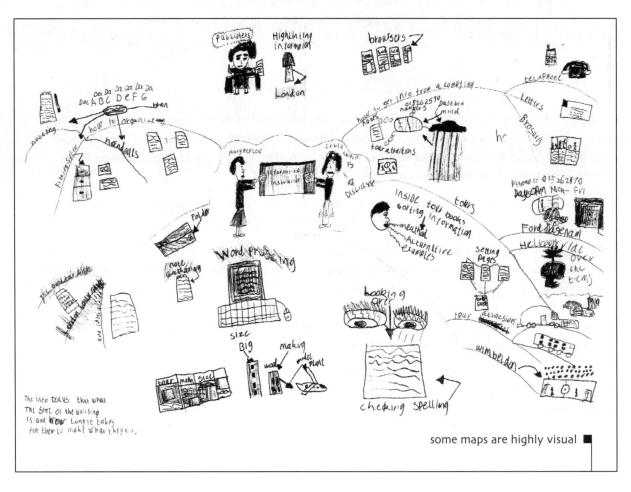

some maps are highly visual ■

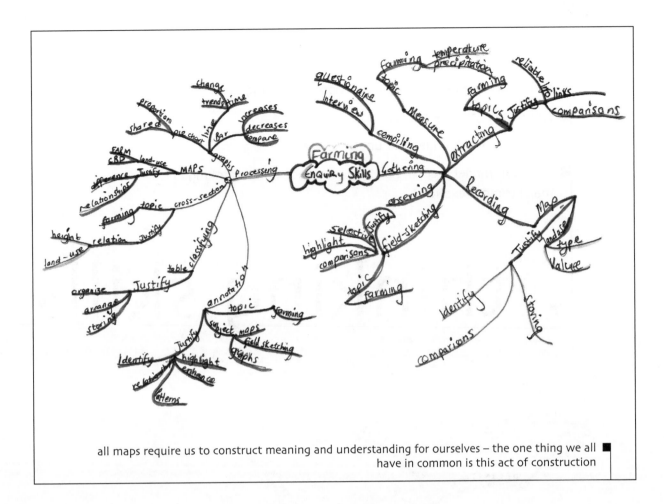

all maps require us to construct meaning and understanding for ourselves – the one thing we all ■
have in common is this act of construction

review

Do I understand the commonality that underlies the different learning styles? ■

Can I identify whole–part and part–whole opportunities in teaching? ■

How can I use the model mapping process to support these ■
teaching and learning situations?

Can I see now why model mapping is relevant to all learners of all abilities? ■

■

■ What do we mean when we talk about 'thinking skills'?

■ How do we think – really?

■ How does thinking lead to understanding?

■ How can model mapping be used as a tool to aid thinking and make it more explicit?

thinking skills

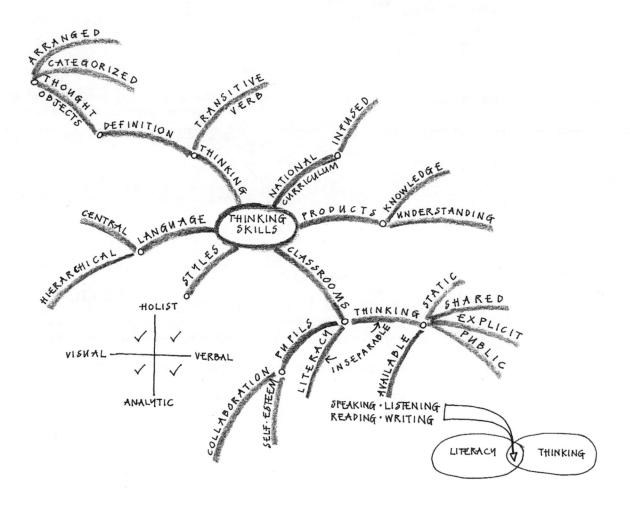

Thinking is the ma
of subject

What do you think about thinking skills?

Talking to a group of advanced skills teachers (ASTs) recently, one of them commented that her colleagues seemed to take on a glazed, distant look whenever she mentioned thinking skills to them. 'It was as if' she said 'they thought I was talking in a different language, about something that had nothing, but nothing to do with them.' Before we could respond, another AST cut in and said 'My problem is the opposite. Whenever we talk about thinking skills, I have a problem with reaching any agreement or clarity over what it is we are talking about – the term "thinking skills" is so vague and all encompassing.' These views may be familiar to you. You most probably have others, but how happy would you be to go on a live education programme and be 'grilled' about thinking skills?

 'How can I tell what I think till I see what I say?'

E. M. Forster

Few, if any, teachers would argue with the ideas that all learners should be independent, creative thinkers; that they should be able to analyse and create and be responsible for developing their own frameworks of knowledge and understanding. You could add your own ideas of what thinking is, or isn't, about. The interesting thing about the plethora of thoughts about thinking is the fact that they tend to be just this – thoughts 'about' thinking or 'descriptions of' different types of thinking. This can be interesting, even exciting, to some but we would argue that its practical usefulness is limited because it doesn't give us any insights into the very nature of thinking. To do this we need to get beneath the surface descriptions and dig a little deeper.

So where would you start?

We start by acknowledging the obvious. You cannot think about nothing. Thinking is a transitive verb; you have to think about something. The 'something' we think is overwhelmingly expressed in language. In the previous two chapters you found out about the interdependence of visual and verbal processing.

'Thinking springs from language. It is by mastering language that the child has the potential to change and reorganize his perception and memory. It is through language that he is able to master increasingly complex forms of thinking related to objects in the world at large. It is through language that he is able to make deductions and draw conclusions from his observations. It is through a mastery of language that the learner acquires the potentiality of thinking.'

Bill Tindal, author and trainer in private correspondence to the authors, 2003

nipulation
language

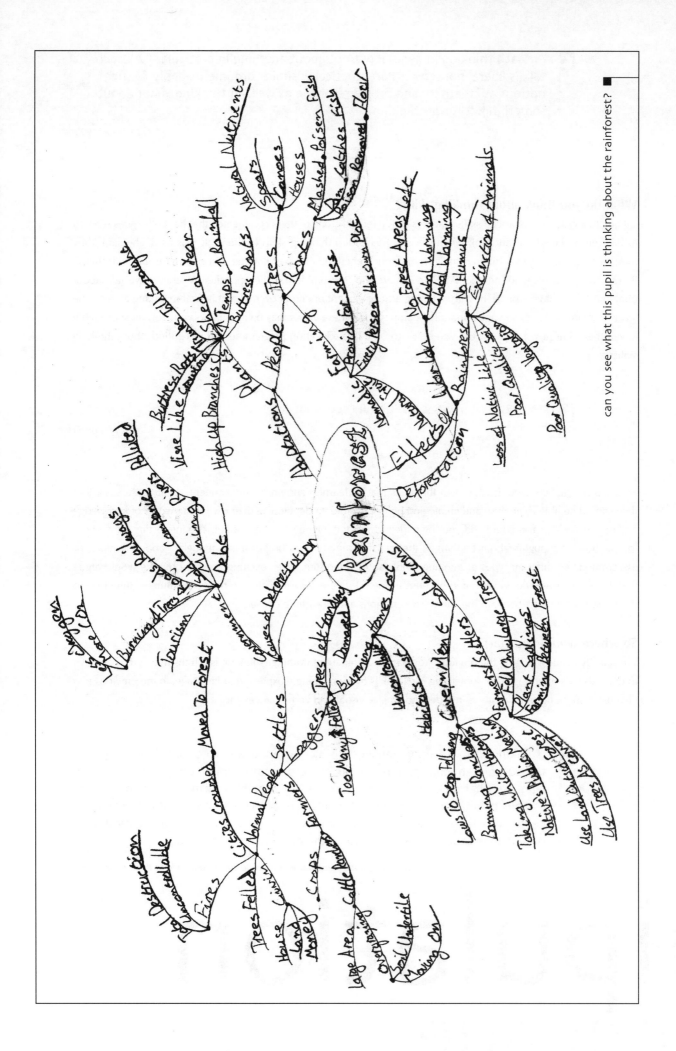

can you see what this pupil is thinking about the rainforest?

Try this. Write down 50 words that are specific to your subject. Now throw the words in the bin, pretend the words did not, do not and will not ever, exist. What has happened to your subject? Where has it gone? Put another way, where or how does your subject normally live or happen? Through words!

What has this got to do with thinking?

You will see then that you cannot separate the language of your subject from your subject. You will also realize that what you think within your subject *is* the language of the subject. We don't just mean language in terms of vocabulary lists. As you saw in chapter 1.4, Language Triangles, language is organized in certain ways – in hierarchies. Understanding that some words are more important than others, that some contain or organize others, is crucial to learners being able to understand your subject. In mastering the linguistic structures of the subject, learners are mastering the thinking of the subject.

 'Language is not the garment but the incarnation of thought'

William Wordsworth

But what has that got to do with knowing and understanding?

This question is dealt with more fully in the next chapter but briefly, we can say that both knowledge and understanding are the products of thinking. When we understand something it is because we have thought or 'thinked' and arranged information, stimuli and data in a way that leads us to the 'ah, I get it' moment.

So what has this got to do with model mapping?

Our ideas and thinking about the vocabularies of our subject material can be expressed in model maps, which are no more and no less than the arrangement of a series of language triangles around a central point.

Model mapping can make the processes of knowing and understanding explicit, and therefore available, to all. Imagine knowing exactly and explicitly what it is that you do cognitively when you understand! Model mapping makes it possible for learners to be very clear about why they do not understand and what they need to do to understand.

 'If students are to become better thinkers – to learn meaningfully, to think flexibly and to make reasoned judgements – then they must be taught explicitly how to do it.'

C. McGuiness (1999)

What has this got to do with me and my classroom?

Model maps enable you to share your thinking with your learners. You saw in the chapter on schema, how we form models, or schemas, in our heads. When we talk to learners we are sharing the product of these models with them. As you will see in the case studies within this book, sharing your schema with learners has several practical classroom benefits. They are far more likely to understand what you are talking about and are far more likely to ask you relevant and specific questions. These questions give you the information you need to tell them what they need to know. All learning style preferences are supported and the learners are freed from the constraints of having to simultaneously apply short-term memory (in remembering what you are saying) and having to think about or process what you are saying.

Model mapping enables learners to more easily share their thinking with you and with each other. As you saw in chapter 1.3, Holographic–Linear, the inability to explain through talking and writing does not mean that we have not understood. It may well mean that we are finding it difficult to transform our understanding, which is holographic in nature, into linear output. Model maps reflect the internal categorization and thinking processes that learners go though in developing their thinking and understanding. Model maps provide learners with a real alternative to linear text as a form of representing their understanding.

From the teacher's perspective, model maps support formative assessment because the teacher can see what the learner has understood and can comment specifically on areas that are missing or need clarification and development. Marking time can be dramatically reduced when you no longer have to go searching for evidence of understanding. Model maps also support learners in translating their models of understanding (normally hidden schemas) into linear speech or text.

When working in pairs or groups, mapping can transform speaking and listening. This is because the learners can see what they are talking about. Collaborative or paired mapping ensures that learners will be learning through thinking in a co-operative and inductive way. (See chapter 2.3, Collaborative Group Work.)

 'All that we are is a result of what we have thought.'

Dhammapada

review

Do I understand what thinking is? ■

Do I understand the distinction between thinking and understanding? ■

Do I make my own thinking explicit in the classroom? ■

Are my pupils easily able to share their thinking with me and with one another? ■

How can I use model mapping to convey my own thinking
methods and develop my pupils' thinking skills? ■

■

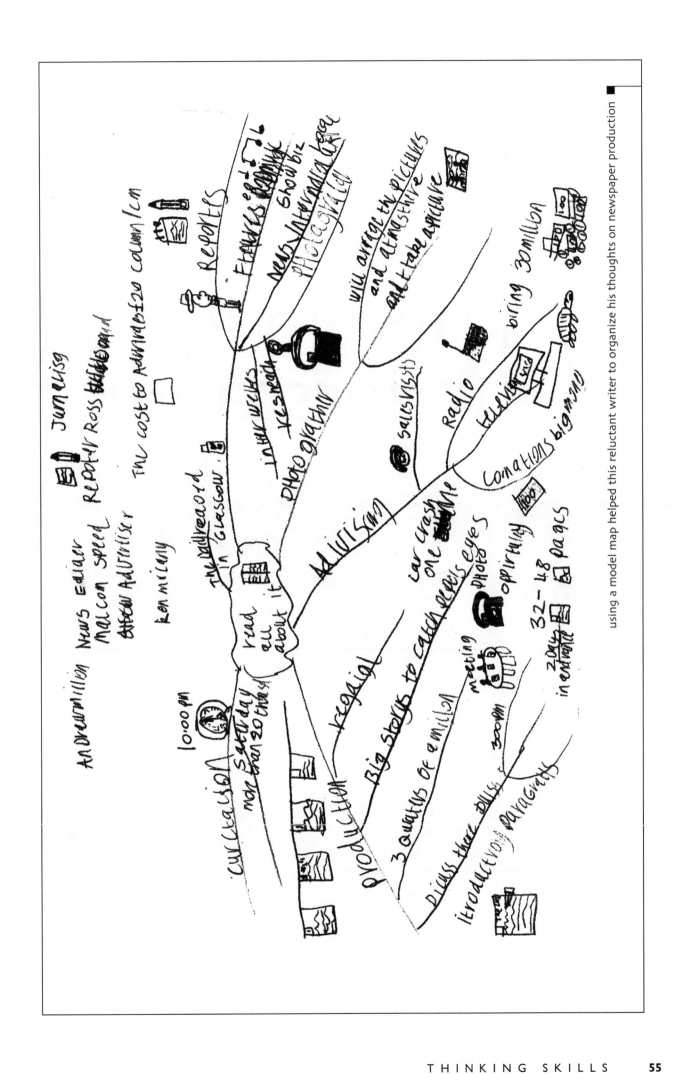

using a model map helped this reluctant writer to organize his thoughts on newspaper production

- Is there a difference between knowledge and understanding? If so what does it look like?
- How can we make the structure of knowledge and the structure of understanding explicit?
- What is 'cognitive subsumption' and how can model mapping help it to happen?

knowledge and understanding

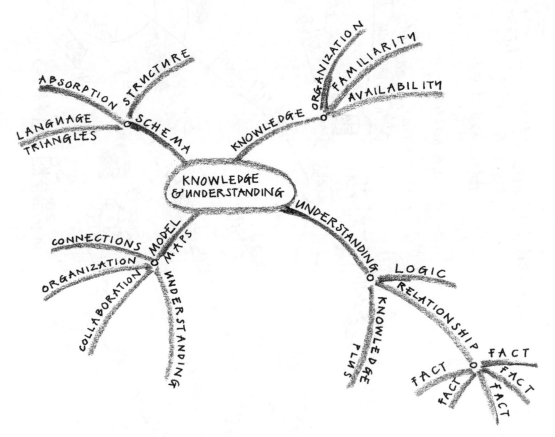

The thinking behin

and understanding

First of all, what's the difference between knowledge and understanding?

For a long time, there has been a raging debate between those who favour learning 'facts', and those who favour a deeper understanding of the facts.

We are going to be controversial and say that, fundamentally, there is no difference at all between the two. It is simply that what we have called knowledge has been devalued as being no more than learning facts by rote. And what we have called understanding has remained a nebulous, undefined mental state. It is no wonder then that behavioural psychologists have mocked this term used by teachers and goaded them into demonstrating what exactly understanding 'looks like'.

OK, so how are they the same?

Let's take knowledge first. When we say that we 'know' something, we have a record of an event, something that has occurred in the past. This record is organized in a particular way. At this stage, we may not be sure of the nature of this organization but we can be pretty sure it is not random. If it were random we would not have ready access to it. Knowledge has to be accessible.

To know, the dictionary tells us, is 'to be acquainted with', 'to be assured of'. Knowledge, therefore, has to be familiar to us – only then can it be available to us when we want it. It also has to be made available to others. For that to happen, it needs to be framed in an organized structure.

Understanding, when closely observed, has the same features as those described above. It is defined in dictionaries as 'grasping with the mind', 'following the logic of'. What this activity consists of is more than merely knowing a series of isolated 'facts'. It is the knowledge of how these single facts relate to one another. So, understanding includes knowledge but suggests something more.

> 'It is important to realise that understanding, as seeing the relation between particulars and generalisations, and understanding, as seeing the tool use of things, are complimentary processes'
>
> *M. L. Bigge and S. S. Shermiss (1999)*

Maybe, we can see it in the following way. If knowledge (of facts) is at one end of a continuum, then understanding (of how facts interrelate) is at the other. And one person's knowledge is another's understanding. It all depends on how much you insist on a learner clarifying and articulating how what they know interrelates.

That's all very interesting, but why do I need to know this?

When you engage your pupils in your schemes of work, you do so with the intention that they will be able to recount the facts. You would also want them to be able to relate these facts to each other in such a way that 'the whole equalled more than the sum of the parts'. You would call this understanding.

For many teachers, hard pressed with targets and levels, simply being able to recount isolated facts has, naturally, dominated their agendas. Understanding is often seen as a luxury, an additional enrichment. It is seen as being different from knowledge, instead of being simply a more explicit and schematized organization of facts.

d knowledge
is identical

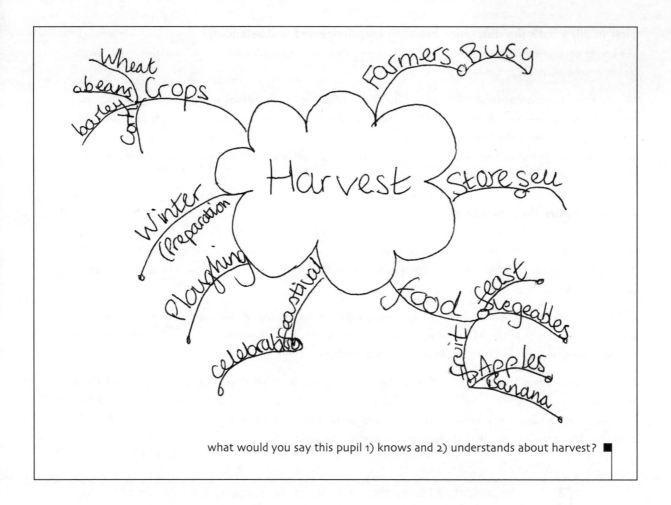

what would you say this pupil 1) knows and 2) understands about harvest? ■

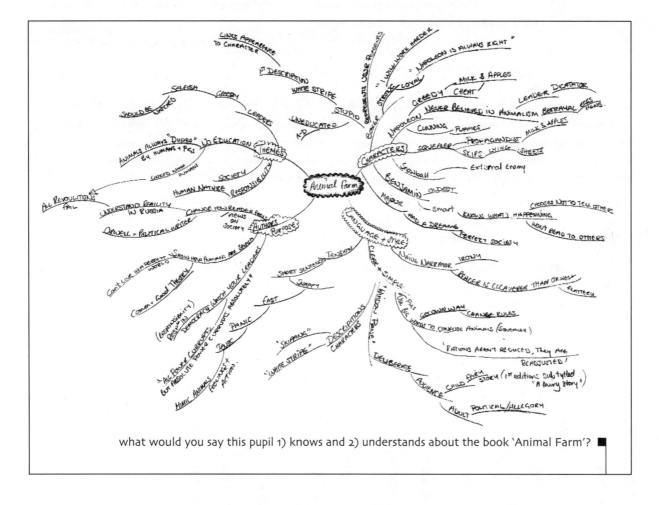

what would you say this pupil 1) knows and 2) understands about the book 'Animal Farm'? ■

'Spatial cognition, in turn, is an important sub part of cognition *per se*, and its understanding is thought to be central to understanding learning and knowing in general.'

R. Kitchin and S. Freundschuh (2000)

So, what if developing understanding promoted knowledge of facts? When the structure of understanding is made explicit, through being made visible, then facts can be related to one another. And an efficient memory, as researchers tell us, is predicated on organization, on structure.

So what's the link between knowledge and understanding and learning?

Every pupil in your class comes into your room with a schema. It is their organized structure with which to hold their understanding and memory of what they know. And when you introduce something new to them, you are introducing it to their schemas. (See chapter 1.2, Schemas.)

If the new information you are presenting is sufficiently related to their existing schema, it has a place in which to lodge. Joseph Novak (1998), who has written extensively on how pupils construct knowledge, calls this process 'cognitive subsumption'. This term refers to the way in which existing hierarchical structures based on language provide the matrix in which new information can be integrated (see chaper 1.4, Language Triangles).

Without this connection, there is no learning. Yes, some pupils may be able to retain new information for a short while – sufficiently long to answer your questions – but unless it finds an appropriate conceptual link, it is lost. It remains fleeting, surface learning with no 'home' in which to exist. It soon disappears.

'In knowledge-based business, learning and innovation are the critical drivers of business development.'

T. Clarke and S. Clegg (2000)

Technically speaking, this process of cognitive subsumption is a description of the learning process. It is not surprising, you now realize, quite why model mapping is making such an impact in classrooms. It makes this previously vague, but nonetheless central, process of 'cognitive subsumption' an everyday reality by being made visible, public and concrete.

But what about thinking?

Thinking is the same process as learning, but can be explained in another way. Thinking is a transitive verb. That means that thinking has to have an object. In other words, you have to think about something. And predominantly, you do that with language.

Language, as you read in chapter 1.4, is hierarchical in structure. So when you engage in thinking, you are engaging with the conceptual meaning inherent in language triangles. The interrelated structures of these language triangles are the building blocks of personal schemas.

'we believe that the effective transfer of knowledge between groups of individuals depends critically upon the creation of appropriate representative frameworks to facilitate the exteriorisation and ingestion of knowledge in different forms.'

P. Barker and P. Van Shank in M. Yazdani and P. Barker (2000)

And so, just as the process of learning can be explained in terms of cognitive subsumption, thinking is equally defined by it. But, in this instance, we have described the place language has in the construction of personal schemas. Schemas are the structure into which new information is 'subsumed'. Model maps, being a graphic way of representing personalized language triangles, offer teachers a very accurate view of pupils' internal thinking processes. These are the very processes that build knowledge and understanding.

How can I use this in my classroom?

Before teaching a new topic, realize that you will be communicating it to your pupils' schemas. This may seem a rather novel way of looking at classroom interaction, but its novelty offers powerful insights. Progressing beyond the glib phrase 'connect the learning', you now know what this entails.

So, how can you see what you are connecting to? Ask your pupils to create model maps of their knowledge and understanding of the topic you are about to introduce. You can get the pupils to work collaboratively on this (see chapter 2.3, Collaborative Group Work). But what if you think the topic is so very new to your pupils that you are pretty convinced they have no existing schema? Well, try it anyway – you may well be surprised. Otherwise, ask them to create model maps of a closely related topic.

> 'Seeing solitary facts in relation to a general principle, then, is the essence of understanding.'
>
> *M. L. Bigge and S. S. Shermiss (1999)*

When you introduce the topic, use the structures of your pupils' model maps as the central reference for the content. As their model maps begin to fill up with the subsumption of new content, consider rearranging them. At this point, it may become apparent to your pupils that their original schemas are ineffectively organized to 'hold' the new information. They will feel compelled to reorganize it.

This offers you an opportunity for more collaborative mapping as your pupils hypothesize, refine and negotiate a new structure for the rational and effective organization and integration of new and old information. Cognitive subsumption will be a practical and known reality in your classroom through the use of model maps – and a really engaging, challenging and compelling one at that.

review

Do I understand the link between knowledge, understanding and learning? ■

Does my teaching enable understanding to happen? ■

Do my lessons communicate to learners' existing schemas? ■

How could I use model mapping in my classroom to bridge the gap between ■
mechanical learning and true understanding?

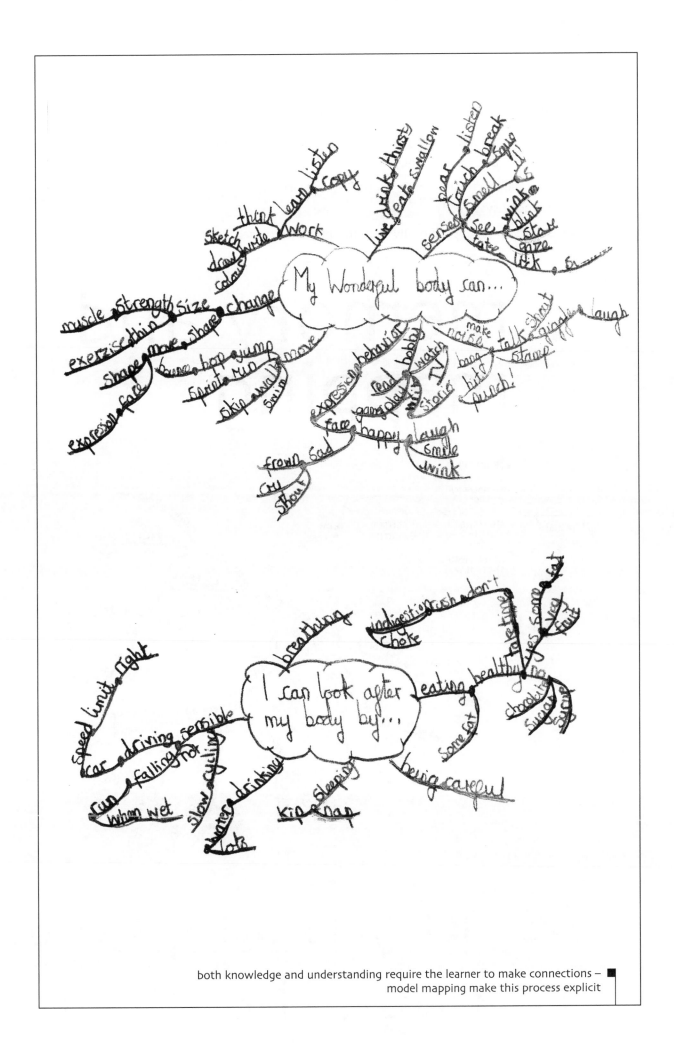

- What makes some things more memorable than others?
- What is the difference between short-term and long-term memory and how do they work?
- How can model mapping support our short- and long-term memory systems?
- Can model mapping really help my pupils to remember?

memory and mapping

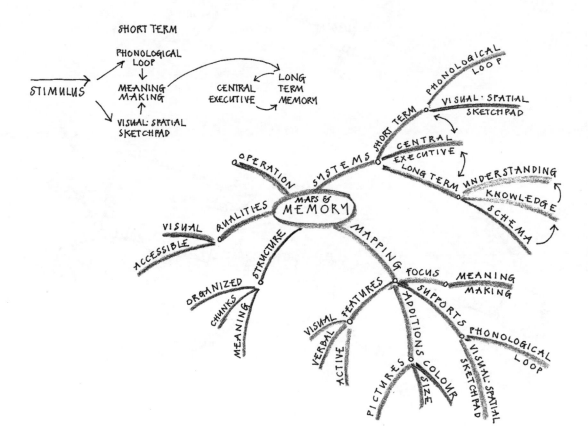

Memory is shaped and through the mapping

What makes mapping memorable?

In June 2002 the UK press ran articles claiming that we recall colour images more readily than black and white and that, when we dream in colour, we are more likely to recall our dreams when we wake up. For years teachers have been telling students to use a highlighter to identify key areas of text, and study guides have promoted the use of diagrams and pictures as aids to memory. Maps have, for many years, been recommended as powerful revision aids. But if you were asked why this is the case, what would you say? Would you say that the brain remembers pictures more readily than words, or that the brain makes connections in a similar way to maps? Would you point to the use of pictures, icons, diagrams, colour and size and promote the idea that maps work the way the brain does? We aim to take your understanding of memory and its relationship with model mapping to a new and more useful level.

Are there different sorts of memory?

You will have realized by now that this book is concerned with meaningful learning. It is about how learners form and modify their schemas or mental models of the world. When looking at memory and meaningful learning it is useful to explore the relationship between short-term or 'working' memory and long-term memory.

The learner receives information through her senses: words through her ears; images through her eyes; feeling through touch, and so on. The learner uses her short-term, or working, memory to work out the meaning of the information she receives. This meaning is then transferred to long-term memory.

Are these memory systems separate and how do they differ?

No, the two memory systems do not operate separately; they are interdependent. Meaning making in short-term memory is established by linking new information and stimulus with what is already known in long-term memory. Thinking processes such as analysis, creativity, comprehension and reasoning take place in our short-term memory. This explains why it is sometimes called our 'working' memory. Unlike long-term memory, our working memory only has a very limited capacity. Once full, we run the very real risk of 'losing' information by its being displaced by the arrival of new information. This has significant implications in classrooms, where learners receive massive amounts of information very quickly.

personalized
process

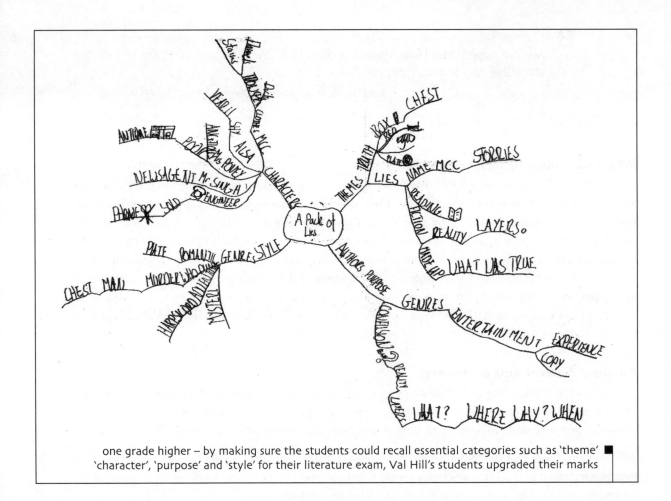

one grade higher – by making sure the students could recall essential categories such as 'theme' 'character', 'purpose' and 'style' for their literature exam, Val Hill's students upgraded their marks

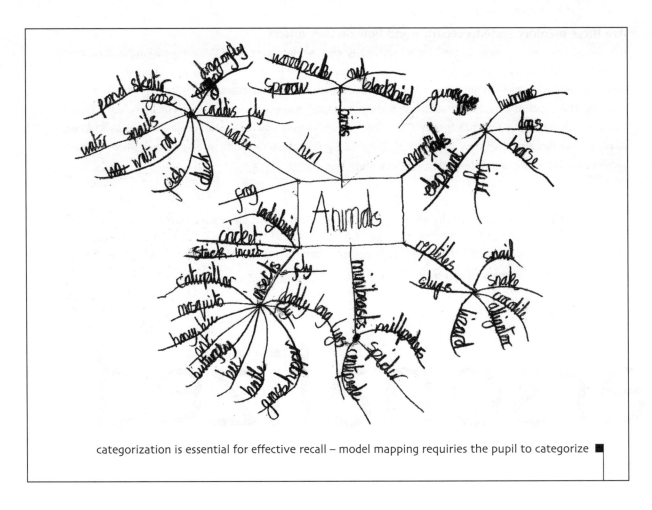

categorization is essential for effective recall – model mapping requiries the pupil to categorize

Can you give me an example?

Think of a time when you were listening to a lecture at college. As you listen you are simultaneously processing, or thinking about, what you hear. While you think about the first batch of information a new batch arrives and displaces the first (the working memory is full up). You are not conscious of this displacement – you are just left with a partial understanding of what has been said because you are not able to access the full story.

Can you say a bit more about how our short-term memory works?

Your short-term or working memory selects and processes information for the short term via two systems, which are co-ordinated via a third, called the central executive. The central executive co-ordinates the flow of information from and to the phonological loop and the visual-spatial sketchpad (your two working memory systems) and your long-term memory. The phonological loop identifies and stores words. The visual-spatial sketchpad selects and stores visual information. Information can be processed by either of these systems or more likely by both. Meaning making takes place within the working memory system. It involves the learner having to call on existing categories of knowledge and understanding and link new information to these categories.

 'Where the information being learned has a framework or structure that can be used to organize both the learning and the retrieval, then the memory is considerably improved.'

M. W. Eysenck (1994)

The workings of your phonological loop can be explained through the analogy of a voice recorder. You can insert tapes of different lengths. Our phonological loops are like internal tape recorders in that they only have a limited 'recording' time. Once full, they start again at the beginning. The sketchpad is responsible for storing and processing visual information and verbal information that has been encoded in the form of images. Both the sketchpad and the loop can be fed information via your direct perception or through recall.

So how is this relevant to my class?

In your classroom communication is going on all the time and memory systems play a vital role in the extent to which lessons are successful. Imagine yourself explaining something to your pupils. As you talk, the pupils' memory systems are being asked to 'kick in' to operation. Their central executive is looking in their long-term memory for what they already know in order to try and connect with the new stimulus. Simultaneously, the phonological loop and visual-spatial sketchpad (short-term/working memory) are processing the information and linking in with the information brought forward from the long-term memory. The problem is this: the short-term/working memory systems only have a limited capacity. Unless the learner is able to create meaning and therefore commit learning to the long-term memory system, much of what you say is lost.

 '...variation in amount of recall depends primarily on the degree of meaningfulness associated with the learning process...Information learned meaningfully (associated with subsumers in cognitive structure) can usually be recalled for weeks or months after acquisition'

J. D. Novak (1998)

How many of you have had wonderful class discussions with pupils and then asked them to write up the discussion, only to find that many of them are unable to recall much, if any, of what has been going on? The situation occurs because learners are being asked to both hold and process information simultaneously. The answer is to free up the processing 'RAM' being used for holding the information. This allows pupils to focus on processing or making sense of it all. This is particularly useful for pupils with specific memory difficulties associated with ADHD and dyslexia.

So what has this got to do with model mapping?

For new information or stimulus to be remembered it has to be 'subsumed' within existing structures (schemas) of meaning or be sufficiently significant to subsume existing structures within itself. Model mapping can support both the short- and long-term memory systems in doing this. With regard to working memory, a model map can relieve the workload of the phonological loop and the visual-spatial sketchpad by doing the work for them. With the verbal and visual information literally in front of them, the learner is freed up from the act of having to remember what she is thinking about and can spend more energy thinking about what to do with it.

> 'the superior playing skills of chess masters stem from their ability to perceive the board as an organised whole rather than as a collection of individual pieces.'
>
> *A. Baddeley (1994)*

With regard to long-term memory, we remember things that are meaningful to us. We could say we remember things we have understood. A model map is a model of the meaning and understanding we have of something. We find that when teachers give learners the opportunity to explain their map to a partner, this both clarifies and extends their understanding. We also find that their ability to recall the map at a later stage is virtually perfect. Do not be surprised if levels of concentration, attention, participation, co-operation and collaboration improve dramatically as a result.

Can you give me some more classroom examples of this?

Have you ever had a situation in class where the learners did not follow the verbal instructions given? Have you ever had a situation where, despite your best efforts, your pupils were unable to retain and recall what you explained to them? Have you ever had learners in your school who find revising, retaining and recalling hard and are perhaps ineffective at it? By mapping out instructions and the content of what you are trying to explain to learners, you can free up the working memory from having to hold information, allowing it instead to work with long-term memory to build understanding. Teaching learners to map and encouraging them to explain their maps to each other creates opportunities for learners to build their models of understanding in a way that supports both the information processing and the social models of learning – arguably the two most effective models of learning.

review

Do I understand how memory works? ■

Do I understand why pupils so often fail to retain information? ■

Do my teaching styles enable pupils to transfer information easily between short-term and long-term memory? ■

How can I use model mapping in my own classroom to work with pupils' natural memory systems? ■

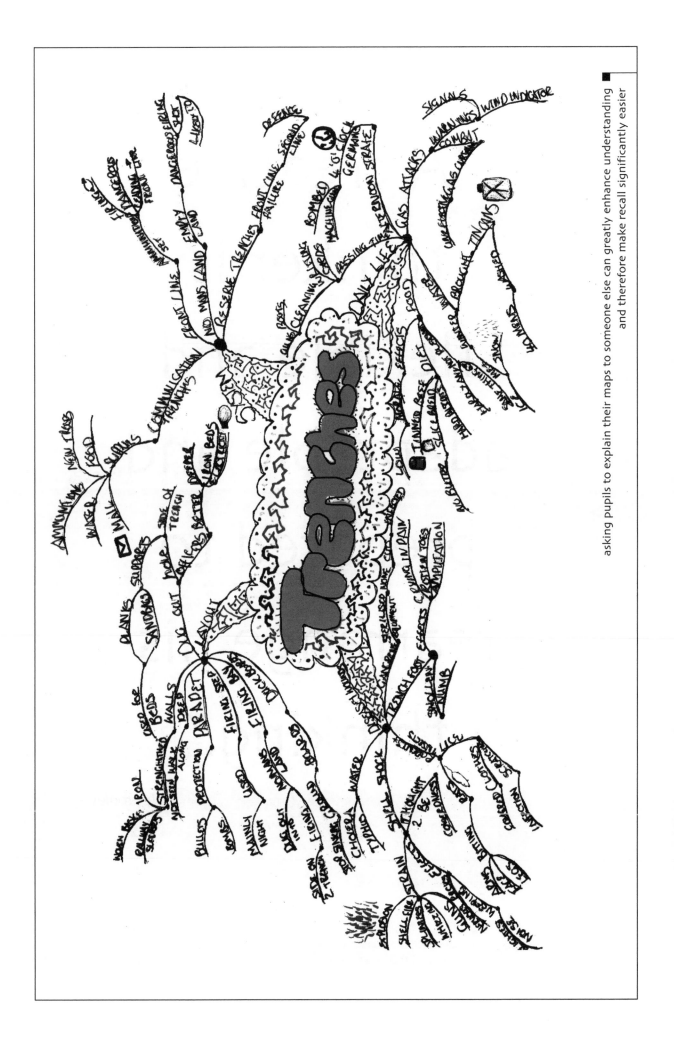

asking pupils to explain their maps to someone else can greatly enhance understanding and therefore make recall significantly easier

'A creative thinker is flexible and adaptable and prepared to rearrange his thinking.'

A. J. Cropley

SECTION

WHEN

2

■ Why is the Big Picture so important?

■ How does this relate to schemas and how learning happens?

■ Why use model maps to present the Big Picture?

■ What type of Big Pictures can be mapped?

Big Picture first

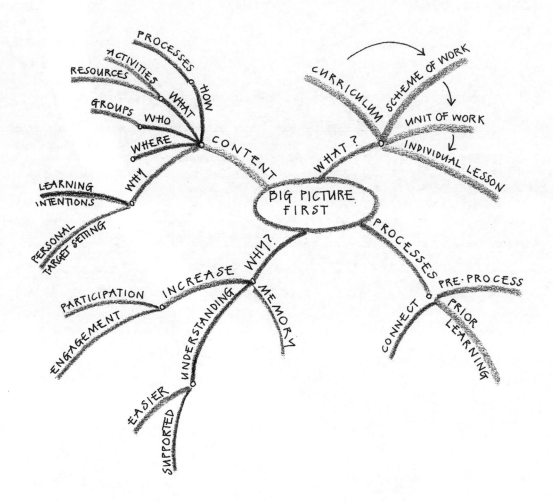

Understanding req
detail in the

> 'Learning needs us to be able to locate the detail in the wider context. The structure and organisation of the brain points us to this basic learning premise: seek and secure connections and constantly locate those connections in the wider context.'
>
> *A. Smith (2001)*

context

Model mapping is a powerful tool that can help pupils realize how it all fits together.

Where do schemes of work live in your school? In the cupboard? On the shelf in the staff room? How 'live' are they for the pupils in your class? At the end of term does next term's scheme of work go home with the pupils? Do the parents in your school get to see what is being covered next term? We don't of course mean the unwieldy National Curriculum schemes of work folders issued by the Education Department. We mean A4 summaries mapped out onto a single sheet.

'Big Picture' mapping is like peeling layers of an onion. You can map out the whole curriculum. Within the curriculum map you have schemes of work; within each scheme of work you have units of work and these can be broken down into individual lessons; and within these there is also a Big Picture or a point that you work hard to communicate. When you stop to consider, pupils, teachers, children, adults, human beings, are all constantly doing our best to work out how the whole thing called life fits together. In school we can help pupils work out at least part of it – their curriculum – by showing them what it looks like.

> 'When designing learning activities or inputs of new information be aware of the need to provide a global context within which local data can sit.'
>
> *A. Smith (2001)*

opportunity

Model mapping can help pupils make sense of the world by giving them access to the 'Big Picture' of what it looks like.

> 'Students learn best by actively making sense of new knowledge — making meaning from it and mapping it in to their existing knowledge map / schema.'
>
> *C. V. Gipps (1994)*

uires locating the bigger picture

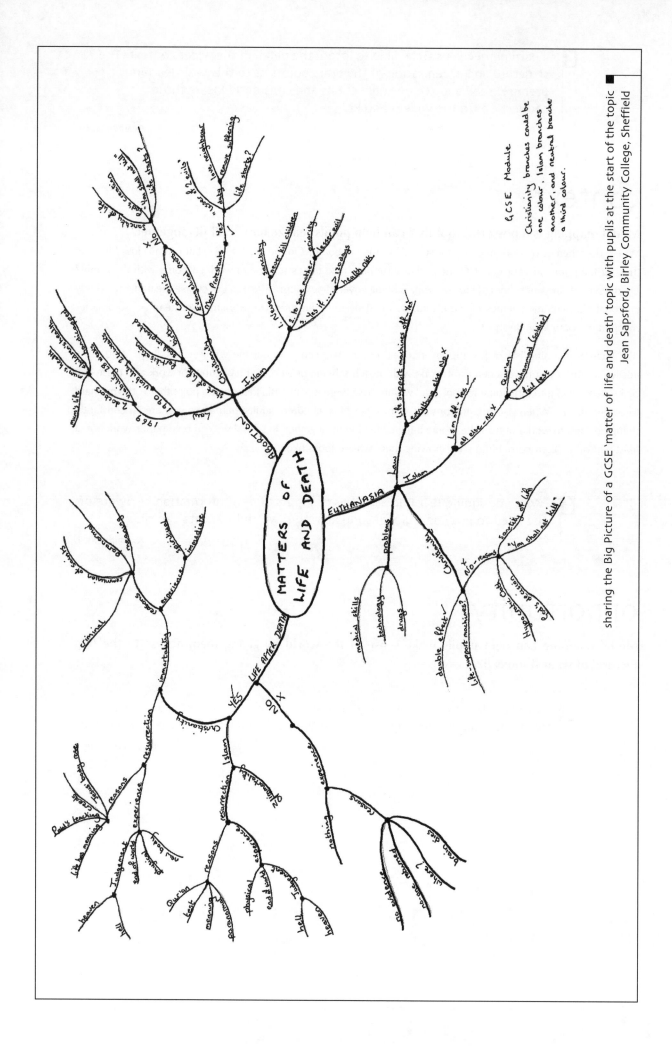

sharing the Big Picture of a GCSE 'matter of life and death' topic with pupils at the start of the topic
Jean Sapsford, Birley Community College, Sheffield

method

You can map the Big Picture in much the same way as you map anything else.

You can use any of the techniques set out in the How section of the book. Big Pictures you can map include:

- schemes of work

- the week

- the topic

- the lesson

- the curriculum

- collective views or opinions.

> 'Knowledge is organised into mental packages that are developed to provide clear interpretations and smooth expertise in familiar domains of experience.'
>
> *G. Claxton (1990)*

Big Picture maps should be produced because they are useful, not just for the sake of it.

Use your Big Picture model maps for a purpose. For example, you can use them: to include learning intentions in the Big Picture of a lesson (see chapter 2.6, Formative Assessment); as part of a revision strategy (see chapter 2.4, Total Recall); or to combine Big Picture thinking with collaborative practices (see chapter 2.7, Development Planning).

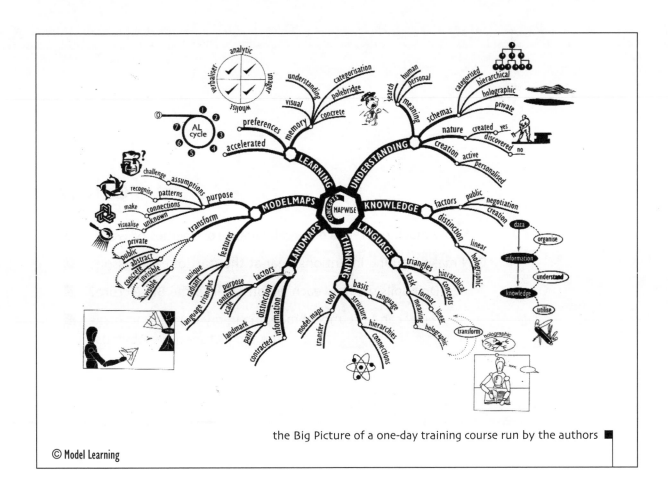

the Big Picture of a one-day training course run by the authors ■

case study

Our day out

I'm in school doing an extra day's supply. I'm taking a class lower down in the school on an educational visit. Although I know the pupils I am not familiar with the class routines. After registration I ask the pupils to gather their coats and make their way to the mini bus. I ask some of the ambulant pupils to support the classroom assistants with the non-ambulant pupils. Silence. They don't move. I repeat my request. No change. I'd been told they were looking forward to the visit. Why weren't they doing as I'd asked? One of the assistants is waving her hands around frantically, drawing lines in the air and one of the boys is standing in front of me holding a piece of card with the Makaton symbol for 'visit' on it. He points to the whiteboard and says 'map'. 'They want you to map out their day,' says one of the assistants.

Two of the pupils are now waiting to hand me new cards to go with the first that is now blue-tacked to the whiteboard. The first says (in words and Makaton) 'where', the second 'who'. Ten minutes later the pupils know not only where they are going, who is going with them and who they are going to meet there but also 'what' they will be doing and 'why' they are doing it. On the board is the Big Picture for our day.

I'd always used model mapping for giving my pupils access to the Big Picture of lesson content and forthcoming schemes of work because I know how much it helps pupils to see how all the bits fit together. This class had now taught me how much I took for granted their willingness to accept whatever was coming up next. Now I had found another way to use model mapping with pupils who have severe learning difficulties.

Carol Hariram, Class Teacher, Woodlands SLD School, Chelmsford, Essex

review

How much reference do I really make to schemes of work? ■

Do I make learning intentions clear at the start of each lesson? ■

Do pupils see how each lesson fits into the Big Picture? ■

How can I use model mapping in my teaching to make ■
the Big Picture more obvious?

■

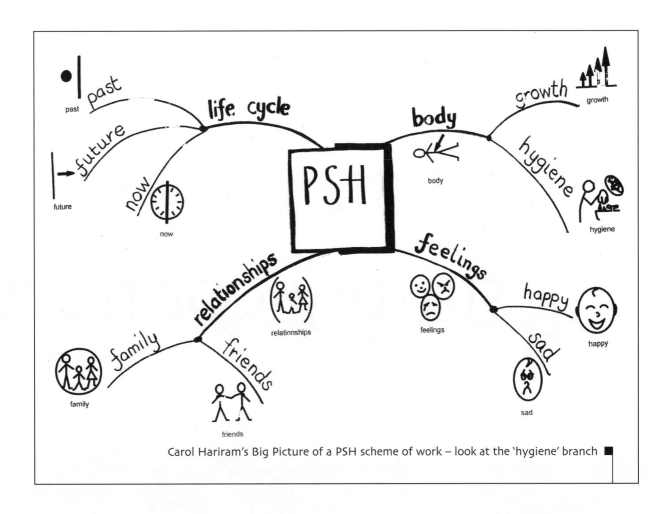

Carol Hariram's Big Picture of a PSH scheme of work – look at the 'hygiene' branch ■

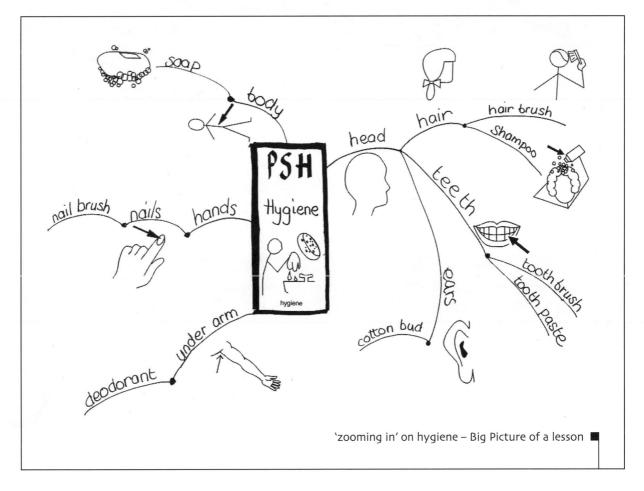

'zooming in' on hygiene – Big Picture of a lesson ■

■ What is meant by 'connecting learning'?

■ Why is this process so important?

■ How can we make such connections more likely?

■ Where do model maps come into this?

■ Can I think of some practical examples from my own teaching?

simply connect

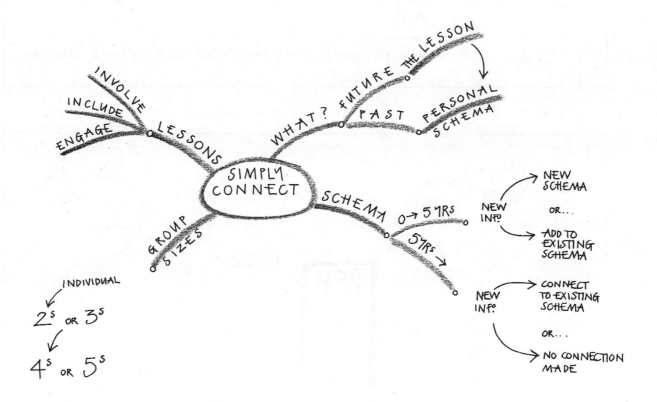

Intelligence is CO
and mapping is

context

It is important to connect the learner to prior learning and experience.
You want pupils to engage and participate in class. To do this they need to connect to whatever is being offered to them. For this to happen you need to connect to what they already know.

 'All learners, irrespective of learning style preferences create frameworks of understanding and interpretation inside their heads which psychologists call schemas. It would seem useful therefore to provide learners with a model to understand what this looks like and show them how to build these models.'

B. Tindall, author and trainer

Making connections is important because, according to the cognitive psychologists, from around five years old we stop forming brand new schemas in our minds. For something to make sense to us we have to connect it to something that is already familiar. One of the characteristics of the human mind is its desire for things to make sense.

If pupils do not connect new stimulus to something that is meaningful to them we can expect them to spend their time doing 'something else' rather than participate in our lessons. At best you can expect them to experience feelings of being lost or unconnected to what is going on.

You can use connect the learning exercises at various stages of the lesson and to help pupils stay on task throughout the lesson.
Within the classroom we may want to connect pupils' learning at the beginning of a topic. We can also use the same technique set out below to pull together and connect all the learning that has taken place at the end of a topic.

Model mapping provides a very straightforward way of connecting pupils to the learning intentions of the lesson. Do you have pupils who:

- shout out inaccurate answers to questions?

- opt out of question and answer sessions in class?

- dominate question and answer sessions in class?

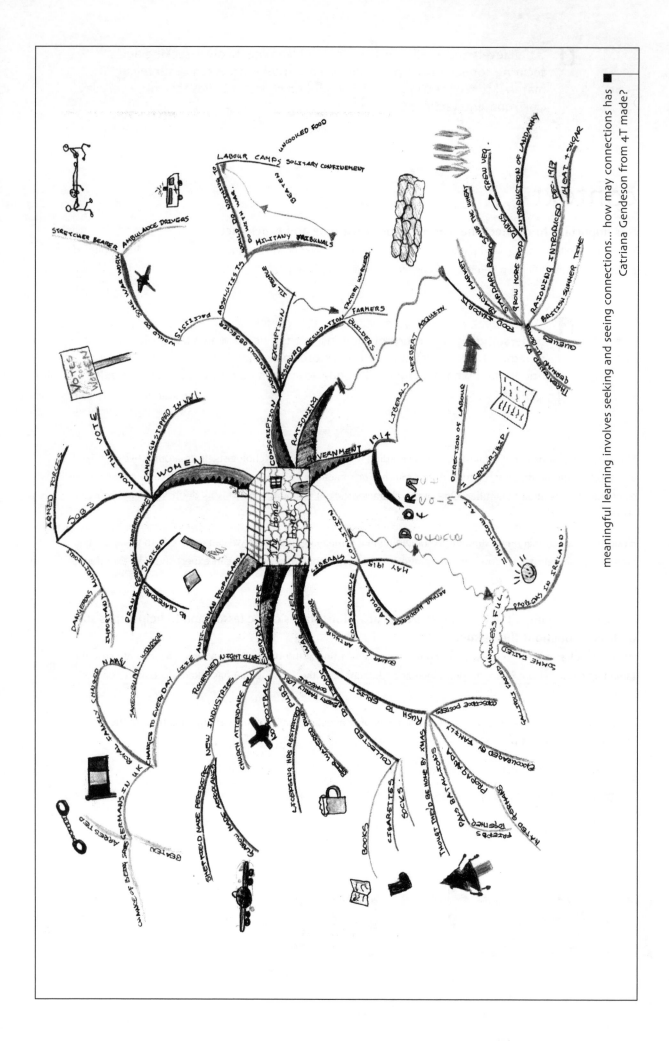

meaningful learning involves seeking and seeing connections… how may connections has Catriana Gendeson from 4T made?

Model mapping can help address each of the above scenarios by enabling all pupils to fully connect with what you are teaching.

opportunity

Model mapping supports you in setting up lessons that involve and include all learners.
Model maps ensure that all opinions and views can be collected and used in a very efficient and effective way. They provide a framework on which further learning or connections can be based.

 'If I had to reduce all educational psychology to just one principle, I would say this: the most important single factor influencing learning is what the learner already knows. Ascertain this and teach him accordingly.'

D. P. Ausubel (1968)

method

Pupils will be asked to work on their own, in twos (or threes) and perhaps also in groups of four or five.
The following sequence is not intended as a straightjacket. The same methods can be used either as a simple information gathering exercise or to promote deeper levels of questioning and communication within the group.

1 Write a key word or question on the whiteboard. For example you may ask pupils to think of the four most important things that they learned last lesson, or four things that they would like to find out or learn about the forthcoming topic. Ask pupils to spend 30 seconds to two minutes on their own, thinking and recording their thoughts and key words on paper.

2 Now ask pupils to spend one to three minutes sharing their thoughts and key words with a partner (or you could ask them to form groups of three). Ask them to add any new thoughts or ideas that emerge during their discussion. At this stage you may want simply to ask pupils to add new information to their own lists or you could ask them to prioritize or select information based on an additional question that you give. For example, using the questions suggested in stage 1 above, you might ask pupils to discuss the points made so far and agree the two most interesting / important / significant ones, then ask the pupils to make sure that they can justify their selection.

3 Now ask the pairs to team up into groups of four and repeat the process that they just did. Label each member of the group 1, 2, 3 or 4 and remind them that you will be asking different numbers to comment on different questions that you will be asking. You could consciously number the less able children 1s and the more able 4s. At this stage give the group four questions that they all need to be able to answer. None of them will know who will be asked to answer which question. Alternatively you may want to allocate questions to specific numbers and ask the groups to make sure that all of them can answer each question.

■ **Note**: For pupils not used to working with a partner you may decide not to move into larger groups. In this case, label the pairs A and B and tell them that As and Bs may be asked to feed back to you at the front of the room.

You can vary your approach depending on the skills and experience of your learners.

When the group work is complete you can take the feedback in from the groups. If this has been a simple information gathering exercise then you could follow route A below. If the exercise has involved pupils considering different questions at each stage then route B may be more suitable.

 'It is only through spontaneously making comparisons that children (or adults) can be modified through the arrival of new stimuli. They have to organise the new experiences according to how they can relate them to, and compare them with, what they already know and think'

Mike Lake, thinking skills guru, in private correspondence to the authors

- Route A: Collect all the key words into a list or around a central point. Ask the pupils if they can see connections between any of the words. You could put all of the words onto pieces of paper and then ask pupils to physically put them into groups before identifying the main categories of words. Sue Palmer wrote up the method in the *TES* three years ago – she called the article 'The art of DOM', DOM standing for Dump it, Organise it, Map it.

- Route B: As you take the feedback you may want to map it onto particular branches that you have already put in place. These branches may represent the different questions that you have asked the pupils to consider. Discuss with the pupils where best to put the information.

case study

Caribbean project

Before I started telling the class about the Caribbean I wanted to find out what they already knew about it. As individuals, then pairs and then groups of four the pupils gathered together their knowledge. We then dumped it all onto the whiteboard. Next we put the information into groups, established what the headings were and then created a model map of 'the Caribbean' on the board. As we looked at and discussed a set of A0 posters on the Caribbean, I asked the pupils to see if there was any information on the posters that was not already on our map and if so, to tell or show me where we needed to add it. Our map grew considerably as we went through the posters. I then put on a 20-minute video and asked the pupils to make a note of any stuff we had not already gathered. I deliberately placed the TV screen next to the map to help the pupils easily look from one to the other. After the video we discussed our notes and by this stage they were all eager to come up to the map and make the necessary amendments or changes.

The significant things for me were that this was a cover lesson, that these kids had moderate learning difficulties, and how amazing it was to literally see our understanding and knowledge of the Caribbean growing. I felt like a tourist guide which, when you think about it, I guess I was!

I. Harris, Year 5 Teacher (Moderate Learning Difficulties)

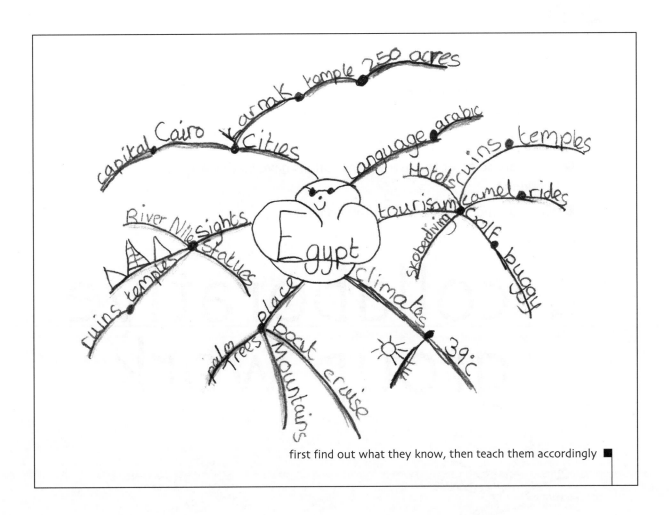

first find out what they know, then teach them accordingly ■

review

Do my pupils really engage and participate in class? ■

If not, could it be because they don't always see connections? ■

Do I start each lesson with a clear idea of what my pupils already know? ■

Can I use model mapping to illustrate connections and so aid understanding? ■

- What are the benefits of group learning as opposed to traditional 'talk and chalk' methods of teaching?
- Why do group activities sometimes 'go wrong'?
- What are some of the barriers that pupils have to this way of working?
- How can model maps help in this context?

collaborative group work

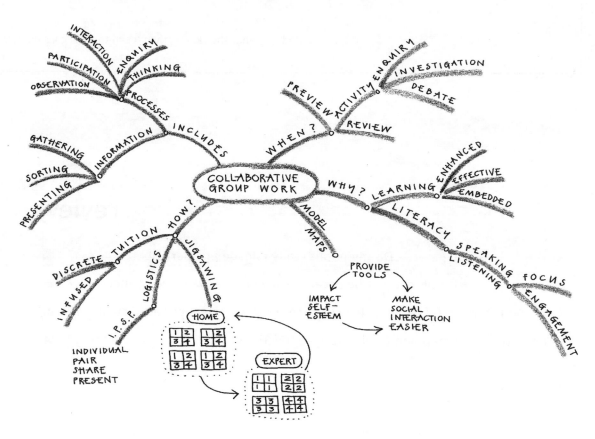

Working together a shared

> ❝ 'What matters most is the modelling process and not the model.'
>
> *M. Lissack and J. Roos (1999)*

> ❝ 'A map provides people with the means to share the perceptions of others.'
>
> *R. S. Wurman (1991)*

context

You can use model mapping with groups for a variety of purposes.

Model mapping can help you to find out what pupils know or what they can collectively remember, to develop understanding or to enquire into a problem.

Collaborative learning, when coupled with information processing, is one of the most effective models for learning.

We have spoken to hundreds of teachers about group work. Here is what they tell us: when it works, it makes teaching the best job in the world; when it doesn't work, it is hard to clear up the mess and it may seem tempting to revert back to a more comfortable mode of delivery – the whole-class approach. Instinctively you know that group work is the way forward but pressures (and instructions) from above provide you with all the justification you need to sell out and class teach. Hang in there! What is needed is a greater understanding of what is going on emotionally and cognitively within the group situation.

We believe that model mapping 'tools up' the learner cognitively.

With the right tools for the job the learner is less likely to enter the scenario feeling threatened. After all, how would you feel being plonked in a group, not knowing what to do and, more importantly, not having any of the necessary tools for the job? For how long would you sit still?

Putting attention on the map.

It is relatively easy for the teacher to pose a problem or set up an enquiry but simply setting up the enquiry may not create the conditions needed for it to succeed. Look at what learners need to bring to the enquiry and how model mapping can support them:

- The willingness and the skills and tools to be an observer and participant simultaneously. We find that the learner is far more likely to participate when there is a map to focus on and the learner knows how to use it.

- The willingness to enquire into the problem. This is made a lot easier if you can actually see what the problem is.

is easier with vision

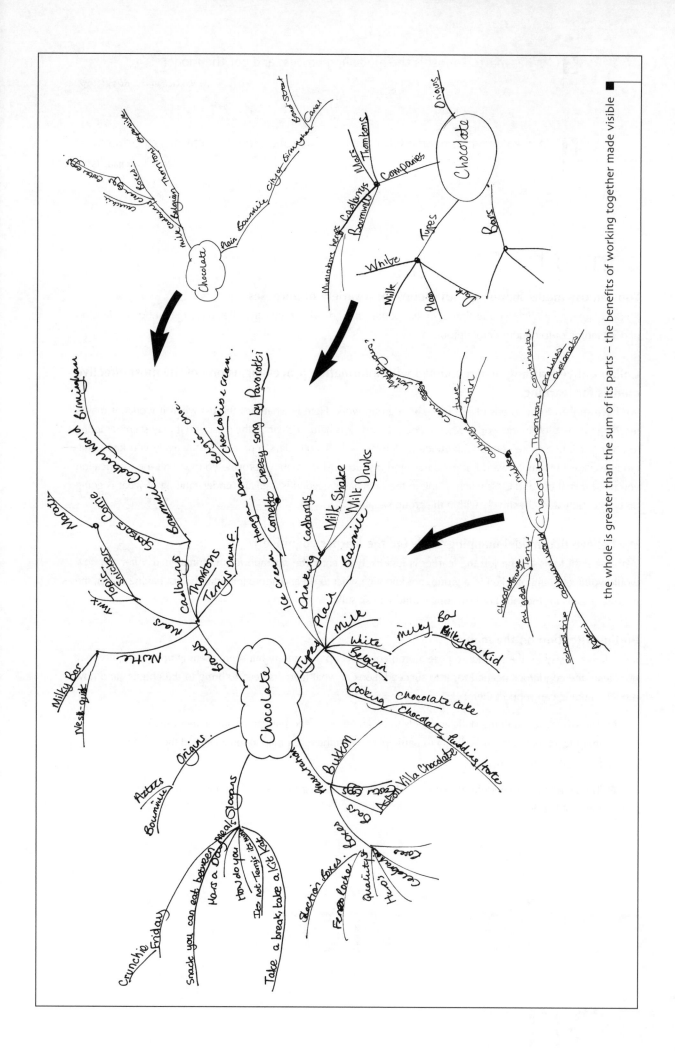

the whole is greater than the sum of its parts – the benefits of working together made visible ■

- The ability to interact with other pupils who may also be puzzled and feeling very self-aware. Using model maps, interaction is supported by the common focus.

- The willingness to consider and utilize conflicting and emerging viewpoints in a way that energizes the enquiry (and does not detract from it). Again, this is supported by having a map as a common focus.

> 'Tacit knowledge is knowledge that an individual is unable to articulate and thereby convert into information. Tacit knowledge is more useful to an organisational system if it can be transferred to others so they too can use it. Transfer of explicit knowledge is relatively straightforward. Transfer of tacit knowledge can be achieved...by first converting it into explicit knowledge and then sharing it.'
>
> *W. R. Bukowitz and R. L. Williams (1999)*

Model mapping provides learners with the skills they need to work effectively in groups or pairs.
Mapping ensures that the learners:

- have a method which they can use to collect ideas;

- have a method which they can use to identify links and associations and categorize information;

- have a method for setting out and sharing these associations as a whole;

- test out and discuss hypotheses, consider consequences and modify their frameworks of interpretation by literally altering the structure of the information in front of them.

At the same time the map helps ensure that pupils are being asked to give conscious attention to the experience, to formulate new ideas and integrate them with existing ones.

opportunity

Model mapping is a tool that overcomes the barriers to learning that can come up for pupils unfamiliar with group work practices.
Model mapping provides a very powerful tool for combining information processing with collaborative learning practices. The method set out below is only *one* way to do it. It is not *the* way to do it.

method

Build up from paired to larger group situations. Before engaging in a curriculum enquiry it is a good idea if pupils experience collaborative mapping on a general topic such as 'happiness' or 'food'. In other words, it is necessary for pupils to be taught specifically how to map and how to use maps in different ways.

1 Using a familiar topic, ask the pupils to individually map out everything they know about the subject. Allocate a specific amount of time for this (three to four minutes). You might want to break up the mapping by giving them a minute to swap ideas with their neighbour. Remind the pupils that icons, pictures and diagrams are welcome so long as they can explain what they mean.

> 'Without human contact, the human brain will not develop.'
>
> *D. Hamer and P. Copeland (1998)*

■ **Note**: There could be a considerable time lapse between stage 1 and 2 – for example, pupils may want to take their maps home with them to discuss and amend with their parents.

2 Next, ask pupils to form pairs (or threes). Allow pupils to find their own partner within given guidelines, for example, 'no one that has sat on your table today' and/or 'someone in the pair will be doing the writing' or, when they are more familiar with the routine, 'someone who you haven't worked or mapped with before'. Give the pairs a period of time to prepare a new map on the same topic. It must be a new map since this will involve more talking and thinking. After the allocated period of time, ask pairs (or threes) to stop and move to stage 3.

■ **Note**: You may want to stop after stage 2 and talk to the pupils about what it was like working together in this way. Try to steer them towards sharing what it was like rather than how they did it.

3 As stage 2, except this time pupils are going to work in fours to combine the maps. We have run sessions with pupils in larger groups but recommend group sizes of five maximum. You can help ensure the involvement of everyone in the group by allocating a number to each group member and informing them that everyone needs to be able to explain the map.

You can break this activity up by inviting one member of each group to visit the other groups to find out what they are doing and report back.

> 'Just as humans have the greatest ability of all the species to think, so they have the greatest ability to communicate thoughts.'
>
> *D. Hamer and P. Copeland (1998)*

The same three-stage format can be used to find out what pupils already know, to enquire into a specific problem or issue and to review a topic that has been completed.

case study

Inductive v. deductive learning – the test.

Picture this: two classes of students. Both are given pre-tests and final examinations. Both groups have a similar profile of students from lower socio-economic status (low SES) and higher socio-economic status (high SES).

Both groups are taught the same material and the same amount of time is allocated to cover it. Only the method of learning differs.

'When the goal of teaching becomes the achievement of shared meaning, a great deal of both teachers' and students' energy is released.'

J. D. Novak and D. B. Gowin (1984)

Group 1 is taught using traditional 'chalk and talk' methods with the teacher explaining things to pupils in a whole-class arrangement. The pupils are being asked to engage in 'deductive' learning practices; they are being asked to 'deduce' what the teacher is talking about.

Group 2 is taught using inductive group work activities. In other words the teacher does not tell the pupils what she knows, she facilitates by providing the pupils with the opportunities to work with the details and build up their own understanding. These activities take the form of investigations and exploration of content and materials. This is what inductive thinking is.

■ **Note**: When we explain, we are asking pupils to think deductively; when we set up investigations or exploratory lessons, we are asking them to think inductively.

Outcomes:

- ■ The pre-test scores of the low SES students in both groups were significantly lower than those of the high SES students.

- ■ The low SES students in Group 2 achieved average gains nearly two and a half times higher than their peers in Group 1.

- ■ All the low SES students in Group 2 exceeded the scores of the high SES students in Group 1.

- ■ The high SES students in Group 2 also outscored the high SES students in group 1.

'The more intensely cooperative the environment, the greater the effects; the more complex the outcomes (i.e. higher order processing of information, problem solving), the greater the effects. The cooperative environment engendered by these models has had substantial effects on the cooperative behaviour of students, on increasing feelings of empathy towards others, on reducing inter-group tensions…, and on building positive feelings towards others, including those from ethnic groups.'

Case study and quote taken from B. Joyce, E. Calhoun and D. Hopkins (2000)

case study

Mastering meaningful texts through mapping.

In this case study, concentrating on three examples of very powerful literary model maps, I describe how model mapping has been very successfully integrated as a key learning strategy across the Secondary English Curriculum in an English Department at a selective boys' school in Essex. Maps of various kinds have greatly assisted our very post-modern Essex boys (and girls) to encounter enjoyably some very significant pre-modern spiritualities and to undertake some advanced (deconstructive but creative) interpreting of A Level, GCSE and Key Stage Three literary texts.

In their recent report of the school, OFSTED stated that 'highly effective teaching of independent thinking skills... promotes confidence and originality in students' work' and that 'students are taught...to consider multiple viewpoints and to adopt them tentatively before arriving at firmer personal conclusions... this greatly extends their powers of concentration and imagination'. Mapping, as a learning strategy or 'thinking skill', was central to this success and to these OFSTED judgements. All of this happened within the context of the school's having promoted a variety of 'learning how to learn' strategies through whole-school INSET over the last several years. Maps have also helped greatly with public examination criteria-related formative assessment.

My class of A2 (final year A Level) students followed the learning strategies outlined here, with one group creating and presenting maps at key points in the following process:

1. Internet research in groups

2. Selection of materials

3. Group map design

4. Group presentations of maps, involving active note making and question-and-answer sessions

5. Written evaluations of other maps

6. Use of mapped interpretations in essays

7. Revision for modular examination paper.

The map itself (originally poster-size) imaginatively displayed the range of possible lines of interpretation for *The Rime of the Ancient Mariner* by Coleridge: the 'Romantic', the 'Freudian', the 'political', the 'biographical', the 'Christian', the 'spiritual-allegorical' and the 'psychological'. Student-designed mini-icons, internet thumbnails, key words and phrases and very short 'Grade A' comments all combined fluently with relevant short quotations from the poem itself. I felt, on reflection, that there could have been no better strategy to open the minds of my students to the rich variety of possible interpretations of the poem than the use of the appropriately divergent model map. My students' insights were of the highest quality, enthusiastically expressed via pole-bridging (even with the OFSTED Inspector observing) – and were, above all, genuinely exploratory. The use of the map as the critical strategy seemed even more fully vindicated when ten out of 14 students gained grade As for the relevant A2 modular examination in January 2002.

If the use of maps can enhance the quality of oral presentations at A level, the scope for improving speaking and listening work in GCSE English is even more significant. Speaking and listening tasks add up to 20 per cent of the overall GCSE grade. We have found the map to be an invaluable tool – quite simply our GCSE English 1 activities have been transformed and renewed through their use. Shown opposite is Rajeeb Dey's (Year 10) presentation of aspects of Tennyson's narrative poem *Morte d'Arthur*. Rajeeb's use of the literature exam criteria-related big ideas 'characterization', 'themes', 'language' and 'setting' meant that his speaking and listening presentation also served as a formative assessment tool, enabling him to organize a later essay on the poem using these same criteria-related areas.

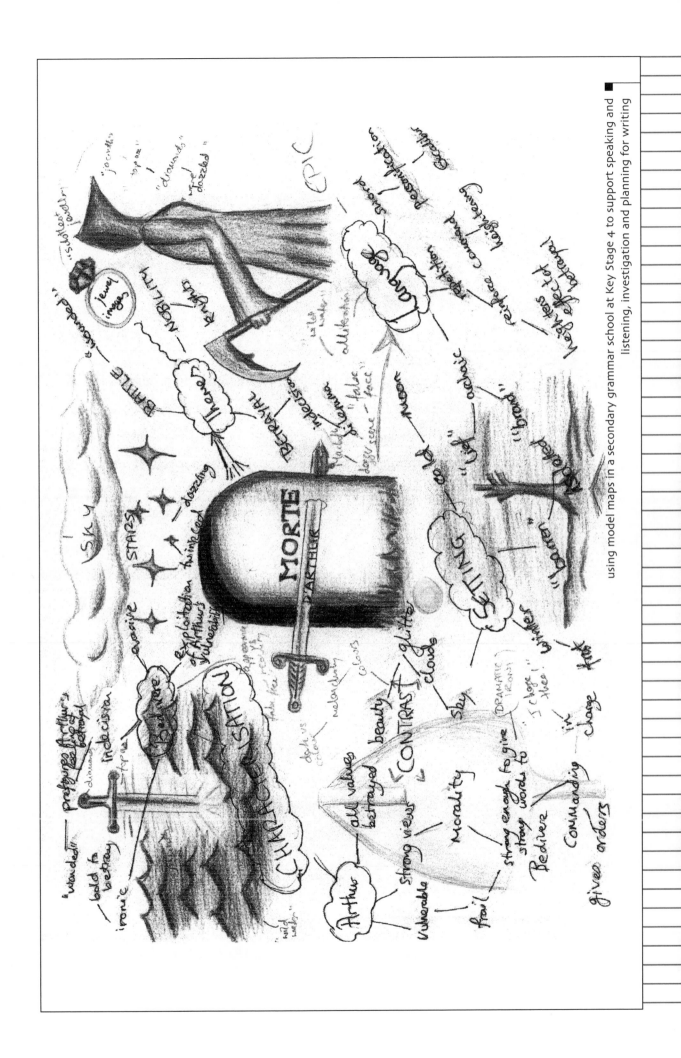

At Key Stage 3 we have recently incorporated mapping into our teaching of Shakespeare. The big ideas of 'theme', 'character', 'plot' and 'language' in the Year 7 map from *The Tempest* (shown opposite) deliberately foreshadow GCSE criteria. Much enjoyment has been had by these 11–12-year-old pupils composing the sometimes comic icons with, for instance, the Harry Potter inspired wizard's hat, designed to help classmates associate J. K. Rowling's hero with Shakespeare's Prospero.

David Greenwood, English Teacher, King Edward VI Grammar School, Chelmsford, Essex

review

How often do my pupils do group work? ■

Do I know how to make collaborative activities a success? ■

Can I identify the reasons why some pupils find group work difficult? ■

Do I understand the difference between deductive and inductive learning? ■

Could I introduce model mapping to help make the learning ■
more inductive and collaborative?

■

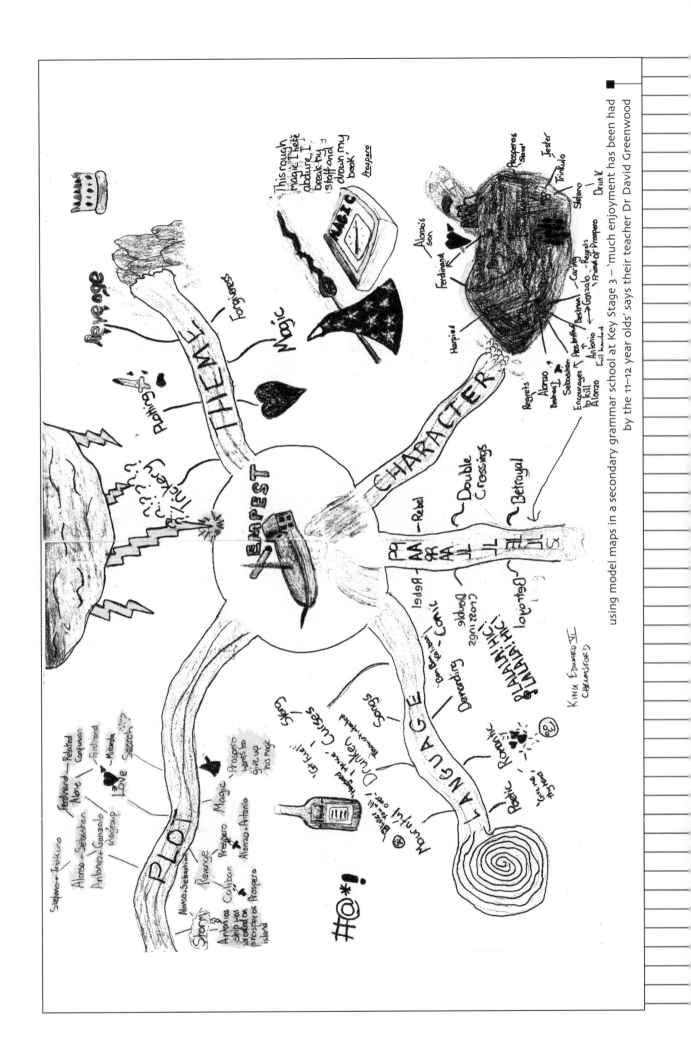

using model maps in a secondary grammar school at Key Stage 3 – 'much enjoyment has been had by the 11–12 year olds' says their teacher Dr David Greenwood

- What makes recall more likely?
- How can recall become total?
- What is meant by pole-bridging?
- Why is model mapping such a power tool for aiding recall?

total recall

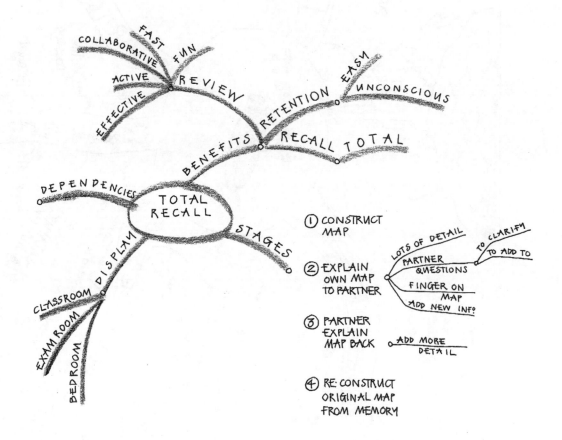

Memory is based on **u** and mapping

context

Pupils need to remember what they learn and they need to be able to recall it.

They need to do this, not just for examinations and tests, but for everyday situations. We remember things that have become meaningful for us. We also remember things that we understand and that have become 'memorable' to us in some way.

Model mapping provides you with a method that can make recall total.

Chapter 2.2, Simply Connect, revealed one set of strategies that you can use to review the work covered with pupils. This chapter reveals how you can teach pupils to use model mapping to help them recall information totally.

opportunity

Model mapping offers you the opportunity to make revision a fun, full and effective activity in school.

It offers an opportunity to take the strain out of revision, retention and recall. It provides a practical methodology that supports and encourages pupils to work collaboratively on revision tasks in pairs and groups.

method

There are three criteria that need to be fulfilled if recall is to be total.

Mapping for total recall works best when learners:

1 are experienced at mapping;

2 are the authors of their own maps;

3 work collaboratively with others.

In this exercise, pupils are asked to pole-bridge a map, that is, explain a map to a partner or group so that the explainer has the opportunity to clarify and deepen their own understanding through an interactive dialogue with a partner. The learner does not need to know that one of the intentions is that she will be able to recall it. For the

nderstanding,
makes it visible

exercise to be most effective it is helpful if the pupils are already experienced at talking about and explaining their maps to others. Once they are practised at this they will not question why they are being asked to do it.

1   Begin by producing maps of the content that has been covered so far and is to be revised so that the learners have in front of them a model of their understanding as it stands at the moment. You could prepare these maps yourself, but in our view pupils benefit far more if they are directly and actively involved in the production of the maps that they are going to learn. They should ideally be the authors of their own individual maps.

2   Ask pairs to explain their maps to each other. This can work using maps authored by others (if the pupils were party to their production and if they understand them) but, as stage 1 sets out, we recommend pupils have their own maps.

This stage is done in pairs although threes and fours can work, time permitting. The pupils take it in turns to explain their maps to each other. The partner (or group) *must* be able to see the map clearly. If the partner does not understand anything that the explainer is saying, he stops the explainer and seeks clarification, stating exactly where (pointing to the map) he did not understand. The explainer should go into lots of detail about his map. He always has his finger (not a pen or pencil) on the part of the map that he is talking about. He can follow branches outwards, or he can jump around from one branch to the next (depending on where the conversation goes) but wherever the conversation leads, the finger follows… All the time the explainer is heightening his visual awareness of his map by noticing the size of print and the bits he has rubbed out; any diagrams or pictures become alive for him.

During the course of the conversation the explainer may want to add something to his map. This may be because his partner has asked a question that cannot be answered from the information contained within the map. It may be that during the explanation he realized something for himself. When this happens, the explainer may want to add to or delete parts of his map (if so, remind him to put the pen down afterwards and carry on explaining using his finger).

If some pairs finish within the time allocated, ask the pupil who was listening to explain the map back to the original explainer. This allows the explainer to hear how effective his explanation was. He can even ask the new explainer questions about his own map. (You may want to use this as an additional exercise.)

Make sure that both (or all) pupils have enough time to explain their maps to each other.

3   Now take the maps away. After a break away from them, you are going to ask the pupils to redraw the maps they explained from memory. You could take their maps in and set this part of the exercise as homework or you may want to ask pupils to do this after break or after lunch. Pupils may only need to do this recall exercise once to realize how effective it is. When pupils really engage in the explanation and listening part of this exercise the recall is truly amazing. Pupils will redraw virtual photocopies of the maps they have explained. It really is total recall – as the following case study testifies.

Ideally, pupils will be familiar with the benefits of the exercise before they use it for revision for exams. Combine this with the exercises set out in chapter 2.3, Collaborative Group Work and chapter 2.2, Simply Connect and you have a very powerful technique for pupils to use in the weeks leading up to their tests.

■ **Top tip**

Involve parents and guardians by asking them to listen to their son or daughter explaining their maps.

case study

Recalling history.

Having attended the MapWise course I was impressed by the practical applications we experienced and was keen to try them out – especially the pole-bridging. The topic (the Union Act of 1707) had already been taught but the pupils had found it difficult to understand the relationship between the political and economic causes. I gave each pupil a copy of my map that set out the areas that I wanted to explain and therefore wanted them to understand. I told them that, by the time we had finished, they would be able to redraw the map and explain it to someone else without looking at the original. The level of disbelief was high. After the general murmuring of 'she's finally lost it' died down I talked through the map. I then asked the students to put their fingers on their own copies of the map and move them along the lines as I explained things to them. As they had generally accepted that I had 'lost it' they played along, happy in the knowledge that it wouldn't work.

Then I asked them in pairs to talk and walk (with their finger) through the map to each other – turning off my OHP copy of the map so that they had to concentrate on the paper in front of them. I walked around the classroom and had to take one pen away. From the course I knew it was important that they used their finger! They now *knew* I had gone mad. I then collected in their maps, gave them a blank sheet and asked them to redraw the map. No one spoke as they quickly and diligently redrew the map. Having asked them to swap maps with the person sitting next to them, I switched my OHP back on.

The response was less one of incredulous disbelief and more one of amazement. Jaws dropped, groups that it can be very hard to impress were dumbfounded. Their recall was perfect. The first thing I did at the beginning of the next lesson was to ask them to redraw again. Again perfect. Their results in the end of year tests were consistently higher than the previous year's.

Since this initial trial I have continued to use mapping. Some pupils have asked me if it is easier to get a high level in history than in other subjects – our levels being that much higher.

Ruth Rogers, Head of History, Danley Middle School, Maidstone, Kent

case study

Mapping to revise.

I introduced model mapping to one 15-year-old girl called Laura and encouraged her to use this method to help her revise. I was genuinely surprised by her almost immediate degree of involvement with the mapping process. Laura's map notes for a biology exam can be seen on the following page. In order to produce this map she worked between textbooks and jotters and a computer mapping program. She subsequently added colour to the main branches of her model map. Laura also used this method to help her with other exams.

Revision maps can also be re-created in exams to serve as the basis for essay writing, and Laura used them in this way too. In another exam a hearing impaired boy had received some signing support at the start of the exam when the various instructions are issued. His support teacher had been really worried about whether or not he would cope with the exam itself but told me later that, as soon as she had seen him mapping out his plan for the first piece of writing, she knew he was going to be okay.

Gerry Dolan, SENCO, Dingwall Academy, Scotland

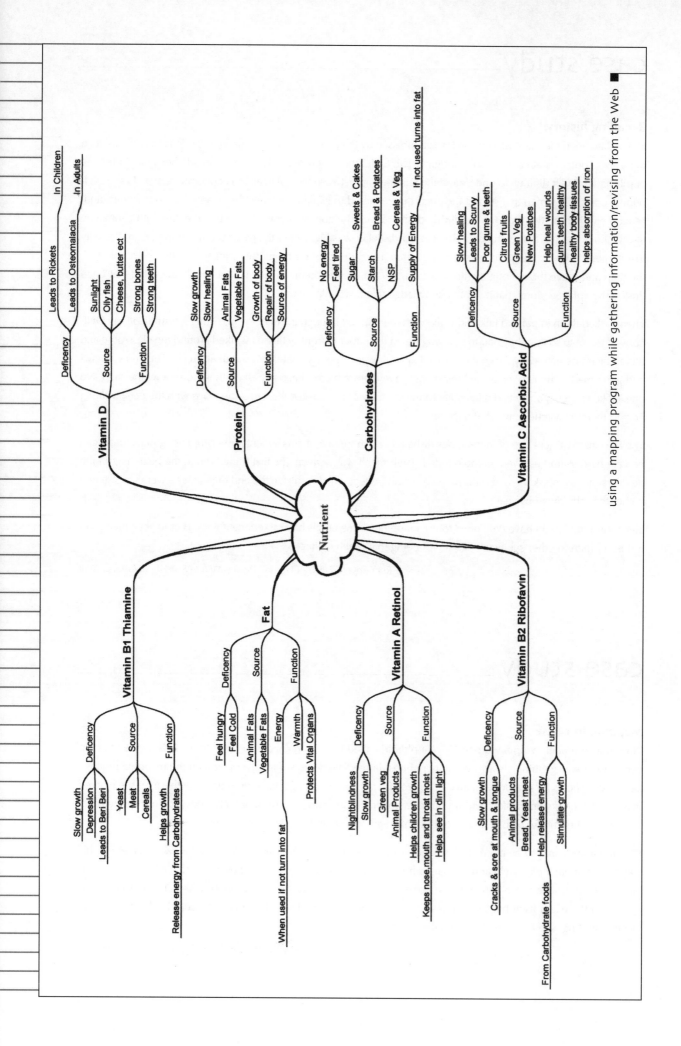

using a mapping program while gathering information/revising from the Web

case study

Remembering language techniques.

We used model maps to remember language techniques for SATs examinations. The map shown below was constructed collaboratively in class, pooling our knowledge. All pupils contributed, coming up to the board and justifying the placement of each stem as part of the hierarchy. Pupils used the map in their SATs practices and reproduced it from memory each time on their planning page. They all claim it gave them great confidence when faced with the dreaded language question, which carries the marks. Their results seem to bear out their conviction.

Val Hill, Advanced Skills Teacher, Stewards School, Harlow, Essex

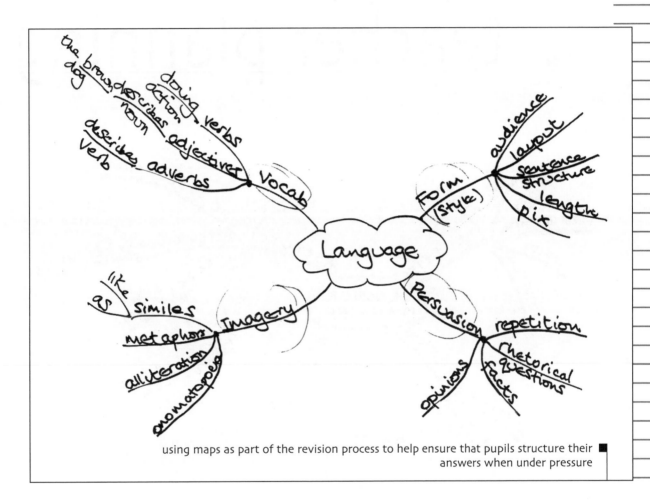

using maps as part of the revision process to help ensure that pupils structure their
answers when under pressure

review

Can I see ways to use the techniques outlined in this chapter as part
of review / revision work in my classroom?

How can I build in more opportunities for speaking and listening in my classroom?

Do I give pupils the opportunity to explain their work to others?

■ How can planning be made more useful?

■ Why does model mapping make planning more flexible and creative?

■ Can mapped plans be multifunctional?

■ Can mapped plans be used as part of the lesson's delivery?

teacher planning

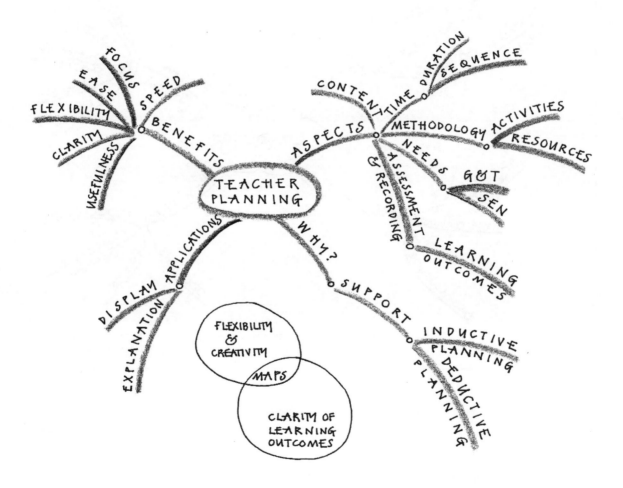

Plans that are map
pupils what

context

You are asked to think about and plan carefully what you are going to teach in the classroom.
You have to consider aspects such as content, methodology, activities and resources, time and sequencing of task, the needs of individuals and of the class, assessment and recording. This can understandably seem an arduous task. Some of us may find it hard to think about what to write in the boxes.

opportunity

Model mapping provides an opportunity for your planning to be more flexible, useful and creative.
Model maps can support you in identifying and being clear about what your learning intentions are – they support you in working out what to do and in being clear about why you are doing it.

Using model maps as a planning method, you are simultaneously producing teaching resources and/or display posters (see chapter 2.8, Displays).

Plans produced in model map form can therefore become an integral part of the lesson's delivery. They can also be used for, and provide a record of, ongoing self-assessment. Schools can agree to use model mapping as the official school documentation or the information in them may be transferred onto school planning templates. In our experience, school inspectors have no problem accepting model maps as planning documents. In both instances there is the opportunity to make planning easier and to save considerable amounts of time.

'I hated using formal lesson planning templates and used to really struggle working out what to put in the boxes. If I'm honest I'd have to admit that I sometimes made stuff up just to fill in the bloomin' things. Often my lessons would have very little to do with my planning. Now planning is easier and, more importantly, I find it useful. It informs my teaching, I am more confident with my materials and more flexible in my approach.'

Carol Hariram, Teacher, Woodlands SLD School, Chelmsford, Essex

ped show you mean

method

Model maps help you successfully combine a clear idea of learning outcomes with a creative approach to delivery.

Some of you may like to plan in an inductive way and go through the dump it, organize it, map it (DOM) routine. This is a good method to use if you are not clear initially what the learning intentions are. Others of you may be clear about what the main branches of your model map will be and will be happy to map from the centre outwards. Certainly, once you have mapped a few lessons or schemes of work using the DOM method, you will have identified these main headings. Once you have your main headings, mapping a lesson or a scheme of work is no different from mapping anything else. Using planning templates involves selecting and arranging all your thoughts in your head and then putting the finished product onto paper. By using model mapping you are putting your thoughts onto paper first and connections and links literally show up in front of you. (Mapping techniques are explained fully in the How section of the book.)

> '…maintain an open window on your own thinking processes. Reveal— vocalise—your own thinking…'
>
> *G. A. Woditsch (1991)*

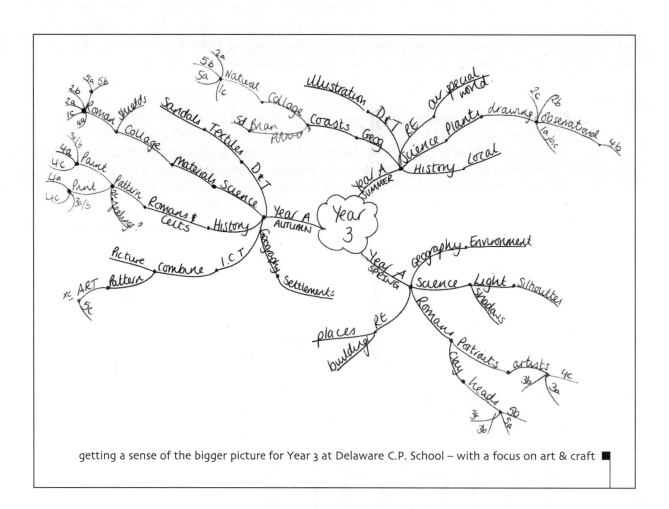

getting a sense of the bigger picture for Year 3 at Delaware C.P. School – with a focus on art & craft ∎

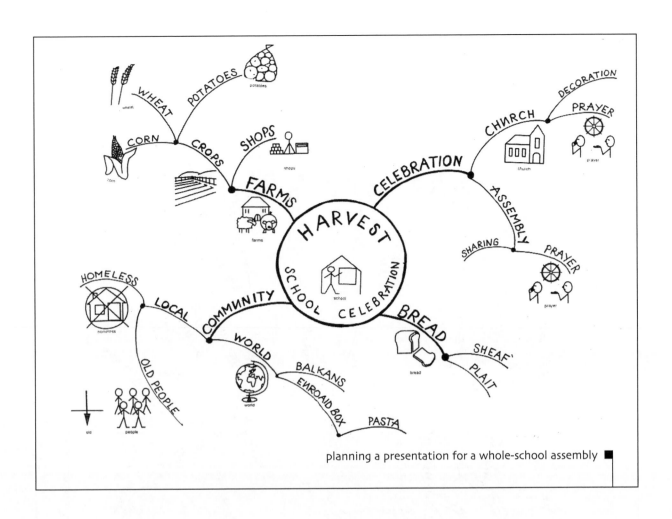

planning a presentation for a whole-school assembly ■

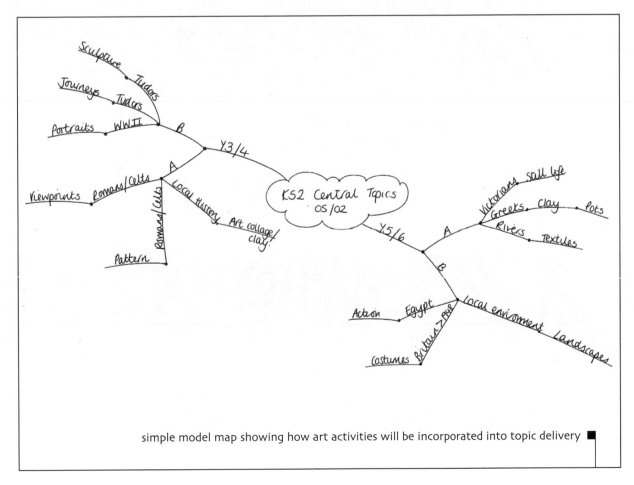

simple model map showing how art activities will be incorporated into topic delivery ■

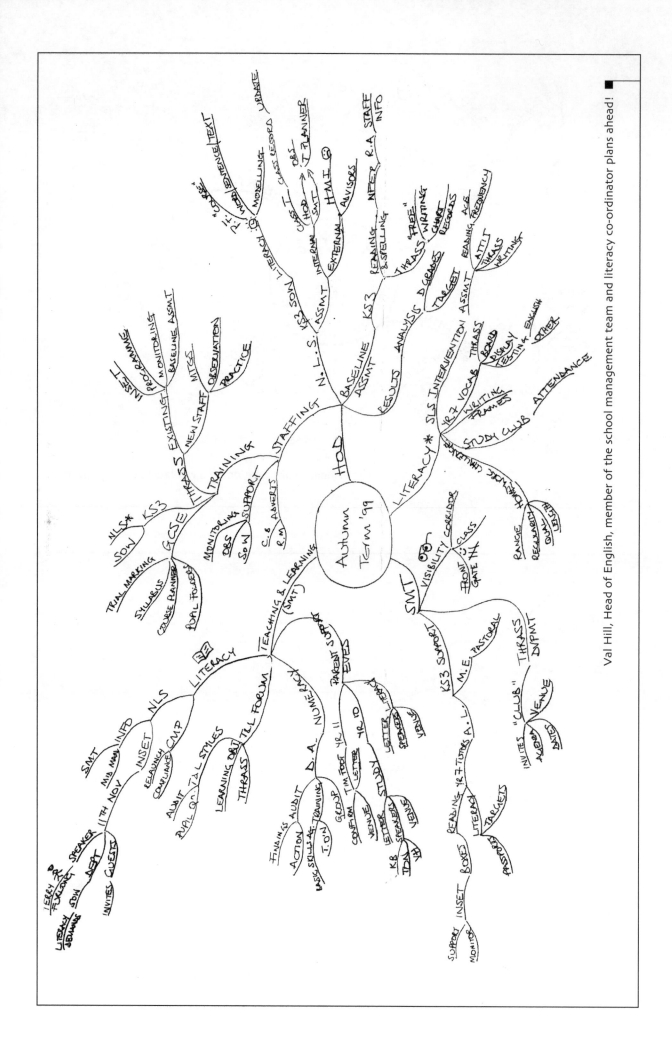

Val Hill, Head of English, member of the school management team and literacy co-ordinator plans ahead!

review

Do I enjoy planning? Does it seem like a useful activity? ■

Am I always clear about my ideas and learning intentions? ■

Does my teaching link directly to my lesson plans? ■

Could I use model mapping to ensure that my planning relates
more to my day-to-day teaching? ■

- How can model mapping help me give more immediate and useful feedback?

- How can model mapping help with evaluation and target setting?

- What are the benefits to teachers and learners of using model mapping to monitor pupils' progress?

- How can model maps help pupils to demonstrate their understanding?

formative assessment

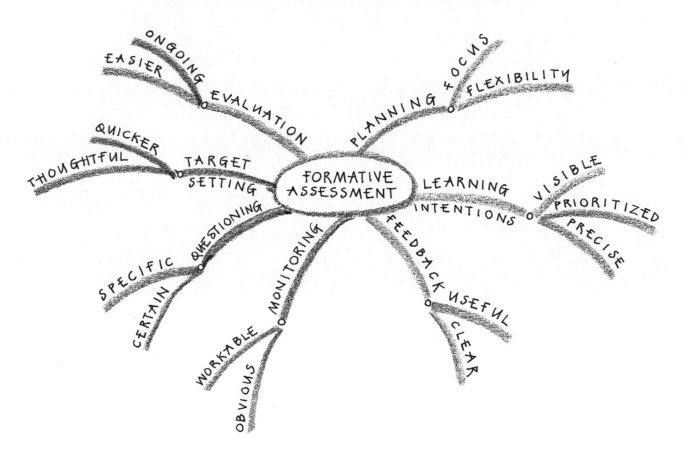

Show what they kn
see what

context

Formative assessment is not just about marking pupils' work.

Formative assessment concerns:

- planning

- the setting and sharing of learning intentions

- helping pupils to evaluate their own work

- target setting

- feedback

- questioning

- monitoring.

opportunities

Model mapping offers practical and time saving support in many areas of formative assessment.

In areas of the curriculum where pupils would normally be required to set out their understanding through linear text (with or without pictures and diagrams), mapping can offer considerable support to the teacher and learner.

- Planning

  Model mapping offers a practical way to make teacher planning quicker and easier. More importantly, it helps ensure that planning is focused on what is to be learned in addition to how it is to be delivered. (See chapter 2.5, Teacher Planning.)

- Setting and sharing learning intentions

  Model mapping offers the opportunity for learning intentions to be set inside the bigger picture, which contains the more specific issues of 'how'?, 'why'? and 'who'?

- Target setting

  Model mapping provides an easy way for pupils to see all of their own personal targets on one page and for them to complete self-evaluation exercises.

ow and
they mean

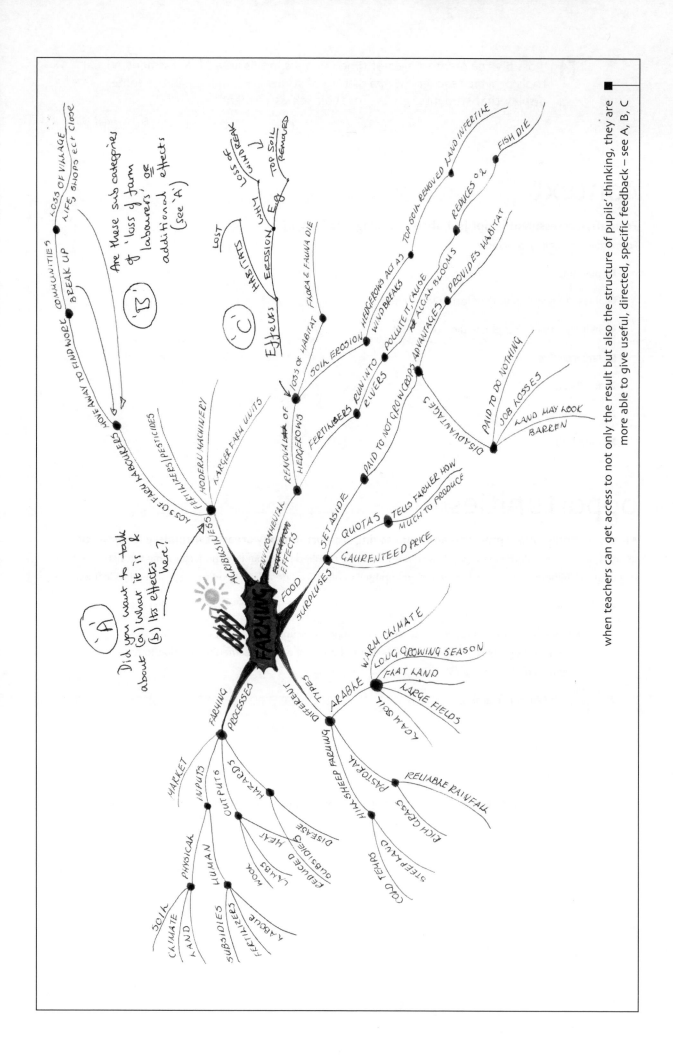

when teachers can get access to not only the result but also the structure of pupils' thinking, they are more able to give useful, directed, specific feedback – see A, B, C

■ Feedback

When pupils use mapping as a means of demonstrating their understanding, teachers can see how they have organized the information and can give clear, precise feedback on it.

■ Questioning

When you use model maps as part of their explanation or instruction, pupils are, of course, far more likely to see and understand what you are talking about and are therefore far more likely to ask you questions that clarify and further their own understanding. When pupils use maps to demonstrate their understanding it is far easier for you to give them specific feedback and ask them questions that will deepen their understanding.

■ Monitoring

Both you and your pupils can use model mapping to support monitoring of pupil progress. An inability to demonstrate understanding in a linear (spoken or written) way does not mean that a pupil has not understood. No longer hindered by having to turn his understanding into linear text, the pupil is more likely to show you what he knows and understands. For your part, it takes less time to appraise understanding and your monitoring of progress is likely to be more accurate. The pupil is also far more likely to succeed in linear writing and speaking with the model map in front of him. (See chapter 2.11, Planning for Writing.)

method

■ Planning

See chapter 2.5, Teacher Planning for ideas on how to use model mapping in your planning.

■ Setting and sharing learning intentions

The method is best illustrated by the case study on page 74.

■ Helping pupils to evaluate their own work

Assuming the pupil has produced a map as a representation of her understanding, you have a model of her thinking in front of you. Ask her to explain her map. As she does this, ask questions that help her evaluate the work.

■ Target setting

Target setting may arise as a result of the self-evaluation process described above. In all cases targets set should be negotiated with, and agreed with, pupils. Subject-specific and cross-curricular targets can all be displayed and set on a single map. Comments relating to the targets can be added as pupils go through the week. The collection of these target sheets provides an easy way of monitoring pupil progress.

Aspirational wall maps can be set up. Pupils can use these to display their individual targets. Personally writing down targets and displaying them where others can see them helps pupils own and be responsible for their achievement.

■ Feedback and questions

Feedback should be specific and useful. Teachers and learners can provide very focused feedback to each other by using maps to enhance the communication between them. When teachers or learners use maps to help them explain something, the listener's short-term memory is freed up from having to try and capture, hold and think about, what is being said (see chapter 1.8, Memory and Mapping). The map does the holding job for the listeners, who are subsequently freed up to think about what they are listening to. The listeners can see where things are going and they can see where things are coming from. They can see how it all fits together. Feedback and questions can now be very precise and extremely useful to both the teacher and the learner.

> 'My students will happily produce a map of their understanding for me. I can see what they have understood and I am able to give them specific, useful feedback in a fraction of the time. Boys will willingly redraft. The time spent learning to use the tool has been paid back with lots of interest!'
>
> *Val Hill, Advanced Skills Teacher, Stewards School, Harlow, Essex*

■ Monitoring

You can now see that pupils who can map are more likely to be able to give you an accurate representation of what they have understood. (Remember an inability to explain through linear text or speech does not mean the pupil has not understood – only that they are unable to turn their understanding into written text or speech.) Mapping can therefore not only increase monitoring effectiveness, it can also make it easier and faster for you since you no longer have to go wading through the text to see evidence of pupils' understanding.

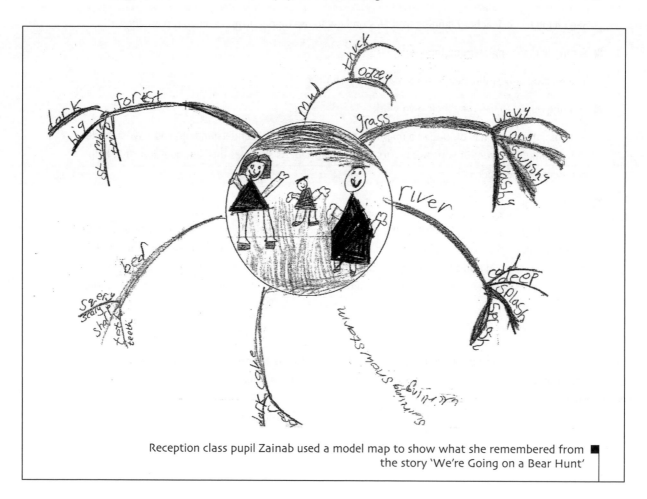

Reception class pupil Zainab used a model map to show what she remembered from the story 'We're Going on a Bear Hunt'

case study

Animal Farm

Model mapping is a fantastic aid to communication both within group situations and between teacher and learners. The *Animal Farm* maps below and over the page were produced during a lesson when I was being observed as part of an AST (advanced skills teacher) assessment. The structure of the map guided the discussions between learners and between them and myself as I circulated the pairs who were sharing maps with each other. The resulting detail that was added as a result of these discussions was phenomenal. Not only detail but depth.

Val Hill, Advanced Skills Teacher, Stewards School, Harlow, Essex

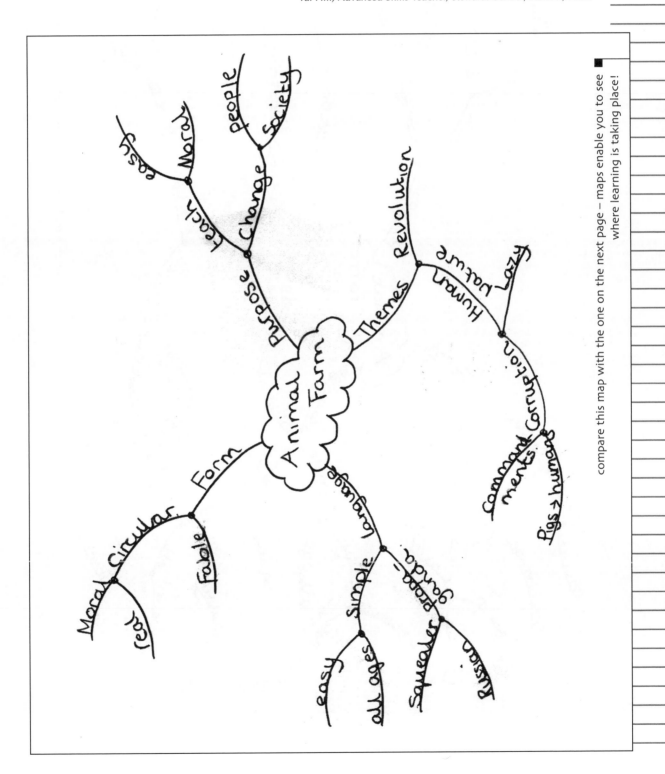

compare this map with the one on the next page – maps enable you to see where learning is taking place!

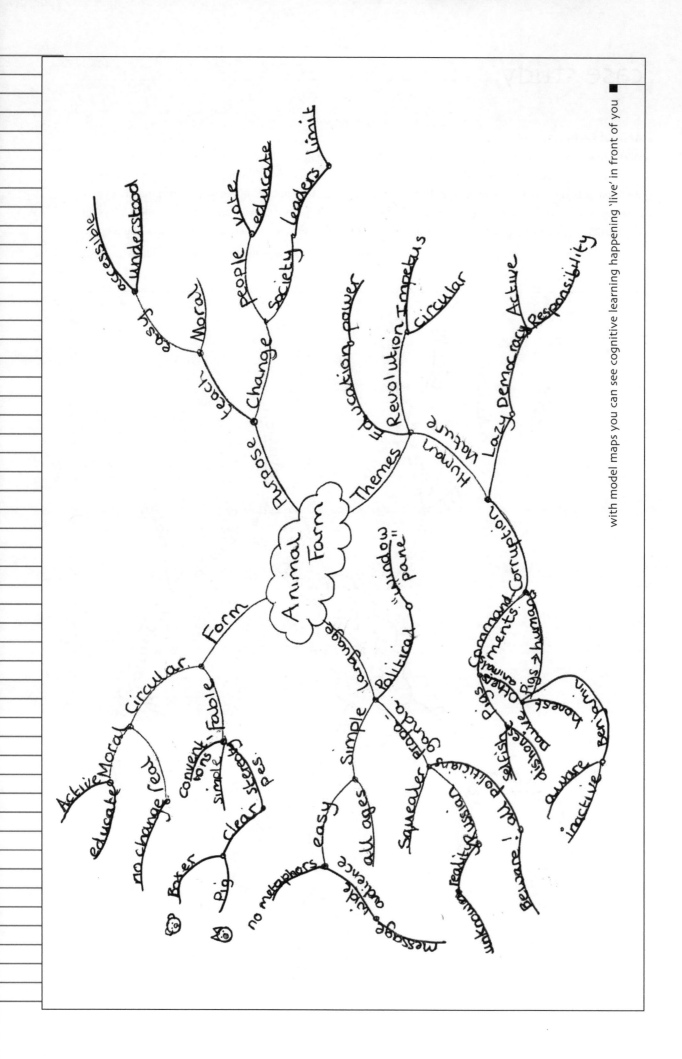

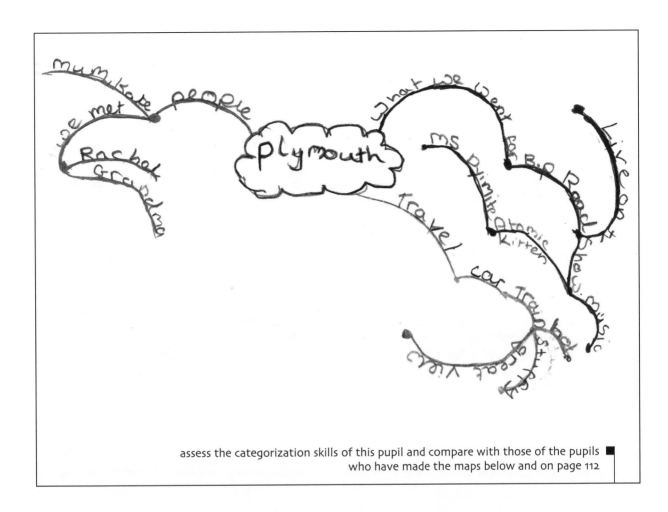

assess the categorization skills of this pupil and compare with those of the pupils ■
who have made the maps below and on page 112

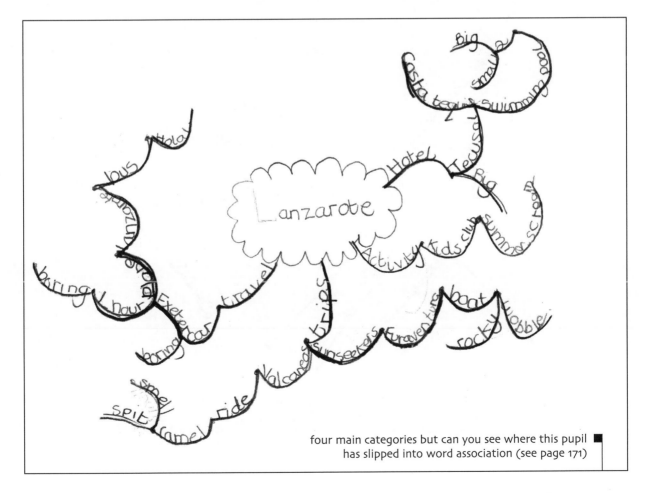

four main categories but can you see where this pupil ■
has slipped into word association (see page 171)

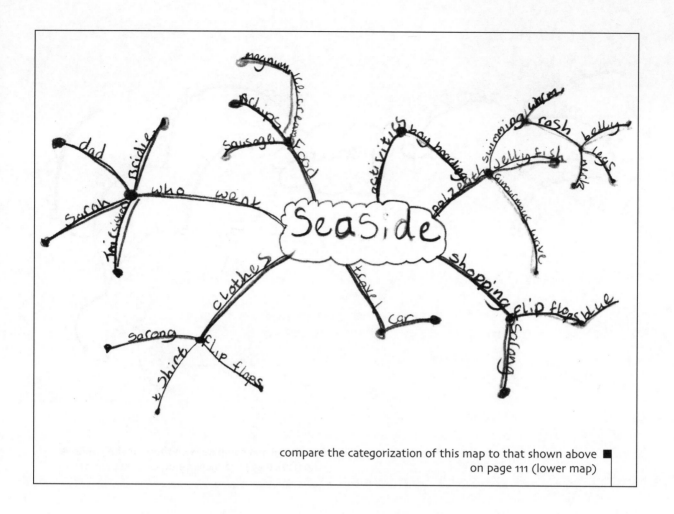

compare the categorization of this map to that shown above ■
on page 111 (lower map)

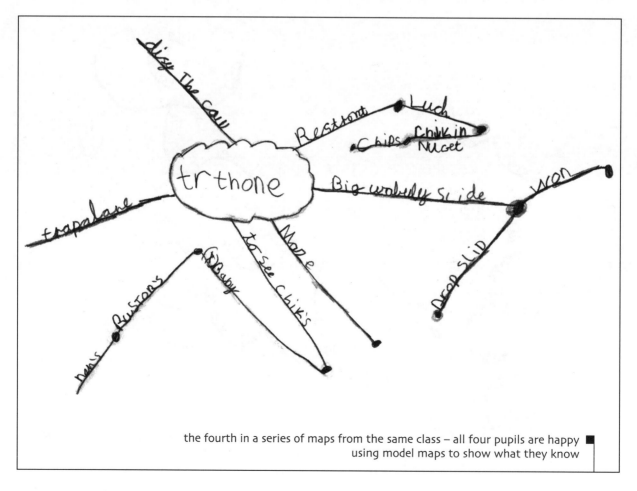

the fourth in a series of maps from the same class – all four pupils are happy ■
using model maps to show what they know

review

What are my current methods of formative assessment? ■

Do they provide a clear and accurate picture of attainment? ■

Are learners able to easily demonstrate their understanding? ■

Can model mapping make formative assessment a more beneficial
exercise for my pupils and me? ■

■

■ How often do I look at my development plan? Do I know what's on it?

■ How can development plans be made more useful and accessible?

■ How can the planning process be more inclusive?

■ Where in this process can model mapping be helpful?

■ What are the benefits of this method of planning?

development planning

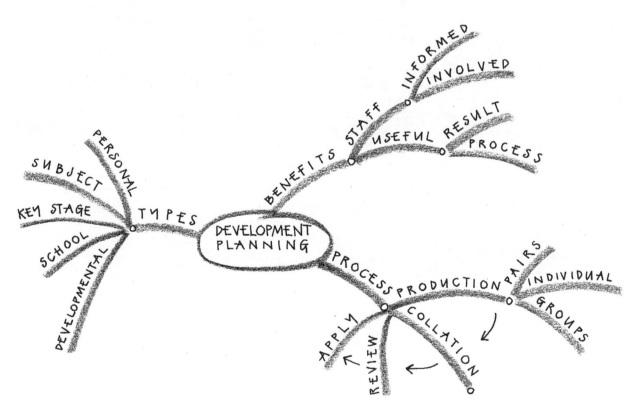

Visions need to be to be shared

'The diagram serves as a focus of attention to which everyone in the team can relate and see to decide whether or not the diagram adequately captures their own views.'

D. Sherwood (1998)

context

Improvement, or development, plans are not always aligned to reality and can be viewed as being a waste of time.

What are the main objectives of your school improvement plan? What part did you have to play in its production? What role do you see for yourself in making the plans happen? Ask yourself these same questions for your departmental or subject or key stage improvement plans.

We find that many teachers don't know what is on their school's improvement plans. Often the plans are not seen as particularly useful documents. Many teachers we speak to relate to them as yet another piece of paper that simply adds to their workload. It doesn't have to be this way…

Plans should be useful documents and everyone should contribute to them.

Whether they are subject, departmental, key stage or whole-school development plans, they should be useful and accessible. Ideally, everyone who is going to be involved in implementing the improvement plan should be involved in its production. Everyone should also understand it and be in agreement about what it means. Are we agreed – in theory at least?

 'As a leadership group we can use model maps to share and merge individual ideas. They also help us to communicate ideas to staff and to help involve and include them more in the development planning process. Across the school they support middle managers, such as department heads, in communicating their plans, priorities, needs and ideas more effectively.'

Barbara Hutson, Headteacher, Woodlands SLD School, Chelmsford, Essex

opportunity

Model mapping offers the opportunity to create improvement plans that everyone finds useful and refers to regularly.

The opportunity is there to have everyone involved in improvement planning and to ensure that everyone is clear about what the improvement plan means to them.

visible

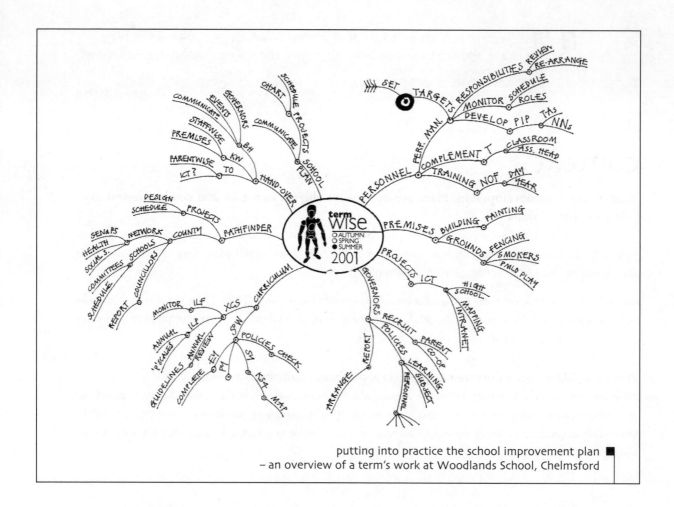

putting into practice the school improvement plan ■
– an overview of a term's work at Woodlands School, Chelmsford

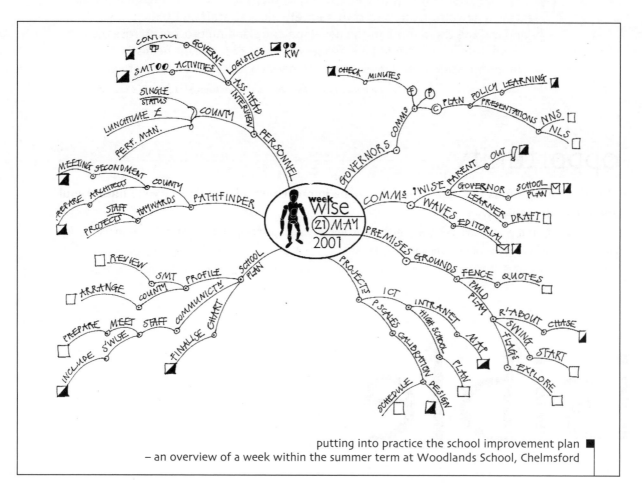

putting into practice the school improvement plan ■
– an overview of a week within the summer term at Woodlands School, Chelmsford

method

The method below builds on the one set out in chapter 2.3, Collaborative Group Work.

1 Teachers map out their own school department key Sstage improvement plan and then form groups of four to share their ideas and combine their maps.

2 Copies of the combined maps are made and the people in the groups are numbered 1–4. Each participant takes a copy of their group map and makes up a new group with three other people who have the same number. They then collate these four maps.

'I use model mapping to organize my thoughts and ideas and to help me communicate them to my leadership group and whole staff.'

Chris Yates, Headteacher, Rodings Primary School, Dunmow, Essex

Collation may involve:

- subsuming several headings into one (for example, 'office', 'teaching' and 'management' might be subsumed under the heading 'staffing');

- fitting information into agreed categories;

- using one word consistently where lots of different words meaning the same thing have been used.

3 At this stage it will probably be necessary to nominate a group of people who will take in all the group maps and collate them onto one map. This map could then be discussed at a further whole-staff meeting with everyone being given the opportunity to stick Post-it notes on to a poster-sized map on the wall.

'Model maps helped me to communicate my ideas and priorities to my department. They helped us engage in constructive dialogue about potentially contentious issues and helped us to reach a consensus that we all see and share clearly at the next stage of the development planning process.'

Alistair Spode, Mathematics Teacher, Brisbane, Australia

■ **Note**: In small schools it may be possible to involve everyone in collating the group maps into one main map. The whole staff could then break away into groups again, with each group taking a main branch to research and develop further.

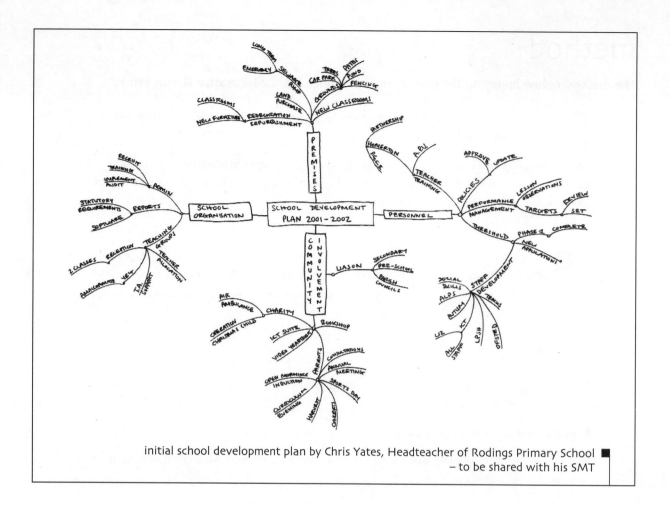

initial school development plan by Chris Yates, Headteacher of Rodings Primary School
– to be shared with his SMT ■

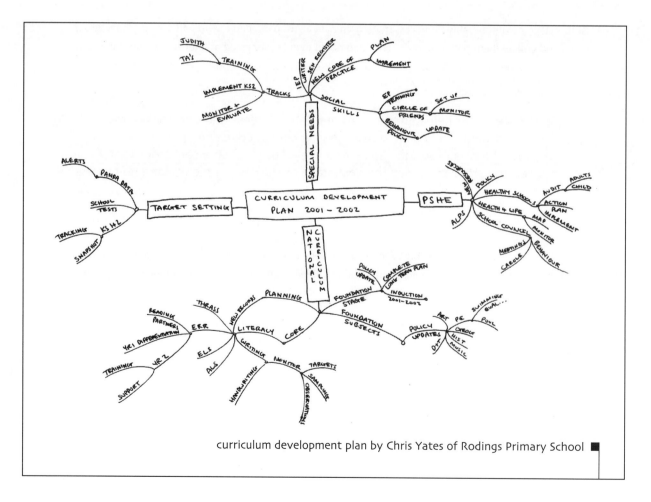

curriculum development plan by Chris Yates of Rodings Primary School ■

review

What methods does my school currently use for development planning? ■

Are these plans used and referred to regularly? ■

Do all the relevant people contribute to the planning process? ■

Could mapping techniques make our development plans
more meaningful and accessible? ■

■ Why do I display children's work?

■ Where do I display children's work?

■ Can displays be used more powerfully as aids to learning?

■ How can model maps be used to this effect?

■ What sort of model maps work best as displays?

displays

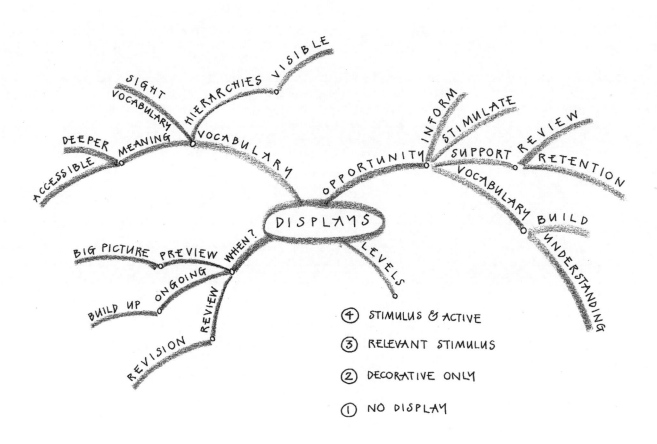

④ STIMULUS & ACTIVE

③ RELEVANT STIMULUS

② DECORATIVE ONLY

① NO DISPLAY

Mapping displays are inspiring and

'With model maps you can literally watch your class's understanding grow in front of your eyes. They are THE best revision tool but don't forget to take them down when the pupils do their SATs!'

Lyn Caviglioli, SENCO, Stanford-Le-Hope Primary School, Essex

context

We need to think about why we display children's work and how we can make best use of our displays for teaching and learning.

There is no statistical evidence that we have seen or heard of suggesting that displaying pupils' best work or 30 examples of hand prints or fake historical documents raises pupil performance in the classroom. If, as we are sometimes told, the purpose of displaying such work is to raise self-esteem, use public areas such as hallways and entrance halls where parents and visitors can see them. Save at least some of your classroom for learning displays.

Displaying key words as part of their contextual hierarchies can help pupils develop vocabulary and access deeper levels of understanding.

Do you already display key words in your classrooms? Have you considered how much more meaningful these words would be if they were displayed as part of a model map?

'It is the spatial relationship between words that conveys and carries deeper levels of meaning. Making these relationships explicit via displayed model maps can support language development and enhance understanding for all children of all ages.'

Bill Tindall, author and trainer

opportunity

Model maps used as displays can stimulate, inform and be an active part of the learning process.

method

There are several ways in which model maps can be included in classroom display arrangements.

■ Big Picture

Model maps can be displayed to give pupils the Big Picture of the work to be covered. You could choose to display only the main branches (or just the title) initially and then, as work on this particular topic progresses, branches can be added to it. In this way the class has a map that reflects its own growing understanding of the topic being covered. The class maps could also represent the end of a collaborative mapping exercise (see chapter 2.3, Collaborative Group Work.)

illuminating,
instructive

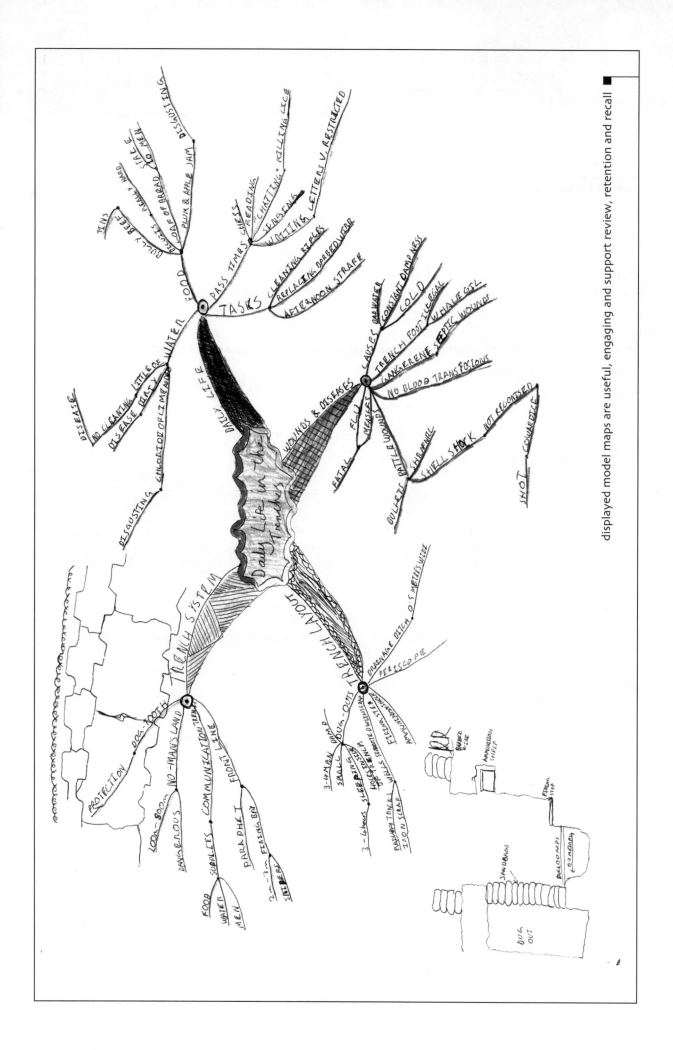

displayed model maps are useful, engaging and support review, retention and recall ■

■ Key words

Key words can be displayed as part of a model map. Pupils access a deeper level of meaning when they can see the relationships between words.

■ Language development

Model maps can be used to help language development in early years. Used alongside pictures, model maps can be used to help pre-readers develop their sight vocabulary (see case study on pages 145–6).

■ Summative displays

Using model maps as summative displays can help pupils to review, retain and recall information for tests and examinations. Work with the pupils to produce and display maps that summarize the work that pupils have covered and need to remember. Ask pupils to point to and refer to them in the weeks leading up to their tests. Model this for your pupils by pointing to and referring to the maps yourself.

■ Pole-bridging

Produce smaller versions of the maps displayed and ask pupils to pole-bridge them to each other. (See pages 93–4.)

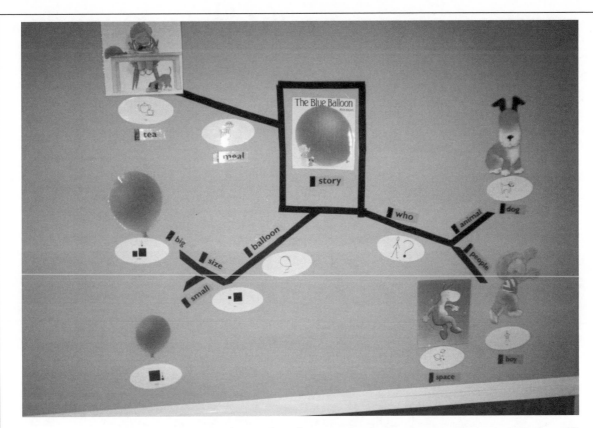

you can perhaps imagine the pupils in this SLD school using the story display to help them ■ show their understanding

raising awareness of the characteristics of different cultural festivals – in this case Diwali ■

raising awareness of the characteristics of different cultural festivals – in this case Chinese New Year ■

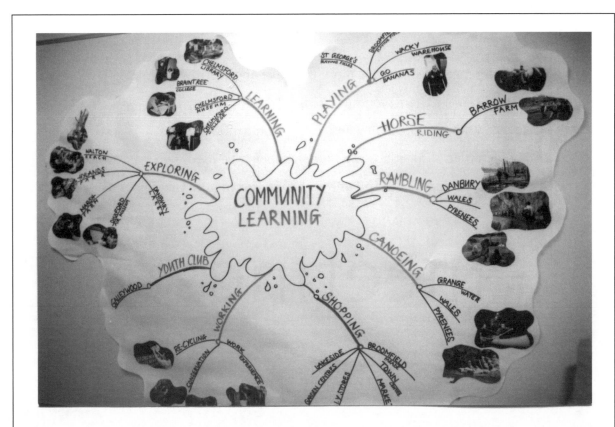

using model maps to show visitors how the pupils in Woodlands SLD school get to the heart of the community

review

What is currently on my classroom walls?

Does it aid learning?

Do I display key words? If so, how?

Do I understand how model maps can make my classroom a richer learning environment?

- How can meetings be made more effective and worthwhile?
- What can make them more inclusive?
- How can model mapping facilitate communication?
- In which type of meetings can model mapping be used?
- Can model mapping be used as a technique for minute taking?

meetings

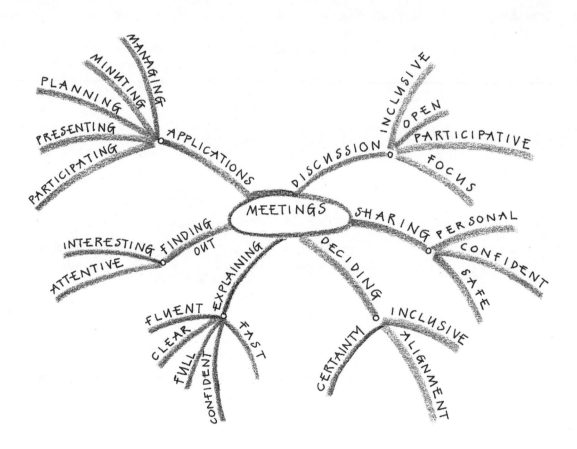

Interactive and effe
happen through map

'We want meetings that are to the point and useful; where individual opinions are included and encouraged within a framework that ensures that we all end up singing from the same hymn sheet. Model mapping has made this so much easier for us.'

Barbara Hutson, Headteacher, Woodlands SLD School, Chelmsford, Essex

context

Whatever the purpose of our attending meetings, model mapping can contribute to their being more worthwhile and effective.

How many meetings do you attend during the course of a year? How many different types of meetings? Whole staff meetings, key stage meetings, subject meeting, governors meetings... Whatever the context, we are always meeting to do one or some of the following:

- to discuss

- to share

- to find out

- to explain

- to decide.

Model mapping can be used in meetings as part of the planning, participation and delivery process.

This chapter will show how model mapping impacts on all of the areas listed above. It will look at how model mapping can be used for:

- minuting discussions in meetings;

- preparing and delivering presentations;

- managing feedback and questions.

opportunity

Using model maps as part of the communication process in meetings can transform the level of involvement and participation.

The reasons for a meeting can all be subsumed under the category of 'communication'. Communication is easier if you can all see the point about which you are communicating. Model maps open up the opportunity for everyone to see what others are talking about and they therefore facilitate a real meeting of minds. They support an open and collaborative atmosphere since what is under discussion or being presented is out in the open where all can see it. In such an atmosphere people contribute more fully and feel more involved.

ctive meetings
ped understanding

method

■ Minuting a discussion

1 The agenda is mapped out on the whiteboard. Each person attending the meeting has a copy of the mapped agenda centrally placed on a sheet of A3 paper to enable them to make their own notes as the meeting progresses.

2 As discussions develop, so key words are identified and placed on the map on the whiteboard. People's contributions can be seen. You don't worry too much about structure since you know that, by getting the ideas out into the open, associations and links will show up; a model of mutual understanding will emerge on the whiteboard.

3 The minute-taker copies the emerging map from the whiteboard and, with five minutes to go, you all go through the map together, checking that it is an accurate model of the meeting. With all agreed, you arrange for the map to be copied and distributed.

■ Preparing a presentation

1 Draw a model map of the area you are going to cover in your presentation. Copy it in black and white. Put rings of colour around the key concepts, decide on the order in which you will present them and label these areas accordingly.

2 Make up a less detailed model map using the same shape and colours but fewer words. Now practise the presentation using this second model map. If you find yourself stumbling, add a few more words to the relevant section and repeat that part of the presentation.

3 Once you are confident that you have sufficient words on which to base your talk, copy your map onto acetate or a computer presentation package (if you want the audience to see what you are talking about). Also photocopy your map onto the centre of A3 sheets of paper (if you would like to help your audience make full and accurate notes as you are talking).

■ Making presentations at meetings

Most of you will, at some time, find yourself delivering a presentation to your colleagues or at an interview. Everyone knows that you should not write a script and read it out, but many people find presenting to a group without some kind of written cues a daunting prospect.

The model map can help you to give a full and fluid presentation. With a map you can flit around the different sections or deliver each section in order. If the audience can see what you are talking about (because you have the map up on a screen) then so much the better; this will enable them to see the connections and follow where you are going – even if your presentation jumps about. By using the model map, you have tailored your material to your own personal style.

■ Managing feedback and questions

If participants have a paper copy of your mapped presentation it can help them ask questions that are relevant and useful. Invite them to write questions that emerge during your presentation next to the relevant sections on the map. Alternatively, invite them to write their questions on Post-it notes that can then be posted on a poster-sized copy of your map at the front of the room.

case study

Mapping a presentation

'All ready for the meeting?' asked the headteacher's secretary in the school corridor. The look on the SENCO's face told her that he did not have a clue what she was talking about. 'You're presenting your plans to the Senior Management Team and governors... in the conference room... in 20 minutes.' After a brief period of panic the SENCO ran into the reprographics suite, found a seat and mapped out what he wanted to say to the SMT and governors. When he had completed the map he copied it onto acetate and onto enough sheets to ensure there would be a copy for each person attending. He also enlarged the map to poster size. He grabbed a new packet of Post-it notes on his way out.

In the conference room the governors and SMT were gathering. The SENCO quickly blue-tacked the poster to one side of the whiteboard and distributed the copied maps around the conference table. Above each map he placed a small pile of Post-it notes. Before he started the presentation he invited the governors and SMT to add any thoughts and notes to their maps as he went through the presentation. Any questions, he suggested, should be written on the Post-it notes, which should then be placed onto the poster when they broke for coffee. This would give him time, he explained, to think about his response to their questions, which he would address one by one after coffee. (It would also allow those present to record their thoughts and to be involved without interrupting what was, in reality, a hastily prepared presentation.)

The SENCO was thanked for his full, clear, useful presentation. He received a letter of thanks from the headteacher commenting on his 'thorough and thoughtful presentation'.

Ian Harris (SENCO at Stewards School, Harlow, Essex from 1997–9)

 'I love having all my notes on a single page when I present at staff meetings. No more flapping about looking for the right sheet – and the way it supports me being able to dip into areas at different levels and answer questions clearly.'

Val Hill, Advanced Skills Teacher, Stewards School, Harlow, Essex

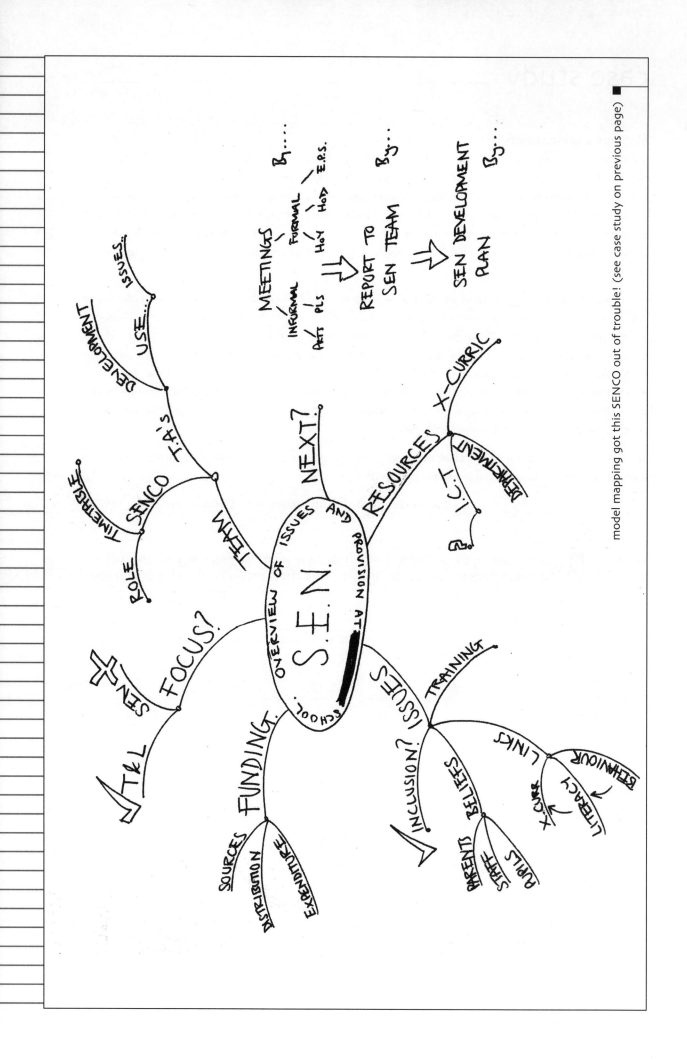

model mapping got this SENCO out of trouble! (see case study on previous page)

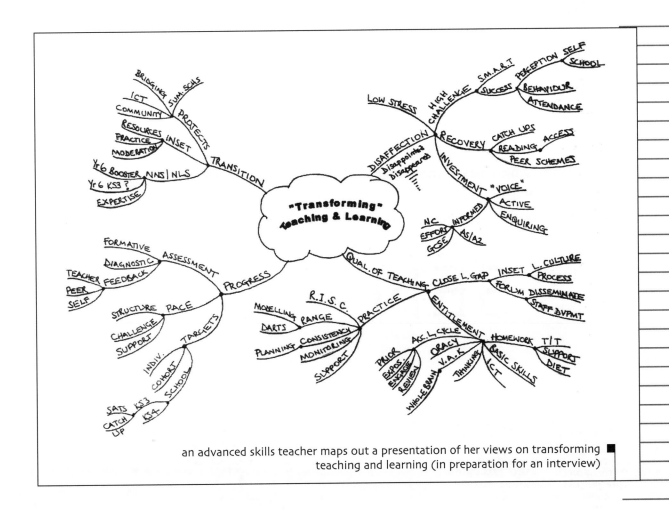

an advanced skills teacher maps out a presentation of her views on transforming teaching and learning (in preparation for an interview)

review

Are the meetings I attend as helpful as I would like? ■

Are everyone's views taken into account? ■

Are the minutes accurate and useful? ■

Can I see ways in which model mapping could improve meetings in my school? ■

- Why is model mapping such a powerful tool for SEN pupils?
- How can mapping help with inclusion in the classroom?
- How can model mapping make learning more likely to happen?
- For which part of the learning process is model mapping most helpful?
- Why does mapping improve co-operation?

SEN

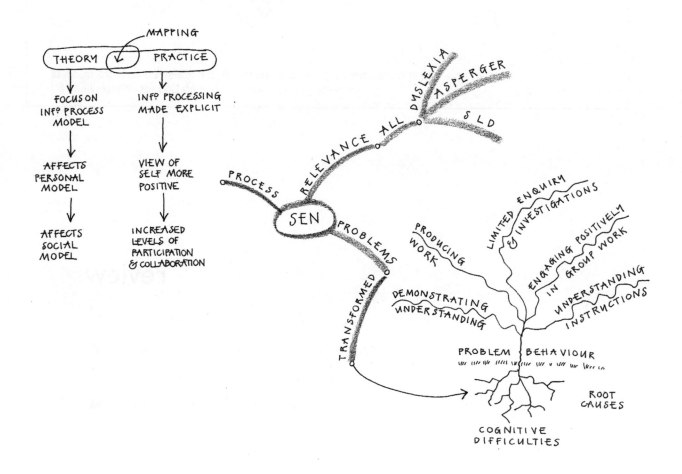

Inclusion happens
see the missing

context

The benefits of mapping are not to be viewed as being exclusive to SEN pupils.

However, mapping has been recommended as an effective tool for SEN pupils for as long as the authors can remember (at least 20 years) and probably beyond that. This chapter explains why.

We have deliberately avoided focusing on particular categories of SEN; those of you who work with special needs children will recognize enough in what we say to make the links to your own practice. Those of you who do not work specifically with these children will benefit from simply realizing that the difficulties outlined below happen to all of us at times – for SEN children they just happen a lot more often than for most.

Both authors have extensive SEN experience at classroom and management level, in mainstream and special schools. We do not think that model mapping, or any other effective teaching and learning strategy, is the 'property' of special needs teachers. Model mapping, like every other 'special needs strategy' we have ever come across, supports all pupils.

opportunity

Model mapping offers you the opportunity to 'disappear' everyday difficulties and empower SEN pupils in special schools and mainstream classrooms.

Do your pupils (or do you) ever have difficulties in the following areas?

1 Understanding and following teacher explanations and instructions.

2 Engaging positively and actively in investigations and exploratory scenarios in class.

3 Demonstrating understanding with clarity and confidence.

4 Working co-operatively and collaboratively.

Model mapping provides a practical way of addressing cognitive difficulties that may arise in all these scenarios.

1. Model mapping can make sure your explanations are effective.

In your classroom you explain things to pupils. When you explain you are transforming a holographic model of understanding that you have in your head into a long string of words (see chapter 1.3, Holographic–Linear). Pupils are being asked to capture this string of words and transform it into a model of understanding in their own minds. We have all had the experience of wondering what on earth someone was talking about. What would your life be like if, day in, day out, you were not able to understand instructions or explanations? Surely your ability to follow instructions and understand explanations would be significantly enhanced if you could *see* what the other person was talking about. In our experience, many 'unwelcome' behaviours result because pupils do not understand their instructions or verbal explanations. Model mapping significantly reduces the chances of this happening. Can you afford to not make your explanation effective for all pupils?

when teachers
connections

Year 1, lower ability child beginning to organize her learning: using this simple, teacher-supported ■
'bubble' picture allowed her to do this

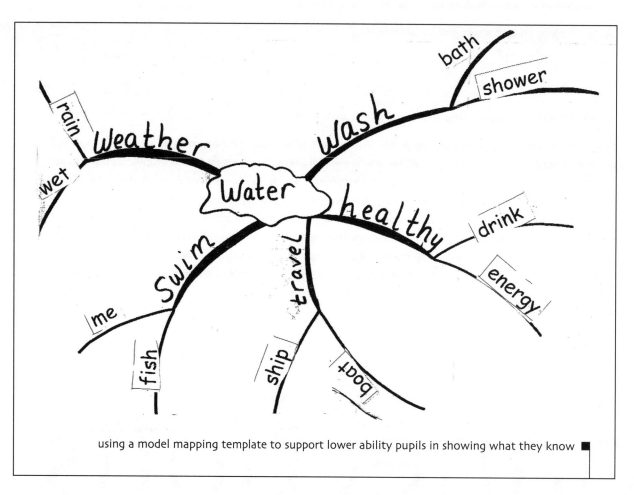

using a model mapping template to support lower ability pupils in showing what they know ■

2. Model mapping makes explicit to pupils how they think, learn, and ultimately develop, models of understanding in their minds.

For how long would you sit still and behave yourself if you had no idea what to do in order to understand? Model mapping can reveal to pupils of all abilities what it is they do cognitively that leads them to the 'ah ha' experience associated with knowing and understanding. We argue that successful pupils do not know what it is they do that leads them to be successful. By 'successful' we mean they experience working in a way that leads to understanding and knowing. Similarly, less successful (SEN?) pupils do not know what it is they are *not* doing that leads them to *not* understanding or *not* knowing what is going on. Model mapping makes the process that leads to understanding and knowing explicit.

3. Model mapping supports pupils in demonstrating their understanding.

Have you ever understood something but been unable to articulate this understanding or found it hard to express your ideas on paper through linear text? The inability of a child to explain through linear speech or text does not necessarily mean that they have not understood. It may actually mean that they, like you when this happens to you, are experiencing difficulties in transforming the holographic models of understanding in their heads into linear representations of this understanding. It may also be that the pupil is experiencing difficulty in building up her holographic model. Model mapping offers the opportunity for you to do both.

4. Model mapping develops the three Cs: concentration, co-operation and communication.

When you communicate with another person you are sharing your schemas with that person and they with you. Your schemas may be modified by what you hear and vice versa. When pupils work collaboratively and co-operatively, we are asking them to do the same thing. How often do you drift off when speaking to someone else? How often do they drift off when speaking to you? How often is this experience mirrored in the classroom? We cannot realistically expect a meeting of minds to take place unless all parties can see what they are talking about. When people's schemas are revealed to each other in the form of model maps, levels of communication, inclusion and co-operation are transformed. (See case studies at end of this chapter.)

Model mapping reveals the inside story of 'how to learn' and makes it accessible to pupils.

The opportunity is here to contribute positively to levels of pupil satisfaction. As a profession we understand the importance of 'developing' pupils' self-esteem such that they are okay about not knowing. (We use inverted commas here because children are born okay about not knowing – so much so that they do not even know that they do not know.) When pupils know how they know, they are far more likely to be okay about not knowing. Why? Because they know what they need to do in order to reach the point of knowing. Get it?

methods

Model mapping can be used at all stages of the learning process.
Below are some ideas for using model maps in your classroom. (See How section for teaching pupils how to map.)

- Map out your lesson and give pupils a copy of your map, or at least have a copy on the whiteboard of flip chart for them to look at. Build up the map as any discussion develops. Let the pupils see what you are talking about by mapping the key words and ideas as you go along.

- Teach pupils how to map and, more specifically, how they can think and learn in an inductive way.

- Allow pupils to build up and demonstrate their understanding by producing model maps. Build in opportunities for them to explain their maps to each other. Let them use maps to plan out pieces of writing or oral presentations to groups and to the class. (See chapter 2.3, Collaborative Group Work.)

- Make mapping an integral part of paired and group working activities.

case studies

Classy talk

In Scotland, S1 and S2 students (Years 7 and 8 in England) are encouraged to give whole-class talks on a subject of their choice. For many students, including those with SEN, this can appear daunting. Not only do they need support in delivering their talk, they also have to gather and organize information prior to delivery! I find mapping helps them to do both.

All my students now use maps to help them discuss various topics with a partner and to support them in delivering a formal presentation to the class. I find that using model maps has various advantages over the use of flash cards or scripts. There is less paper for the students to manage. Using a map emphasizes to them that the talk is not simply a matter of reading a script. In addition the fact that both the speaker and the listener can see the detail and the Big Picture simultaneously helps focus attention, supports active questioning and sets up the conditions for two-way dialogue. As a bonus, the fact that the SEN pupils are using the same strategies as the more able definitely helps develop an atmosphere of inclusion.

This approach is now pretty much the norm in my classes and has led to some interesting insights relating to different areas of SEN practice.

Asperger syndrome: getting through; seeing progress

Michael, aged 13, formed part of the small group who were asked to walk and talk their way through their maps prior to delivering their talks to a larger audience. Michael produced the map shown opposite (top). Michael is diagnosed as having Asperger syndrome and in many ways displays what are considered to be classic AS symptoms: he prefers to work alone; his attempts to befriend others are clumsy and he fails to read social signs; he is also obsessed by a single interest, namely trains.

While much time is spent trying to broaden Michael's interests it is also important that he has the opportunity to share his special interest with others and this type of talk situation is ideal for this. However, as is obvious in his map, the area he has focused on would really bore a general, non-enthusiast, audience: the details he has selected are too similar and narrow and basically employ an inappropriate register.

Trying to explain to Michael what is 'wrong' with his talk map is quite difficult, especially when one adds a stubborn, inflexible nature. However, I felt we made great progress when we compared maps and Michael watched and listened to the other students talking and walking through their maps. I felt he could actually see what was wrong with the content of his talk, as it was obvious that the other students had presented different types of information and that there was some variety in what they would talk about. To emphasize this, I placed an OHP sheet over a couple of the maps and, using different coloured pens, coloured map branches according to the type of information presented. On Michael's OHP, all the lines I superimposed were the same colour so we agreed it would be boring to give a talk in only one colour. In his final presentation Michael added a couple of anecdotes based on things he had done when helping ticket collectors on trains, something he spends his weekends doing. I felt this was real progress.

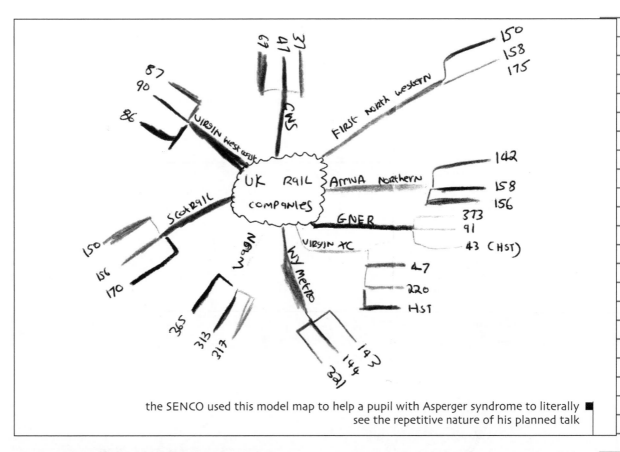

the SENCO used this model map to help a pupil with Asperger syndrome to literally ■
see the repetitive nature of his planned talk

Literacy difficulties – relieving the pressure

The map below shows a fairly typical talk map, which was produced by a boy called Roy when he was 13. Roy has major literacy problems and struggles to do basic things like hand out jotters or folders because he can't read the names. Roy talked through his map on the subject of motorbikes, first with a friend and then to the class – something he had never had the confidence to do before.

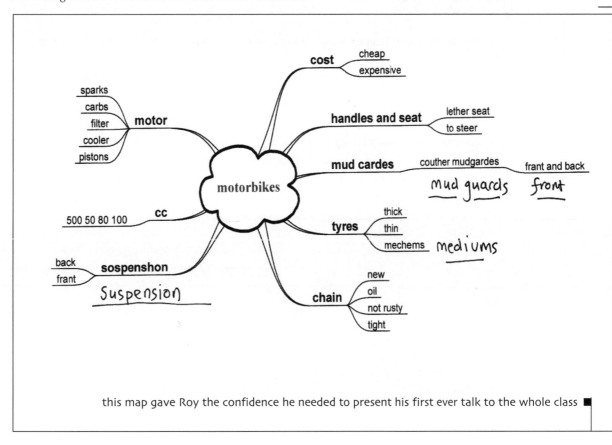

this map gave Roy the confidence he needed to present his first ever talk to the whole class ■

ADHD – a flexible focus

Also part of our group was Max who produced the map below Max has ADHD problems and, while being very articulate, humorous and intelligent, he struggles with literacy work too, particularly in terms of organization of ideas. He chose to give his talk on his life. As is evident from the map Max made, he enjoys mapping because it means he doesn't have to write everything down. He can organize his ideas in a coherent, straightforward way without being limited by the constraints of language.

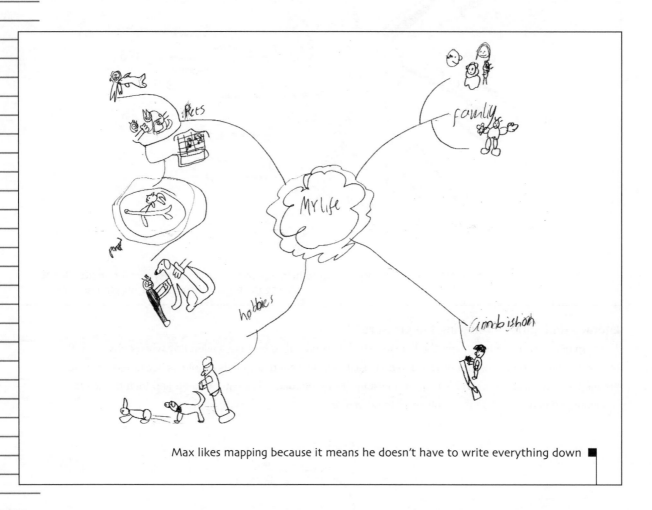

Max likes mapping because it means he doesn't have to write everything down ■

Talking with Max's parents at a parents' evening we had a long conversation about Max and his problems. His parents, both able professionals, were keen to hear about alternative strategies that would help their son to develop and overcome his difficulties. We discussed at some length the need to move away from more traditional methods: there is nothing wrong with Max's thinking or his intellect… he simply needs a teaching and learning approach that supports him in focusing on learning. Model mapping would seem to be part of the solution.

Gerry Dolan, SENCO, Dingwall Academy, Scotland

review

Does my teaching best support the inclusion of SEN pupils? ■

Do I understand why learning is more difficult for those pupils? ■

Could model mapping enable my SEN pupils to participate more in lessons? ■

Could mapping help develop their understanding? ■

■

- Why is writing so unpopular with some learners?
- What mental processes does writing involve?
- How can model mapping turn reluctant writers to enthusiastic ones?
- What are the particular benefits for boys?
- How can mapping develop language skills?

planning for writing

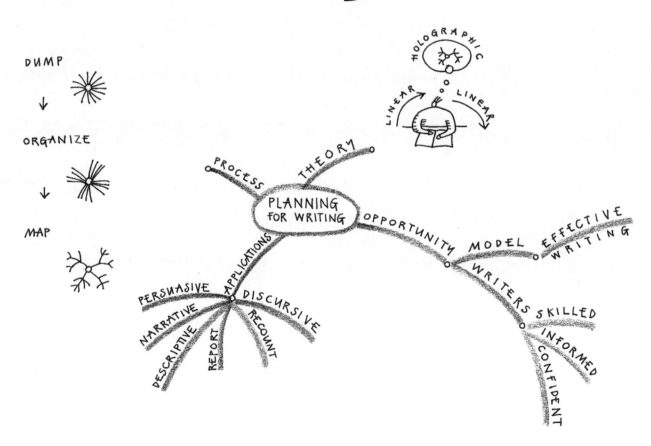

Writing is clear
when thinking

context

Writing is not every learner's favourite classroom activity.
We ask pupils to write in a variety of styles and text genres. For many – but not all – pupils, writing can become a chore and you the teacher can be left to deal with the behavioural consequences of the pupils' feelings of inadequacy.

When you ask pupils to write, you are asking them to engage in an act of transformation.
You are asking pupils to transform a holographic model that they have in their minds into a long, linear string of words. (See chapter 1.3, Holographic–Linear). This act normally takes place without the learner being conscious of it at all. Successful pupils do this without knowing what it is they do; unsuccessful pupils don't do it and they don't know what it is they are *not* doing.

opportunities

Teaching pupils to map can help develop informed, skilled and enthusiastic writers.
Imagine boys willing to redraft their writing plans! Imagine yourself having access to a method that can deepen all pupils' understanding of the writing process. Imagine pupils who are positively disposed towards writing. Teachers who teach their pupils to map do not have to imagine all this – it becomes a reality.

Model mapping offers the opportunity for you to model to pupils exactly what it is that successful writers do when they write.
You can make the planning process explicit and help pupils to organize and talk through their thoughts before turning these plans into linear text.

Model mapping offers you the opportunity to provide all learners (and boys in particular) with the means of building and organizing their thoughts before committing to linear text. Our experience is that boys will willingly complete and redraft maps and have no difficulty in turning their maps into linear text.

method

The following case studies illustrate two ways in which mapping can be used to develop pupils' writing skills.

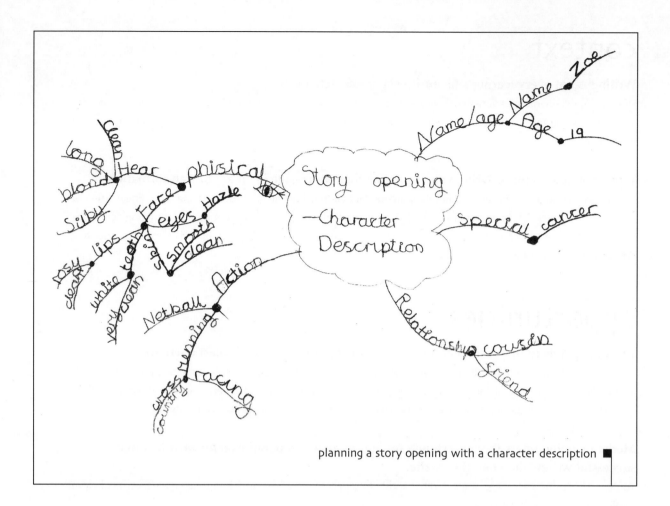

planning a story opening with a character description ■

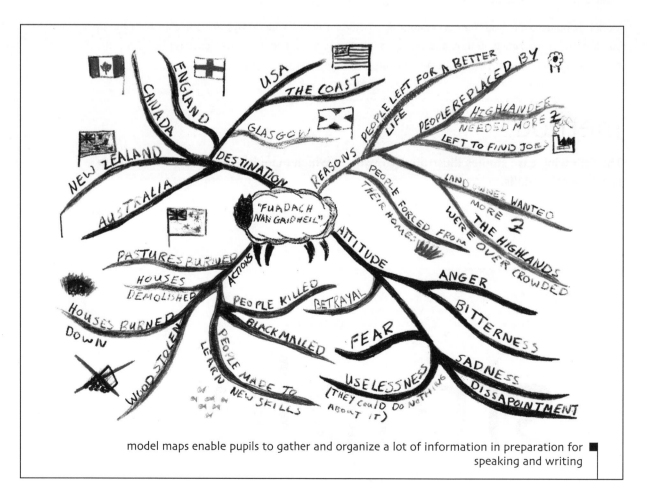

model maps enable pupils to gather and organize a lot of information in preparation for ■
speaking and writing

case study

Using mapping in the Literacy Hour

I started to use mapping as a technique when teaching a Year 6 class in an inner-city primary school. The school had been removed from Special Measures the previous year and was now undergoing major building renovation that involved moving classrooms on a regular basis – it was an unsettling time. The class of children came from a variety of cultures and backgrounds, but generally from an area of high social deprivation.

At the beginning of the new school year I spent time talking to the class about their perceptions of school and learning. It soon became apparent that they did not perceive themselves to be part of a learning culture. Already, many of them had decided that education had little relevance in their lives and could see few positive benefits from their schooling. This was a general trend but particularly related to their feelings towards literacy – especially their attitudes towards writing. Children did not enjoy writing; they viewed it as a chore and had little motivation to improve their skills. This, then, was the challenge at the beginning of the school year – I needed to shift these negative self-images and make learning, especially writing, relevant, exciting and – dare I say it – fun.

For the first two weeks of the term we collapsed the traditional curriculum and spent the time looking at different learning styles and how we learn best. Within this context I taught the class the principles of mapping. This was an enjoyable activity – all the children became involved, quickly deciding that here was an activity that was not based on traditional academic achievement. They all immediately grasped and used the technique, understanding that mapping was a visual representation of their thinking and, as such, had unlimited potential.

Together we began to explore different ways of using maps to support thinking and learning. The literacy focus for the first half term was non-narrative writing. If I was to improve attitudes towards writing it was vital that this work was to be lively, fun and relevant. I started the unit by mapping out our existing knowledge. The children had some idea of different genres but the map also showed huge gaps in understanding. This was a powerful start – the children could see what they already knew, but could also appreciate what they now needed to find out.

Using the map as a starting point we started to explore the characteristics of different non-fiction genres; during the Literacy Hour we analysed texts, identifying common themes. As we uncovered more information we were able to add it to our map, providing a visual representation of the Big Picture. Children could see that learning was taking place as we added more information each day. I utilized display boards around the classroom; our map became a huge display which incorporated examples of texts we had analysed. All the class were able to refer to it at any time and in doing so they reinforced their knowledge and understanding.

Once the children were clear about different genres and could identify and discuss key characteristics we moved towards composing our own texts. Initially we focused on discussion texts: in this context we held class debates, chaired by the children. I took the part of an impartial observer and mapped out the debate. I used different colours to demonstrate clearly which points were in favour of the subject and which against. When completed, the maps became a record of the debate – but, more importantly, gave a structure to the discussion. The children could see this and embraced it easily.

We moved on to looking at constructing our own discussion texts – at this point I explained we would use maps to plan the discussion, although the points would not have to be written down, but rather presented orally. The impact of this was amazing; freed from the constraints of writing down their thoughts, the children were able to exploit their creativity and imagination. In the whole-class sessions of the Literacy Hour we brainstormed factual evidence related to the topic and linked each fact to supporting and opposing opinions. These were mapped out using colour to provide visual reinforcement. As we did this the power of using mapping became apparent – not only did it structure thinking but writing too, as each main branch became a clearly defined paragraph.

I developed a 'scaffold map' – demonstrating that the genre had a structure which could easily be followed. Independently, children began to use this scaffold to map out their own discussion. They were able to use symbols, pictures, colour and words to communicate their thinking – it was continuously stressed that the thought process was the important issue. Once the thought process was complete, and represented visually, the children orally presented their discussion to a partner using the technique of pole-bridging (see pages 93–4). The pairings became critical response partners, asking questions to extend ideas and providing immediate feedback. The children enjoyed the activity and were keen to take it further.

This unit had been so successful that I was keen to see if other non-fiction genres could be displayed in a similar way. Together, the children and I began to explore. To our delight we realized that each genre had its own characteristic map – these could easily be translated into a 'scaffold map' which became the starting point for planning any writing. Children began to plan out different genres with increasing confidence, knowing that they had a clear structure to follow. Initially we presented the completed plan orally, restricting the need to write and so taking much of the stress out of the activities. Over time however, I was able to introduce more formal recording methods. To my delight the majority of the class took this huge step with ease; they wanted to communicate their ideas and were happy and confident to do so. This was an amazing transformation within a short space of time.

It became apparent that the biggest impact of using mapping was to divorce thinking from the activity of writing.

 'It's easy to write when you don't have to think at the same time!'

Jessica, aged 10

Once their ideas were mapped out, children were able to focus on the conventions of writing, concentrating specifically on grammar, punctuation and spelling. Quickly their confidence and enjoyment of using the written word began to increase – this was reflected in the end product of which they were justifiably proud.

In order for this adventure to be successful it was important that the children were aware that their attempts would always be valued – there is no right and wrong when mapping! This very fact helped to create an environment where the children were prepared to take risks and 'have a go'. For many children it also opened their eyes; it took the mystery out of learning. For the first time pupils were able to see how concepts linked together, they could suddenly understand what they were learning, and why. One of the most significant changes mapping brought about was that teaching became much more of a partnership – children confidently contributed their own knowledge and I learnt as much, if not more, than they did.

At the end of the year, we spent time as a group evaluating our work and our learning. The feedback from children was that of enjoyment – mapping was not seen as 'work'; it was fun, it was easy, you could use words or colour or pictures – all were valued. As a teacher, the most rewarding feedback was that, as this group of children left our school, the most enjoyable subject – almost unanimously – was writing. These children were also equipped for future learning and the skills they had learned would continue to support them in years to come.

Jo Grail is now Headteacher of Delaware Primary School, Gunnislake, Cornwall

■ **Note:** The text genre maps that Jo Grail devised with her pupils are available as a set of posters, published by Network Educational Press.

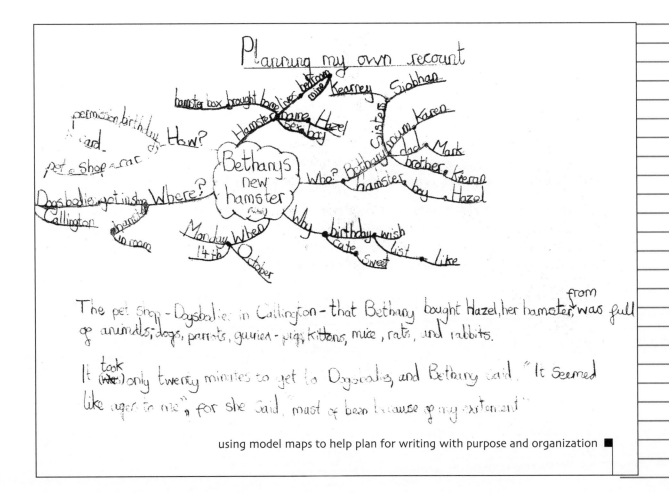

The pet shop — Dysbolies in Callington — that Bethany bought Hazel, her hamster, was full from of animals; dogs, parrots, guinea-pigs, kittens, mice, rats, and rabbits.

It took only twenty minutes to get to Dysbolies, and Bethany said, "It seemed like ages to me", for she said, must of been because of my excitement"

using model maps to help plan for writing with purpose and organization ■

case study

Early years language development

Janet Tindall retired from teaching at the end of July 2002. A strategy that Janet would use as part of her literacy work emphasizes the need to understand about the structure of language and illustrates how language hierarchies are the essential organizing structure of our schemas; of our maps. (See chapters 1.2, Schemas and 1.4, Language Triangles.) Janet is teaching a topic 'living things'. She has blue-tacked a picture on the whiteboard and she asks the children to tell her what they can see in the picture. The children call out the things they can see and Janet draws lines from the 'living things' they are describing to the whiteboard and writes the words on the line. 'Birds', 'men', 'foxes', 'boys', 'dogs', 'cats', 'cows', 'women', 'tortoises', 'daisies', 'roses', 'trees' and so on. are all labelled. One of the children says 'pets' and Janet asks the children to explain what pets are. One of the children says that pets are animals, and immediately another one says 'not all animals are pets, some are farm animals'. Another child says there are also wild animals. Janet asks if anyone can see a wild animal in the picture. One of the children points to the fox, another says that it may be wild but it's not dangerous like a tiger… Similar things happen as the children instinctively categorize the words and images in front of them and say words like 'flowers' or 'people'. Janet draws a line from the words 'women', 'boys' and so on. to a single point where she writes the word 'people'. She uses different colours to represent the different categories that are emerging.

When the children think they have finished, Janet covers up the picture and asks the children to see if they can read the words without looking at the picture. When they are unsure, the pupils instinctively try to work it out by looking to see which group of words the single words belong to. If they remain uncertain, Janet reveals the picture and the children track the concrete words back to the picture and track the higher level organizing words to the concrete words and then back to the picture. Janet then asks the children if they would like to see if they are able to read the words without looking at the pictures. Janet has prepared a set of all the concrete words (she sometimes asks the pupils to do this on the computer) for groups of four to work with. Their task is to put all the words into groups and make sure that everyone within their group can read all of the words. She says that they can go back to the picture to check and they can even add a little picture above the written word if this helps. As they are sorting the words into categories the children point out that the organizing words are missing. They ask if they can write them down on new sheets of paper to show how the words go together...

The class is familiar with this inductive learning process and when Janet asks them to make up a poster map with their words, they collect some A2 sugar paper and prepare their display by blue-tacking the words onto it. The visual information represented an hour or so ago in a picture has been transformed into another visual format, only this time it is one based on a developing understanding of language.

Janet Tindall, Former Reception Teacher, Radwinter C of E Primary School, Suffolk

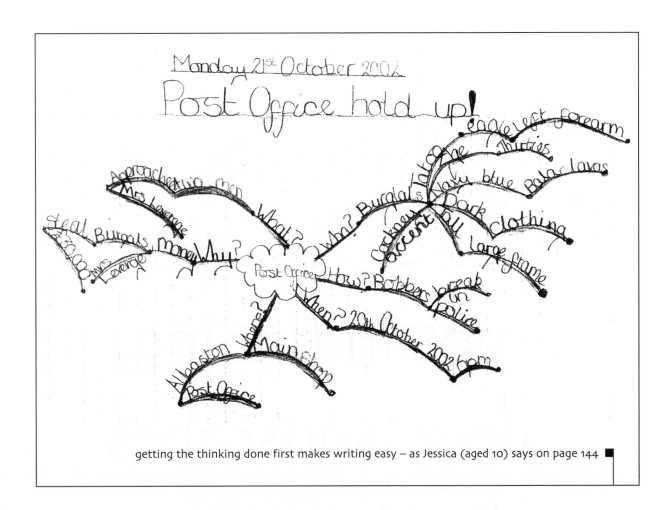

getting the thinking done first makes writing easy – as Jessica (aged 10) says on page 144 ■

review

Can I see how model mapping can support all my pupils
at the planning stage of writing? ■

Do I see the connection between schema and
holographic–linear, and the writing process? ■

Can I see how model mapping can help me model good practice for my pupils? ■

Do I recognize how and why model mapping will help reluctant writers? ■

'The voyage of discovery lies not in finding new landscapes but in having new eyes.'

Marcel Proust

introduction

about section 3

The first chapter in this section teaches the skill of categorization. When you map you are organizing ideas and information into categories. More often than not, a difficulty with mapping is a difficulty with categorization. To map you need to be able to categorize information. When you realize that we categorize our experiences in order to create meaning for ourselves, you will see the importance and relevance of teaching pupils this skill.

> 'People think in categories like "furniture" and "vegetable"…The categories underlie much of our vocabulary and they underlie much of our reasoning.'
>
> *S. Pinker (1999)*

Once you understand categorization you need to be able to represent information in the mapping format. How many years have you been writing top to bottom, left to right on a page? In the second chapter we teach you how to represent your understanding in a new way.

Basic tuition complete, prerequisite skills in place, in the third chapter we show you some different approaches you can take to produce your maps. In chapter four we show you ways you can develop and further your mapping skills. Finally, in chapter five we take you through a range of exercises that are designed to develop your note-taking skills.

Your part in the matter

By far the most effective way to enrol pupils into mapping and the use of other visual tools is to use the tools yourself. Dave M. is a rugby-playing, self-confessed 'extreme' cynic and a chum, who resisted our invitations for him to attend our mapping course for four years. Dave recently got a deputy headship in a secondary school in the east of England. A few weeks into his new job he came along to do the MapWise training. I spoke to him a week later. 'Unbelievable mate, amazing. The kids love it – I use it all the time,' he enthused. 'Get a cover, in I go, ask them to tell me what they've been doing and I map it out for them. They can't believe it. Few minutes into the lesson the kids are asking if they can have a go.' Our point is this: you are the 'significant other person' in many pupils' lives. When the pupils see you modelling how to map, they will want to do it. Do this and even more miracles will start happening in your class – honest.

■ **Note**: Some of the exercises in this section (marked ©) are used as part of our MapWise training course and have recently been copyrighted. However, if you are a teacher employed by a school you are welcome to use these exercises with pupils in your school role. A more comprehensive resource pack of photocopiable exercises is due to be published by Network Educational Press in autumn 2003.

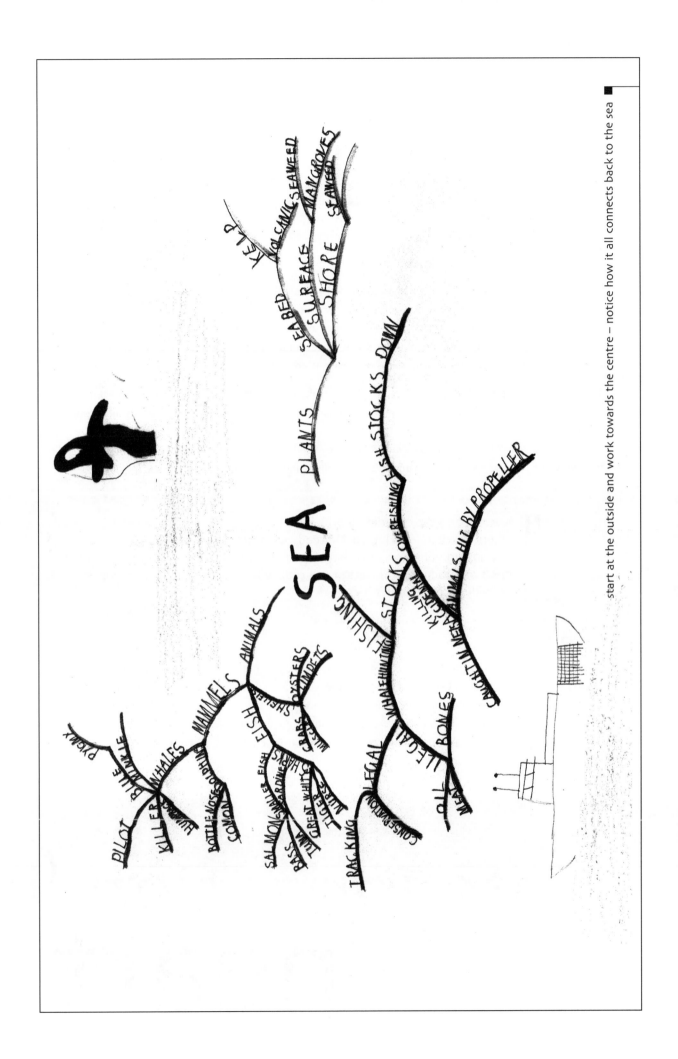

start at the outside and work towards the centre – notice how it all connects back to the sea ■

categorization

This chapter sets out exercises that will help you teach your pupils the basic skills they need to be able to map. You can do them too! We move from working with solid objects, to pictures, to words. Categorization is the essential thinking skill. All but a few of us do it in order to make sense of our world (see chapters 1.2, Schemas and 1.3, Holographic–Linear). Some of us are more successful at categorizing than others; virtually all of us are completely unaware that we do it but, unless we have autism or Asperger syndrome, we do all do it.

The importance of the following exercises is that they make explicit what it is we do with language in order to make sense of the world. When we make this information processing explicit, when we reveal to pupils the processes of knowing and understanding, they are far more likely to be 'okay' about not knowing or understanding. Why? Because now they know what they need to do in order to reach the point of understanding. In other words, they know what 'try harder', 'think about it' and 'see if you can work it out' look like.

> 'Uncovering the organizing principles is like having the ultimate hat rack. It is essential when working with already existing bodies of information as it is in developing your own information. The time spent comprehending someone else's method of organization will reduce the time spent looking for individual components.'
>
> *R. S. Wurman (1991)*

This chapter also serves to question the view that 'some children do not think like that' and that model mapping doesn't suit everyone's way of learning. If this were true, we believe there would be an alternative model of how children understand the world and build schemas of meaning. We haven't found one (although we accept that those on the autistic spectrum have a different way of thinking), and neither have the individuals upon whose work our model is based, including philosophers, cognitive psychologists, linguists and some of the most influential educators of the last century.

Categorization lies
heart of

'children should be at least as self conscious about their strategies of thought as they are about their attempts to commit things to memory. They should be conscious too, of the tools of thought—causal explanation, categorization and the rest.'

J. S. Bruner (1971)

Of course, for it to be successful, mapping has to be introduced in the right way. If it is introduced without proper understanding or support, using the FTH (felt tips and hope) approach, then of course some pupils will fail to pick it up. However, taught well, we believe that all pupils can benefit from using mapping skills – and teaching the skills well is what this chapter is about.

case study

Getting started

When introducing model mapping to students, I generally follow the process I observed Ian and Oliver use at the workshop I attended.

I ask students to imagine that they have been offered one million pounds for their autobiography and request suggestions as to how the students might spend such a fortune. A Ferrari? An island? A boutique or golf course? Unfortunately, however, there is a catch: the publishers require the completed manuscript first thing the following morning. Of course, it would be impossible for the students to write their fascinating life stories overnight and thus they stand to lose the windfall. What can we do to avoid losing this fortune? Hopefully, a student will suggest that one might take an outline or summary of the autobiography to the publisher and thus stall for a little time. If such a suggestion is not forthcoming, the teacher can provide the link. I try to inject much drama and humour into this imaginary scenario.

I then issue A3 paper and explain how to create a model map, demonstrating on the whiteboard or OHP what my own map would look like, explaining that each branch I draw will in fact be a separate chapter about my life. The students quickly pick up on the idea and proceed to create their own maps. We then work in pairs as the students walk (trace with their finger) and talk their way through the maps they have created, telling each other about their lives. The maps created may in turn serve as planning sheets for extended autobiographical writing or class talks.

I encourage a consistent style of mapping and try to touch upon some of the psychological reasoning behind why mapping is successful in all sorts of learning situations. I actively encourage students to use graphics and colour to make their maps more interesting, memorable and personal.

This introductory session serves as a good starting point for the model mapping that the students will be involved in while in my class.

Gerry Dolan, SENCO, Dingwall Academy, Scotland

at the
understanding

the exercises

The exercises on the following pages act as a simple introduction to the art of categorization.

Exercise 1: Categorizing using pictures
Organize these pictures by their colour and length. This exercise combines two organizing principles into one tree diagram.

Exercise 2: Categorizing using shapes
Organize these shapes by their colour, size and type of shape. Here, all three organizing principles are combined into one tree diagram.

Exercise 3: Categorizing using characteristics
Identify the characteristics of the insects and use them as organizing principles to complete the tree diagram.

Exercise 4: Categorizing using concepts
Identify the concepts (the organizing principles) that group together then assemble words.

Exercise 5: Categorizing using sub-categories
Identify the sub-categories (the secondary organizing principles) that subdivide the main categories.

categorization 1

categorizing using pictures

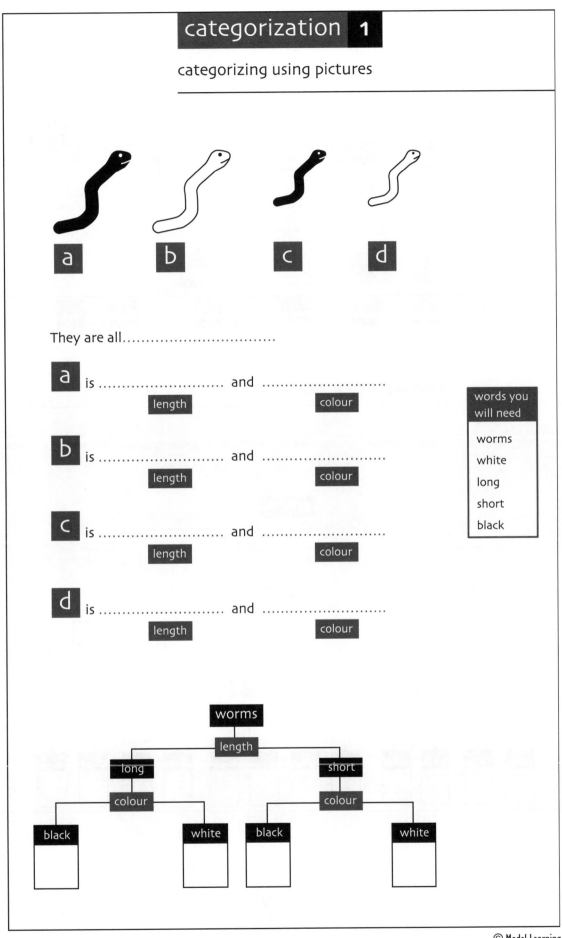

They are all.................................

a is .... and ....
   length   colour

b is .... and ....
   length   colour

c is .... and ....
   length   colour

d is .... and ....
   length   colour

words you will need

worms

white

long

short

black

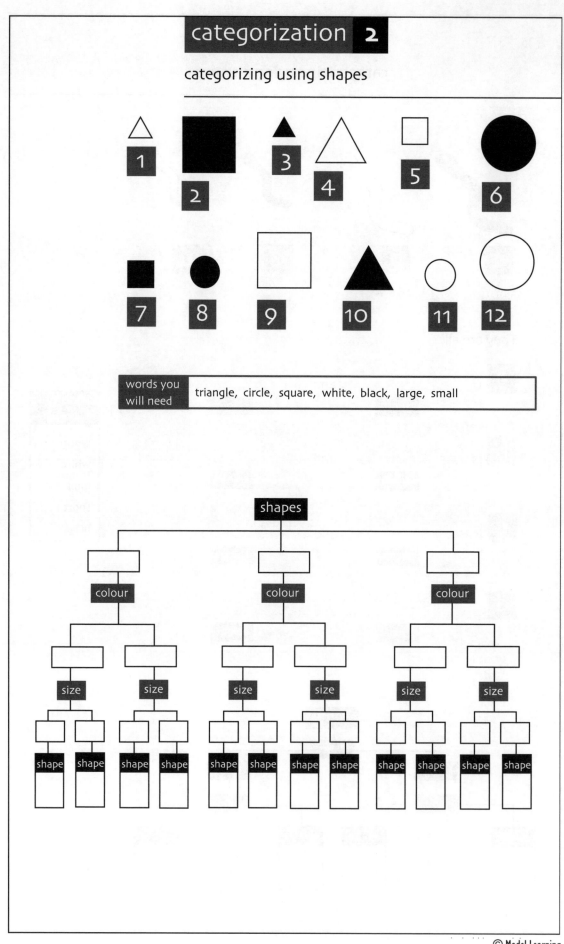

categorization 2

categorizing using shapes

words you will need: triangle, circle, square, white, black, large, small

categorizing using characteristics

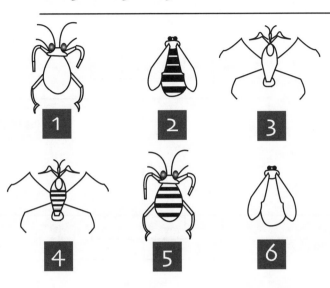

What have they all got in common?

They are all...............................

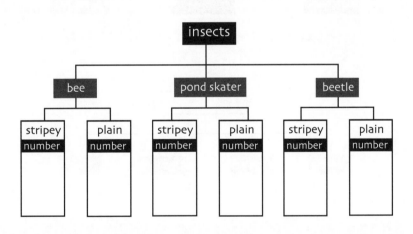

categorizing using concepts

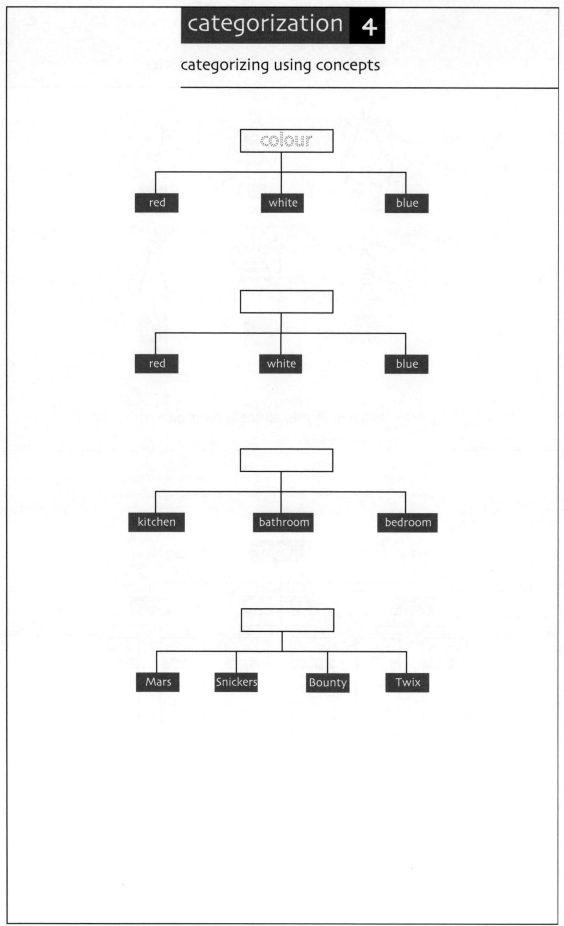

colour

| red | white | blue |

| red | white | blue |

| kitchen | bathroom | bedroom |

| Mars | Snickers | Bounty | Twix |

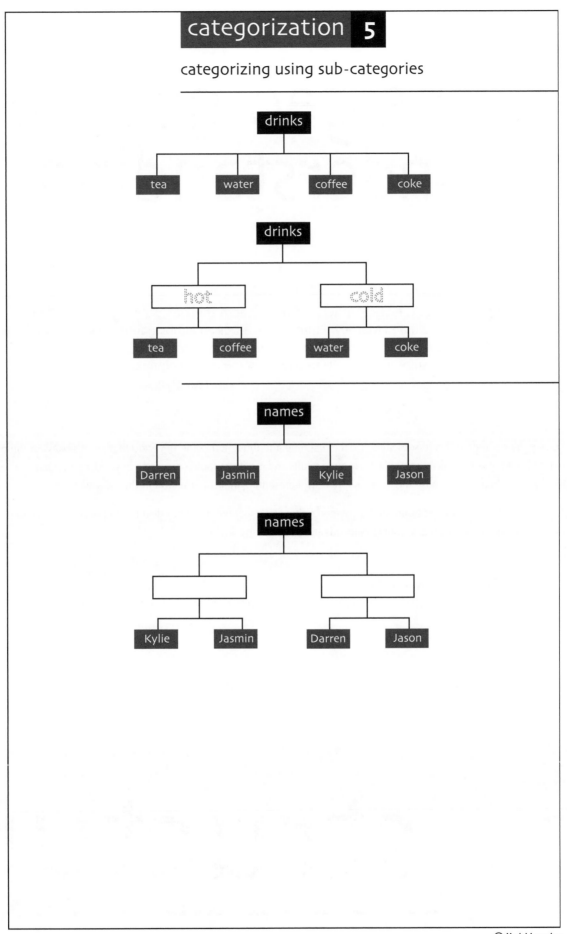

the geometry of understanding

> 'Going to the two "fathers" of the modern thinking skills movement, Reuven Feuerstein and Mathew Lipman, one finds an almost identically expressed answer: that all thinking which leads to the formation of abstract relationships, derives ultimately from the acts of comparing and contrasting.'
>
> *Mike Lake, in private correspondence to the authors*

Have you ever seen or heard something for the first time and thought 'I could never do that' or 'it's okay for them but it's not for me' or something similar? For some adults and pupils, mapping can seem beyond them, not because it *is* beyond them but because they need support in representing their information in this new way.

The exercises in this chapter build on the categorization skills that we started to develop in the previous chapter. In this chapter we work on developing categorization skills using words.

> 'I have always thought it a pity that the world was run by literary blokes because the visual side is so much more powerful and constructive.'
>
> *E. de Bono in B. McAlhone and D. Stewart (1996)*

By the end of the exercises you will see exactly what model maps actually are – a series of tree diagrams tessellated around a central point.

The **structure** reveals the DNA

the exercises

The following exercises are designed to develop skills in changing the graphic format of categories.

Exercise 1
The learner is supported in developing her categorization skills while at the same time she is supported in representing the categories in a different (and often new) graphic format. She has to place the words provided in the correct spaces. For exercise 1 prompts are given.

Exercise 2
As exercise 1 except that there are no prompts and the mapping branches are all empty.

Exercise 2a
This requires the learner to use all three branches from exercise 2 to complete a simple model map on animals.

Exercise 3
The learner is now required to represent his understanding in a model map without the support of the language triangles as provided in the previous exercises. The main categories are provided. The learner has to add detail to these main branches. You may want to ask him to draw this on A3 paper and add further branches with additional ideas on them.

Exercise 3a
As exercise 3 except that sub-categories are provided for one of the branches to make the point that we may sometimes want to further break down main categories before adding detail.

# of understanding
# of learning

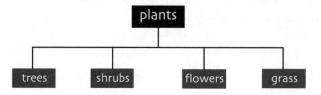

geometry of understanding **1**

changing the graphic format of categories

Flowers, trees, shrubs and grass are all plants.

We can show this categorization like this...

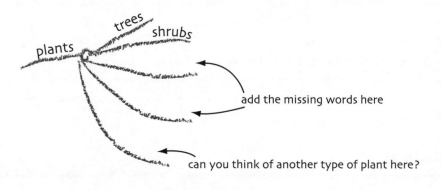

or, like this...

add the missing words here

can you think of another type of plant here?

Robin, thrush and swallow are all birds.

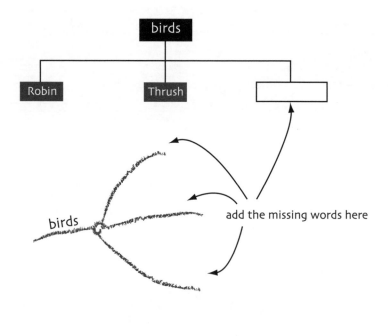

add the missing words here

changing the graphic format of categories

Cows, sheep and goats are all farm animals.

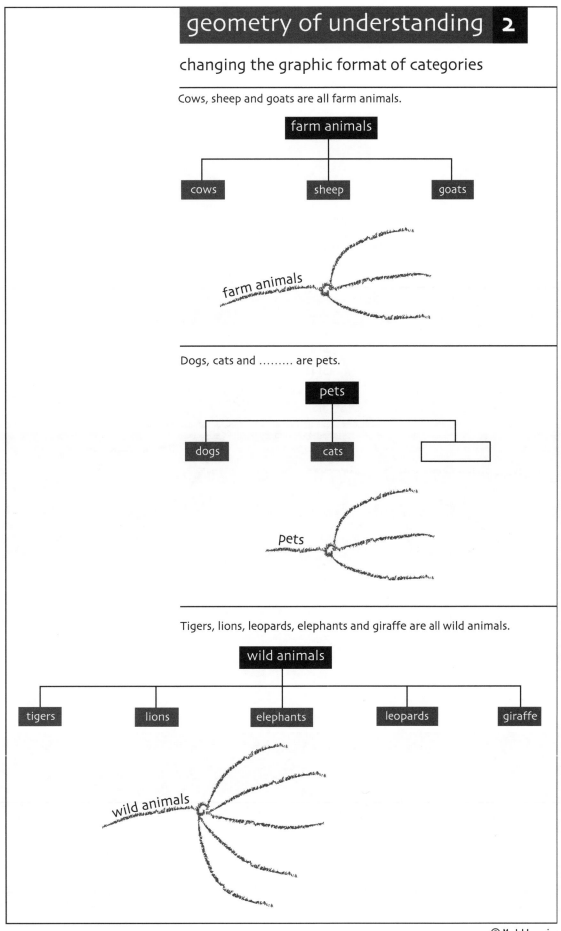

Dogs, cats and .... are pets.

Tigers, lions, leopards, elephants and giraffe are all wild animals.

geometry of understanding 2a

changing the graphic format of categories

Now, complete the model map below

animals
pets
farm
wild animals

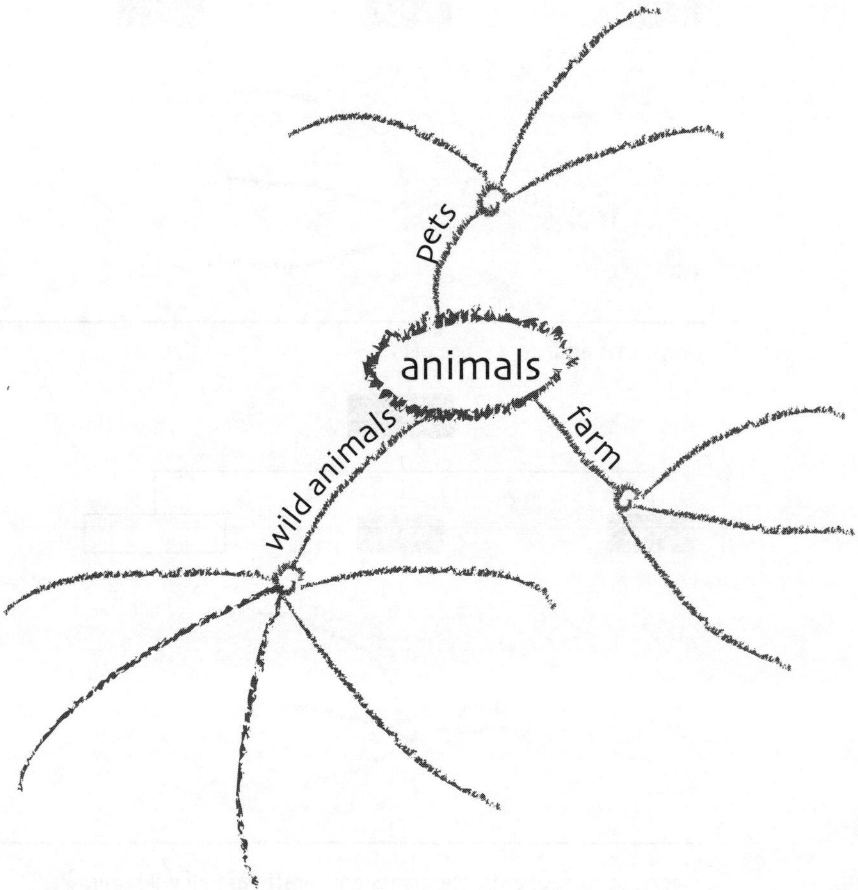

Favourite things

A mind map with "favourites" at the centre, branching out to: sweets, television, games, subjects, people

changing the graphic format of categories

All about me

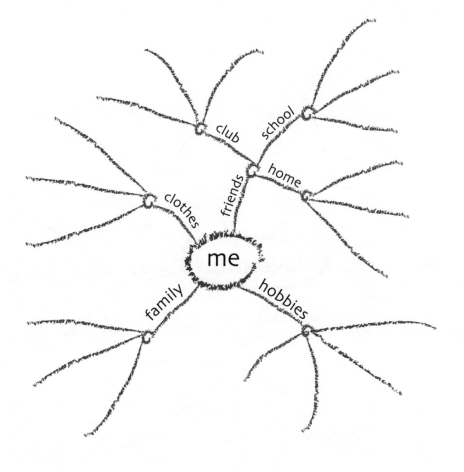

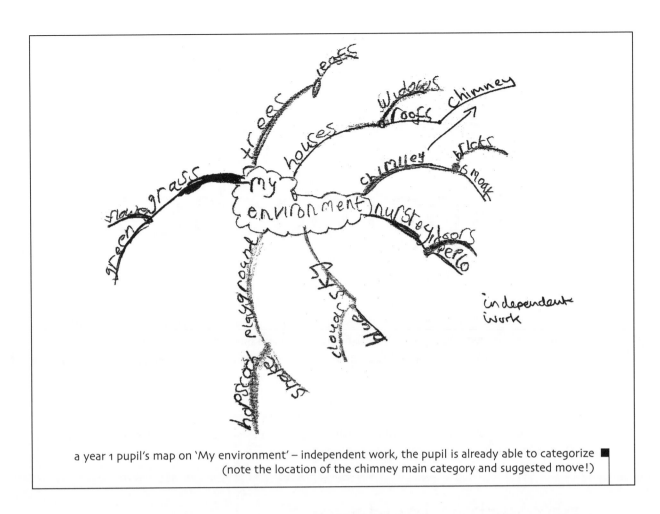

a year 1 pupil's map on 'My environment' – independent work, the pupil is already able to categorize ■
(note the location of the chimney main category and suggested move!)

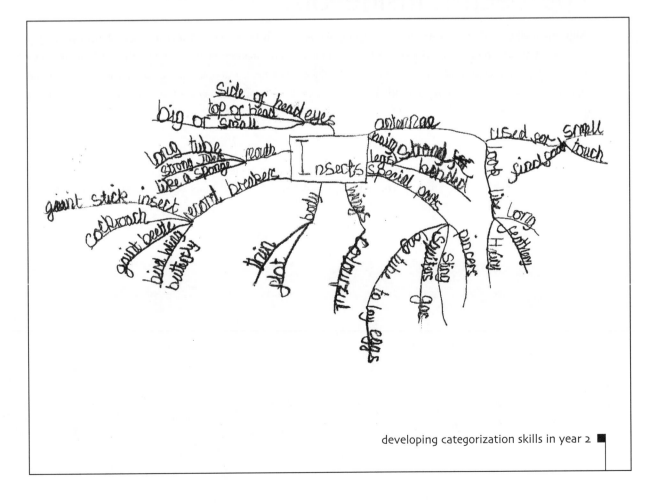

developing categorization skills in year 2 ■

different approaches

This chapter takes you through inductive and deductive approaches to mapping. Some people like to process in a parts-to-whole manner; others prefer to work from the whole to the parts. Put another way, some of us can access the organizing principles of our maps instinctively and are happy working centre outwards from the abstractions at the centre to the details on the outer branches. We call this the 'inside–out' approach. Others among us prefer to identify all the details first and then look for the organizing principles – the 'outside–in' approach. This chapter shows you how to map either way. It also explains the 'clusters-to-map' approach, which encourages free association and supports the mapper in identifying the main organizing categories that can appear anywhere on the cluster.

approach 1: inside–out

With this method you draw your map by identifying your main branches first and then develop them as you proceed. It differs from the outside–in method in that you are making an assumption that you already have information or material to add to the branches. It differs from the clusters-to-map approach in that the initial organizing categories are set out from the beginning. New ones can, and may well, emerge during the mapping process and these can be added at the centre (space permitting).

method

Before you begin, make sure you are clear about what you want to achieve by drawing your map. Make sure you know what the purpose of the map is. The purpose will determine what content you add and will enable you to check that the information you are adding to it is actually relevant. (See also step 5 below.)

1 Put the title of your chosen topic in the centre of an A3 piece of paper.

Whole-to-part or the two routes

2 Write your main organizing principles around the map title on top of lines that radiate from the centre. Make sure your writing is legible and that the lines are as horizontal as possible, as shown in this example.

Lake Garda Map 1

3 Taking each of these branches, consider what your main categories of information for each of them will be and write them on to sub-branches. If a specific detail comes to mind, think which category it belongs to and add that category to your map if it is not already there.

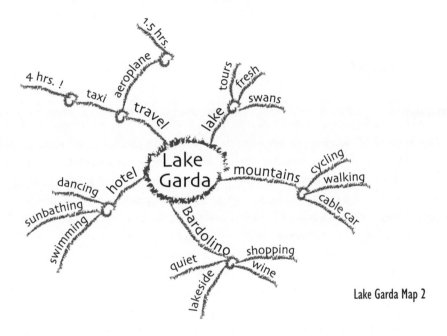

Lake Garda Map 2

For example, when the author of Lake Garda map 2 thought of the main branch words, the word 'tours' came immediately to mind because he and his partner went on tours around the lake. Now look at Lake Garda map 3 on the following page. You will see that the word 'tours' now comes off a family branch called 'activities'. The author obviously knew that the tours were an activity but by making this thinking visible on the map it made it more likely that other activities would come to mind. (See Common pitfalls, on page 171, for more on this.)

part-to-whole are to understanding

4 Repeat the process described above for each of the sub-branches. You do not need to move methodically around the map. You can jump around to whichever branches you wish.

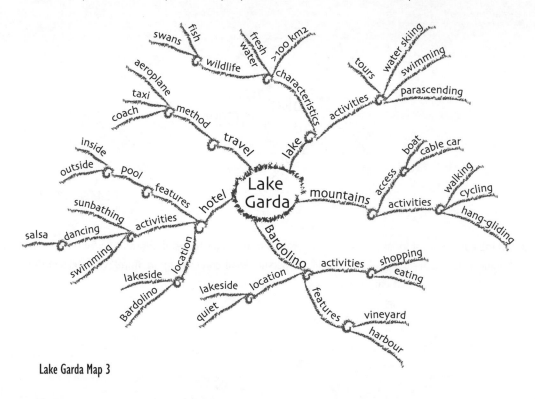

Lake Garda Map 3

■ **Top tip!**

At any stage of the mapping process you can help yourself by asking yourself good questions and then listening to the answers that come up. You can ask yourself the question 'what do I know about this?' or 'what do I want to say about this?' Answer the question by talking to yourself or to a partner. As you do this, listen for the key words and the categories that they belong to. For example, on Lake Garda map 2 the author asked himself the question 'what do I want to say about Bardolino?' The following commentary came into the author's head. 'I want to let my audience know that our hotel was there and that we splashed out on a four-star hotel for a couple of weeks, that it has a quiet lakeside location and that it had good swimming facilities. I also want to let people know about the Salsa dancing club that the hotel had.' Now look at the branches coming out of the Bardolino branch. The words 'location' and 'activities' were implicit categories of information that the author used in his commentary. The words off the 'location' and 'activities' branches are the key words that capture what he wanted to say.

---

5 Keep adding information to your branches in the ways described above until you feel you have added everything you consider important and relevant. As you get further away from the centre of your map, keep checking that the information you are adding to the outer branches is relevant to the title of the map and your initial purpose. If it is not, you have most probably gone into simple word association (see Common pitfalls, opposite).

6 Make sure that there is sufficient detail on the outer branches to support you in explaining the more abstract concepts at the centre. You may find it useful to explain your map to yourself or better still, to someone else. By doing this you will clarify your own understanding and you may well see ways of further developing your map.

Top tip!

Imagine that you have been asked to write a book on the topic at the centre of your map and that the publishers have asked you the following questions:

- What will the main sections be?
  These main sections are your main branches coming from the centre of your map.

- Within each of these sections, what chapter headings will you have?
  These chapter headings become the sub-branches coming off the main branches (see Lake Garda map 2).

- Within each of these chapters, what are the main points you want to make?
  These main points become the minor branches off the sub-branches.

You can carry on with this analogy until you have satisfied yourself that the map has within it everything that you consider relevant and important.

Common pitfalls

1 Word association

Let's take an example. The author's map is based on a postcard that he sent to relatives at home, telling them about his holiday at Lake Garda. His intention therefore was to inform relatives about the holiday. Since the holiday took place in a lakeside location bordered by mountains, you can see that it was relevant for him to have branches depicting information about the lake and the mountains around the lake. More information about mountains – for example, mountaineering and the equipment needed to do it – could easily be added but it would not be relevant to the purpose. This would simply be word association.

2 Two distinctions implied but buried at the node (the bit where the branch splits).

Look at Lake Garda maps 1 and 2 again. At the end of the 'lake' branch on map 2 you can see the words 'tours', 'fresh' and 'swans'. Implicit but not explicit in the node are two categories: 'activities' and 'characteristics'. Put another way, although 'swans' and 'fresh' and 'tours' are sub-categories of 'lake', they do not belong to the same category. Making these categories explicit greatly increases the chances of new connections being found.

approach 2: outside–in

With this method you put all your thoughts randomly down onto a sheet of paper before organizing them into categories and then producing your map. It differs from the inside–out method in that you are not predetermining what the main categories of your map will be. It differs from the clusters-to-map approach in that you do not associate one piece of information with another as an ongoing process.

method

1 Put the title of your chosen topic anywhere on an A3 piece of paper. Randomly write down on the page words that you associate with your chosen topic. Do not try to link or join them (although this may happen anyway).

At stage 1 write the single words onto single pieces of card or paper or ask the pupils to write the single words onto a grid that can be cut up and sorted physically by moving the words around on the desktop.

2   Keep 'dumping' the information until you cannot think of anything else you want to write down (see Curriculum design 1, below). The format does not matter. It could be a list, it could be words randomly spaced all over a page, it could be words written around a central point (as in the example).

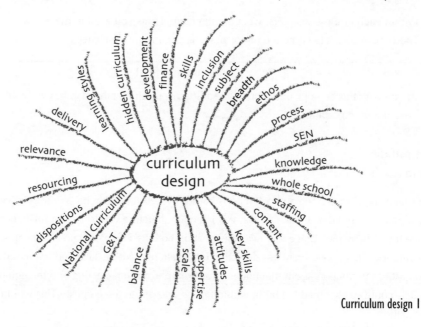

Curriculum design 1

3   Now look for the words that go together and join them to one another. You can do this by drawing lines, by colour coding them or by placing them together as we have done in diagram 2 below. As you do this you could ask yourself the following questions: What do these words have in common? Why am I putting these words together? What category do these words belong to? By sorting the words in this way you are of course starting to categorize the words.

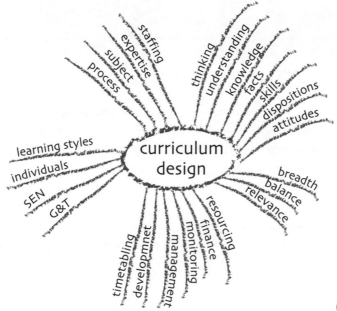

Curriculum design 2

4 Once you have grouped your existing words, you need to first identify the main organizing categories and then see if there are any sub-categories hidden within the words set out so far. When this has been done you are ready to draw your map. Sometimes the word that you need to use as the main category has already found its way onto the page. For example, in diagram 3 below you can see that one of the main branches is titled 'staffing'. 'Staffing' was already available. Now look at the branch titled 'principles'. 'Principles' was not available as a main category; we had to 'find it' by asking ourselves the question 'What category do these words – breadth, relevance, balance – belong to?' Similarly, the main category 'focus' and the sub-categories 'process', 'child' and 'knowledge' were identified by asking the same and similar questions.

As you draw your map you may think of other words to add to it. See how many new words we have added and perhaps consider where you would add some of your own.

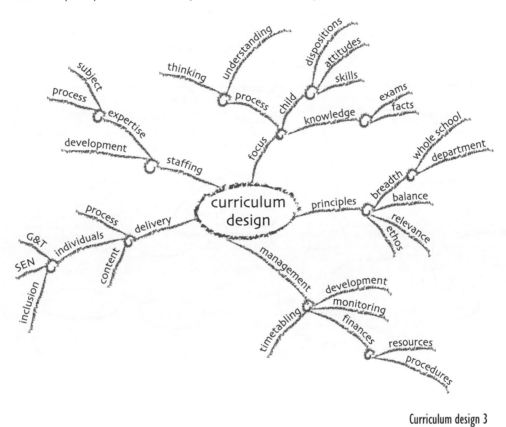

Curriculum design 3

approach 3: clusters to maps

With this method you are putting all your thoughts down onto a sheet of paper in a semi-random fashion. Associations are made and categories for the end product map emerge. It differs from the inside–out method in that you are not predetermining what the main categories of your map will be. It differs from the outside–in method in that you are visually encouraged to make connections right from the outset.

method

1 Draw a circle in the middle of an A3 sheet of paper. Write the title in the circle.

2 Draw circles around the central circle and join them to the centre with lines. In these circle write words that you associate with the title. Do not worry whether they are abstract or detailed.

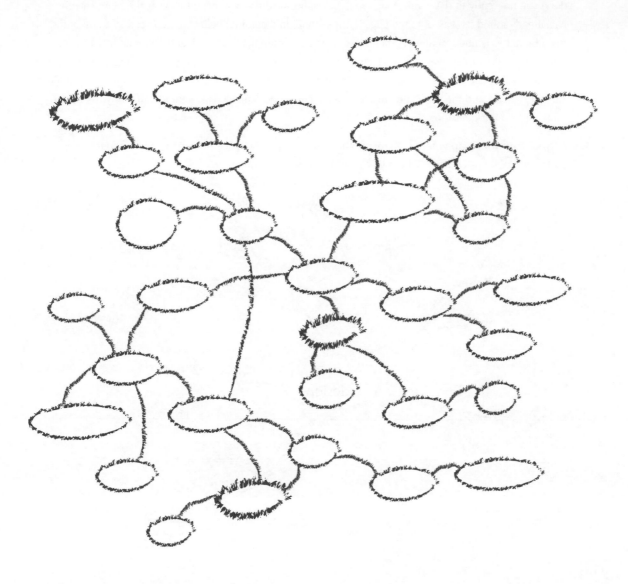

3 Repeat the above process from these outer circles until you have written down all that you can. (See diagram above.)

4 Scan your cluster and, where you see connections, make them visible by drawing additional lines between the words.

5 Use your cluster to help you identify the most important themes or categories of information within it. Ask yourself these questions: Which words occur most often? Which words have most words coming off and to them? Which words can I group together into categories?

6 Once you have identified your main categories or groups you can continue either from stage 1 of the Inside–out method or stage 4 of the outside–in method to produce your model map. (See opposite.)

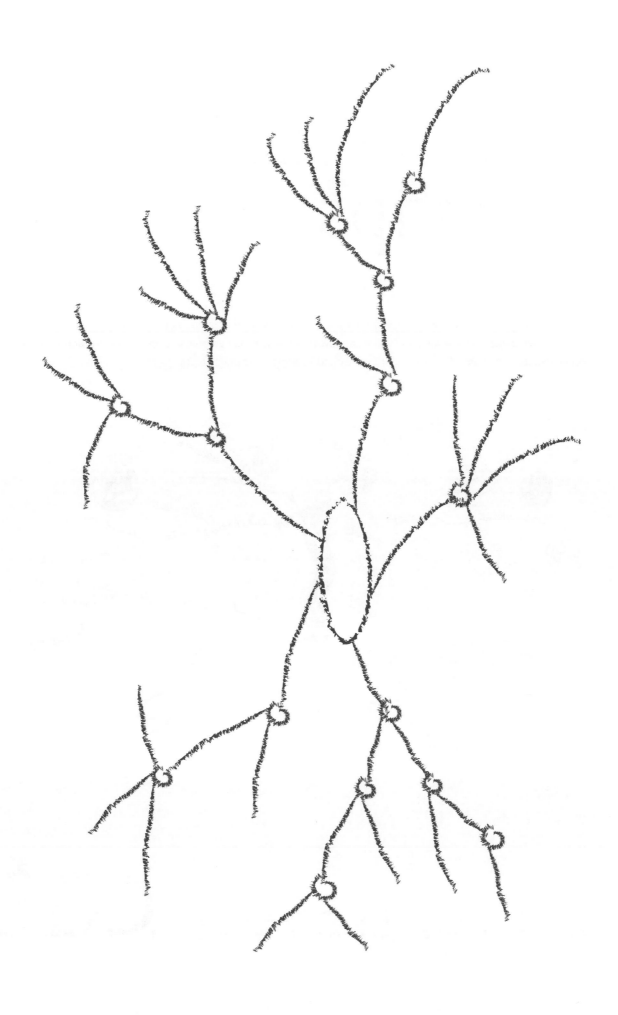

developing maps

This chapter looks at the various ways in which you can develop your mapping skills beyond basic competence in categorizing and spatial layout. You will learn how to achieve greater graphic impact, advance your powers of categorization, integrate other visual tools and extend your mapping practices.

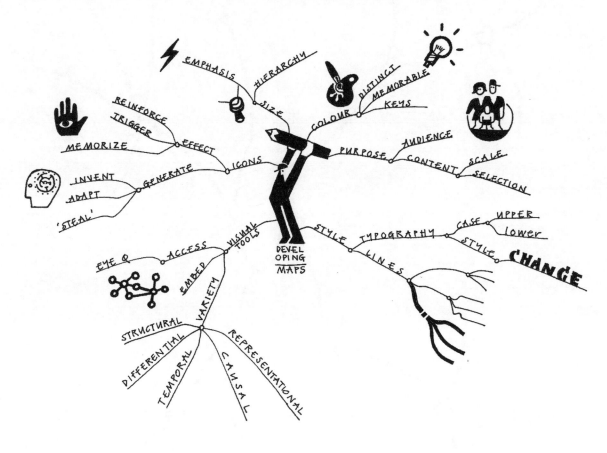

First master **cate**
then bring out the

graphics

Typography

- ■ Lower case v. upper case

There is much debate over the superiority of lower or upper case lettering in model mapping. The advantage of lower case letters is that they are easier to read. Words formed with lower case letters produce a unique shape that upper case words do not. However, as many of the words on a model map are not written horizontally, we can't be sure that this ease of reading transfers to other angles. Also, as we normally write with lower case, words can easily degenerate into our ordinary 'scribbles'. Within the varyingly angled positions of words in a model map this can often make many lower case words unreadable. So, unless you are certain of producing regular, well-formed, lower case text, revert to upper case. The words will not create unique shapes but they will always be legible.

- ■ Size

In model mapping it has become the custom to use bigger sized letters for the more central words. This is very useful as it reinforces the conceptual importance of these major organizing key words. The size of the words can be increased in terms of both height and width. Making the words thicker can add as much significance as an increase in height.

- ■ Style

Another variable open to you is type styles – or fonts. These days there are many different fonts available on most home computers, so spend time noticing the different characteristics and try to reproduce some of them in your handwritten model maps to personalize your words.

The centre

Most books on mapping techniques over-emphasize the significance of a central image. If you have time to embellish your maps, and if you can think of an appropriate image, then use this technique. But, also give it a title. Images can very powerfully capture the essence, or meaning, of a subject. However, they can also be frustratingly vague and imprecise. Try creating an image to represent asbestos – the subject of a talk which one of the authors mapped during a seminar for headteachers! I am sure that the next time you re-read your notes, you will not be able to remember what it was supposed to represent. So, whether you can conjure an image or not, always label the centre of your map.

Colour

When we present our MapWise course, some participants become confused when coloured felt-tip pens fail to materialize. It is not that we don't value the impact of colour, or that we don't use colour in our own maps. It is simply that the cognitive work involved in categorization is the primary part of the mapping process – and *nothing* must stand in its way. It doesn't matter how sophisticated is your use of your felt-tip pens – if you can't successfully categorize the language of the topic mapped and find an appropriate spatial arrangement, you will not succeed in learning or remembering. Colour will not do it for you!

gorization,
coloured felt pens

But, once you have mastered the cognitive skills of mapping, allow colour to enter your maps. If you're producing a quick map, use a four-colour ballpoint pen to map. Then, when preparing the final version of a map, use a fuller array of coloured ink pens. Felt tips tend to be too large and imprecise for accurate lettering or drawing.

Most people use different colours for the different branches of their maps. This is predictable and works very well as it differentiates the major categories of the map. However, don't be imprisoned by this practice. There are no rules concerning mapping – despite what you may read or hear elsewhere. So, if your map has a particular pattern, for example you may have identical sub-categories on all your branches, then see if you want to use colour in a different way. You may, for example, want to highlight the similarity of sub-categories across all the major branches by giving them the same colour.

Exploring further, you may invent other ways of using colour to represent knowledge. So, you may create a system where colours have specific significance. You then need to use a colour key at the margin of your map – or else you may find that you do not remember what the colours mean any more!

Images

Many people feel very anxious about drawing. They think that a model map is a specific technique for 'artistic' people, or at the very least, divergent thinkers. I hope we have dispelled this myth.

Images are very useful. By searching for an appropriate image, or creating it, you will be forced to consider the essential meaning and significance of a concept. This process will focus your mind. Once created, the image will assist rapid and powerful recall.

Clip art gives you a handy – albeit rather crude – lexicon of images. Start collecting images that you find arresting and create your own lexicon. Cut out pictures, symbols or icons from newspapers, magazines and advertising material. Scan junior and visual dictionaries for images.

Images can be very representational (realistic), or symbolic (not realistic). Company logos are a good source of symbolic images. Special visual languages, like the Makaton used in special schools, offer a range of symbols that can depict quite abstract notions. Once you start looking, you will be surprised how many icons and symbols you notice. Safety, cooking and washing instructions, for example, are full of symbols.

You can, of course, invent your own symbols. Above are a few of the icons we have used when mapping our weeks in our time management systems. How many could you invent now you can see a few examples?

Lines

Your model maps will be constructed of many lines. So, this is another feature that can be amended graphically to enhance your maps. Experiment with variations in the thickness of lines, as well as textures (using straight, curved, jagged or dotted), and decorations (adding geometric shapes, shadows, patterns). Also experiment with different types of pen.

When drawing the nodes (the junctions where lines meet), try a variety of shapes. Edward de Bono often emphasizes the importance of 'roundabouts' as they are the place from which actions can evolve. They are where options are considered. Similarly, the nodes on a model map represent the thinking that structures the map, and therefore the meaning. So, rather than minimizing their significance, emphasize them. This reminds you of their importance. You can do this by using a variety of shapes at this junction of lines.

Visual tools

There are a range of visual tools other than model maps. (See our previous book, *Thinking Skills & Eye Q* published by Network Educational Press, 2002, for a full explanation.) These visual tools are suited to specific thinking processes. For example, a double bubble is a better visual tool for the purpose of comparing and contrasting two elements than a model map. A model map could be used for this, but a double bubble would be more effective.

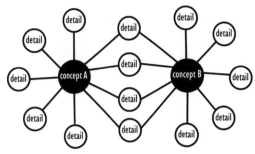

One feature that makes model maps unique among visual tools, is their capacity to embed other visual tools within them. So if part of your map includes a comparison between two aspects, events, persons or thoughts, include a double bubble at that point. The same is true for other visual tools. Their integration will develop your model maps beyond a statement of perception to one that acknowledges other dimensions.

Computers

There are now many software programs available for model mapping. Some can be obtained free (legally) while others will cost a great deal of money. Their main advantage is that they can absorb and integrate a great deal of information in their 'depth'. This means that 'underneath' a map lie further layers of knowledge. For capturing and gradually accumulating knowledge on a single map, computer software is unbeatable.

With new web-based software, it is possible to create your own digital model maps. At Woodlands special school, members of staff have produced digital model maps that contain sound, moving icons and QuickTime movies.

For those of you who want to produce more permanent, print-based model maps, then any industry, illustration-genre software will produce clear, well-designed model maps. This type of software, however, is specialized and unless you are prepared to spend time and effort learning its intricate workings, leave it well alone.

Categorization

We finish with the most important feature of mapping – the ability to create ever more significant and meaningful categories. Whenever you are about to decide what your organizing categories will be, ask yourself what other category might be appropriate if you were able to 'lift yourself' up above your map and your thinking. This is what metacognition is like. It is like flying in a helicopter above your thinking.

What other categories could be super-ordinate? How else could you organize your branches in anticipation of further information? What key conceptual ideas would offer you more choices on how to systematize your map? Ask a friend how they would map the same topic. Continue to explore, and challenge, your thinking via your categorization, and your mapping skills will continue to develop.

Practice

Expand where you use your mapping skills. Don't be content simply to map what you already know, or what you are planning. Map what you don't know! Map what you are reading – how can you summarize the last book you read on one side of A4. In fact, try doing the same on a side of A5, even A6!

Create model maps of each talk, seminar or training session you attend. You will realize that you will become interested in any subject you map. Interest, you will discover, does not lie 'out there' but, rather, within you. The act of mapping will make this very evident and powerfully real for you.

Practise by mapping the news programmes on television. Model mapping is perfectly designed for information structuring. First, there is the overview of what is to be covered – your basic branches. Then, there is a more detailed report – your subsidiary branches. Next, there are the very detailed accounts – the peripheral parts of your map. Lastly, just in case you missed anything, there is the review section – where you can check your map for accuracy.

taking notes

Sixth former at a comprehensive school in Essex to one of the authors in 1988: *'Sir, you keep saying how important it is for us to take accurate notes – what do accurate notes look like sir?'*

Some of us would be forgiven for thinking that this student was 'being awkward'. He wasn't, but I found it frustrating that back in 1988 I didn't have any answers for him. I showed him my college notes (largely linear and nonsensical) and I recommended a study skills book that my head of department had mentioned a few weeks earlier. This chapter is here to save you going through whatever you would go through if and when a pupil were to ask you the same question. It shows you how to create meaningful, memorable notes from linear text.

If you have read chapter 1.3, Holographic–Linear, you will realize that for note taking to be meaningful we need to create our own models of meaning from the linear text in front of us. In this chapter, a series of exercises is provided to help pupils develop these skills. When using these exercises with pupils it never ceases to amaze us how much they enjoy searching out the meaning that is buried within linear text. We can only suggest that this is because the 'meaning making' process has been made explicit.

The note-taking process

1 Read through the text.

2 **Highlight** all the nouns, verbs and adjectives within the text. (See extract on 'sharks' opposite.)

3 Write all the words down randomly. Most pupils will inadvertently start to group (or categorize) the words as they randomly write them down; it's actually hard not to do this!

4 Put the words into groups or categories. Ask yourself which words go together.

5 Find the word(s) that successfully categorize the others.

6 Find sub-categories within the main categories.

7 Set out your work as a map.

Organizing your
key to

Steps 1 & 2: Read the text and highlight the important nouns, verbs and adjectives.

Sharks

Sharks are predatory fish that are found in all the seas but mostly in warm waters. There are around 250 species of shark ranging in size from the 60cm pygmy shark to the 15-metre whale shark, which is the worlds biggest living fish.

Sharks have pointed snouts, crescent-shaped mouths with several rows of sharp triangular teeth.

The whale shark and the basking shark are not predatory. Unlike the other sharks they are harmless plankton eaters.

The most feared shark is the white shark. It can grow to up to 6 metres in length and feeds on other fish and animals. It is known to attack swimmers and boats without provocation.

Shark meat is nutritious and shark oils are used in industry. Its skin, when tanned, is a durable leather.

Step 3: Write down all the highlighted words randomly.

Sharks	fish	250 species
pygmy shark	60cm	harmless
whale shark	15 metres	biggest
predatory	rows	plankton
crescent-shaped	basking shark	pointed
snouts	mouths	teeth	triangular
feared	feeds	
white shark	6 metres	attack	swimmers	boats
animals	meat	
nutritious	industry	sharp
leather	tanned	oils
warm waters	skin	seas

notes is the
understanding

Step 4: Put the words into groups.

seas	snouts	meat	white shark
warm waters	pointed	nutritious	6 metres
species	mouths	oils	feared
250	crescent-shaped	industry	attacks
	teeth	skin	boats
	sharp	tanned	swimmers
	triangular	leather	predatory
	rows		feeds
			fish
			animals
basking shark	whale shark	pygmy shark	
harmless	15 metres	60 centimetres	
	non-predatory		
	plankton		
	biggest		

Step 5: Find words that successfully categorize the others.

As you can see below, sometimes the word that successfully groups the others is one that appears in the text (for example 'species'). Often however, you need to go beyond the text or higher up the appropriate language hierarchy to find the word that groups the others together (for example 'locations', 'products').

Edit your words as you go along, making substitutes if this helps with categorization (changing 'harmless' to 'non-predatory' in this case, for example).

LOCATIONS	SPECIES	PRODUCTS		
seas	250	meat		
warm waters		nutritious		
		oils		
		industry		
		skin		
		tanned		
		leather		

FEATURES	whale shark	white shark	pygmy shark	basking shark
snouts	15 metres	6 metres	60cm	
pointed	biggest	feared		non-predatory
mouths	non-predatory	attacks		
crescent-shaped	plankton	boats		
teeth		swimmers		
sharp		predatory		
triangular		feeds		
rows		fish		
		animals		

Step 6: Find sub-categories within the main categories.

Our map will have four main branches: 'locations', 'species', 'features' and 'products'. Within these main categories however there are sub-categories. These are set out in italics below. As with the main categories, sometimes they are present and sometimes they are implicit and need to be made explicit.

For example 'basking', 'white', 'whale' and 'pygmy' all belong within the category 'species' – they are all species of sharks. The number '250' also belongs inside the category species – there are approximately 250 species of shark. But here the family relationship ends since 250 is not a species of shark. Further categorization is needed...

LOCATIONS	EXAMPLES	PRODUCTS
seas	whale shark	*food*
warm waters	15 metres	nutritious
	non-predatory	meat
SPECIES	plankton	*industry*
250	*size*	skin
		tanned
FEATURES	white shark	leather
snouts	6 metres	oils
mouths	feared	
teeth	attacks	
sharp	boats	
triangular	swimmers	
rows	*predatory*	
	animals	
	fish	
	size	
	basking shark	
	non-predatory	
	pygmy shark	
	60cm	
	size	

Step 7: Setting out your work as a map.

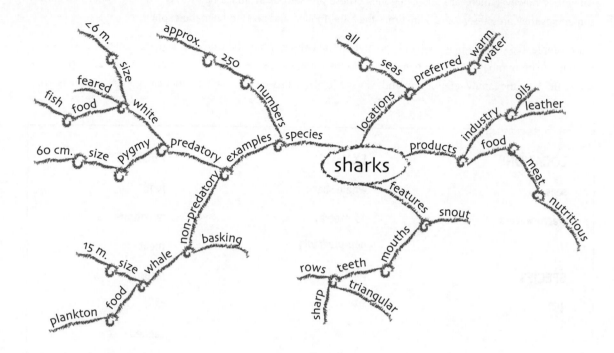

You can see now the centrality of categorization as a thinking and note-taking skill. In order to understand text, learners have to be able to organize information into categories. They have to be able to find the words that group or hold less important words together. This is what successful pupils are good at (although they don't realize it) and less successful pupils struggle with (perhaps because they do not know what it is they are not doing).

You can also see clearly where the 'gaps' in our knowledge about sharks are (according to the short extract used). The white space on a map is as important as the writing itself, if not more so. It seems to 'invite' new ideas and offers a space for them to go into. There is plenty of room for new main categories, sub-categories or details to be added.

■ **Top tip!**

Imagine the map above as a baseline of what the pupils already know about sharks. As they go through a topic, new information can be added. They can see their understanding grow.

Summary maps

The next set of three exercises takes a series of news stories and requires the learner to produce a model map that summarizes the content. We have successfully used these exercises with pupils aged 10–18 years (and more than a few teachers who are a bit older).

Exercise 1. For this exercise the pupils should be given a copy of the map on page 187, which already has its main branches drawn and some sub-branches completed. The pupils have to investigate the news stories on page 186, searching for the words that complete the map.

Exercise 2. Now gather your own news stories. Cut off the headlines and ask the pupils to come up with their own main headings. Then ask the pupils to use these headlines as their central map headings and map out the information contained within the stories.

■ **Top tips!**

- ■ This exercise works well as a paired activity.

- ■ When the pupils have finished transforming the linear text into a map, take away the news articles. Now ask the pupils to choose one of the articles from their map and write it up (turn it back into linear text). They will be amazed how much easier it is to write from a map.

Exercise 3. Now ask pupils to use the same techniques to summarize a page or section of a textbook that they are using in class.

■ **Top tips!**

- ■ It's a good idea if you practise doing this exercise yourself as it can remind you just how hard it can be to extract meaning from text.

- ■ Some pupils at the Exercise 3 stage may need some help or 'scaffolding'. In other words you may need to do for them what we did for you in Exercises 1 and 2 above.

Sicily — Mount Etna erupts

The village of Nicolosi came under threat as lava flowed to within two miles. A religious procession was organized by residents asking God to save their houses. The 5000 residents were ready to be evacuated by security forces that also helped to build a mud barricade to help divert the lava. The village survived but the bubbling lava, travelling at two metres per minute, destroyed lifts on the side of the volcano. A thick layer of volcanic ash closed the airport at Catania.

Shetland Islands

The Shetland Islands have 5000 years of history. They have been home to settlers from the Iron and Bronze Age and have served as stopping off points for Viking raiders. Today their most hardy settlers are their birds. A trip to the island of Noss is well worthwhile. The 150ft cliffs of this 'seabird city' are home to shags, guillemots and gannets. Another Island worth a visit is Unst. The scenery is spectacular and includes kelp wrapped bays, blanket bogs and whitewashed croft houses. You may also see a bus stop that comes complete with television, houseplants and armchair.

A Millennium Dome from prehistory

A hill fort has been discovered in North Yorkshire. Archaeologists claim it is one of the largest prehistoric forts ever found. The fort dates from around 400BC in the Iron Age and was discovered at Sutton Bank, a 700 ft hill, on the edge of the North Yorkshire Moors park at Roulston Scar. A 1.3 mile circuit of limestone has ramparts that are spread over 40 acres. Archaeologists are not sure why it was built. Some say its purpose was military, others say it was built as a symbol to enhance the power of tribal chiefs.

Stimulating gorillas

Attempts are being made at Longleat Safari Park in Wiltshire to stop Sambo and Nico, two ageing gorillas, from becoming bored. Keepers have tried to stimulate them by hiding their food. Now they are going one step further by giving them their own vegetable patch. Carrots and maize are being planted for the gorillas to find and dig up — just as they would in the wild.

Laughing dogs at play

Dogs can laugh. It's official. Patricia Simonet, a psychologist in the US says that dogs produce a range of chuckles, titters and guffaws, many of which are outside of the range that humans can hear. Four sounds were recorded — whining, barking, growling and laughter. She describes the laughing as a "huhh, huhh" pant. Although dogs produce all four sounds during the course of the day, they only laugh when playing. Simonet played the dog sounds to 14 puppies. When they heard the laughter they reacted by approaching a toy or by approaching another puppy. This contrasted with their response to the growl, which evoked no reaction.

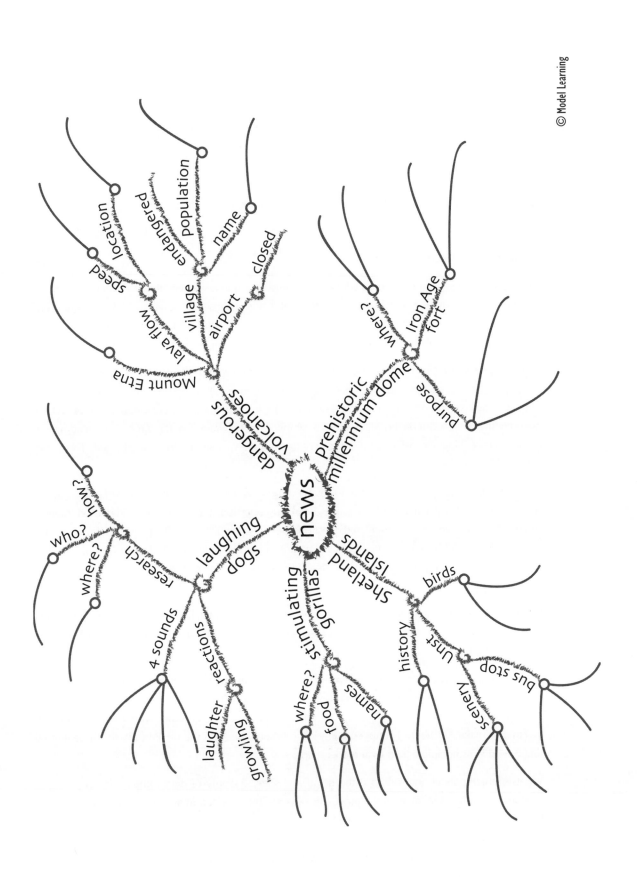

case study

Note taking

In some schools passive learning is the norm. Students need to be encouraged to be more proactive and to be more independent. Model mapping can help achieve these aims.

For some years I have experienced difficulties in teaching students how to be effective note takers. Two of the areas that have caused most concern in relation to this skill are:

1 watching film/video

2 gathering information from sources such as texts or the internet.

■ 1. Watching film/video

Media presentations can be of great educational value for students, especially when they are actively involved while watching and listening. Traditionally this means that teachers make up questions relating to videos so that the students do not sit passively, watching. While employed as a learning support teacher I saw this situation in subjects such as physics, biology, geography and history.

Very often it seemed that the questions asked about the video were pedestrian and seemed to exist to avoid passivity rather than develop learning and questioning. It was also obvious that most SEN students required differentiated question sheets in order to participate in these video activities. Where no such materials existed, the SEN students simply had to watch, as the process of reading the questions, watching and listening and also writing answers was simply too complicated. Thus, they were in effect excluded.

One thing that struck me was the considerable workload involved for the teacher, in that active watching meant the teacher had to watch and make up questions for every single video used in every single lesson; furthermore, differentiated questions were also required. Model mapping eliminates this workload issue and actually creates a holistic means of gathering data from film and video. This also applies to more straightforward didactic teaching where students listen and watch the teacher (hopefully!).

While able students might manage to create an entire map from scratch while watching a video, some students might require support in terms of the teacher supplying some of the titles for the main branches of a map.

The map opposite shows the notes taken by Tom, a 14-year-old SEN student, while watching a 30-minute film about a day in the life of a busy newspaper, as part of a short media course. Normally I issue A3 paper to students; on this day I'd run out and gave out A4 paper which had to be taped together to make A3 sheets. I supplied a few main branch ideas on the OHP but basically requested that the students complete their own model maps.

What is striking about Tom's map is the detail and sheer quantity of data gathered in such a short session. I think his enjoyment in the process is obvious in the skilful, imaginative and expressive way he has organized his map. He subsequently went on to write up a report based on his notes in which he transferred his information from map form to prose form most successfully. On page 190 is a map made by Tom while mapping a similar media video about two journalists who write tourist books.

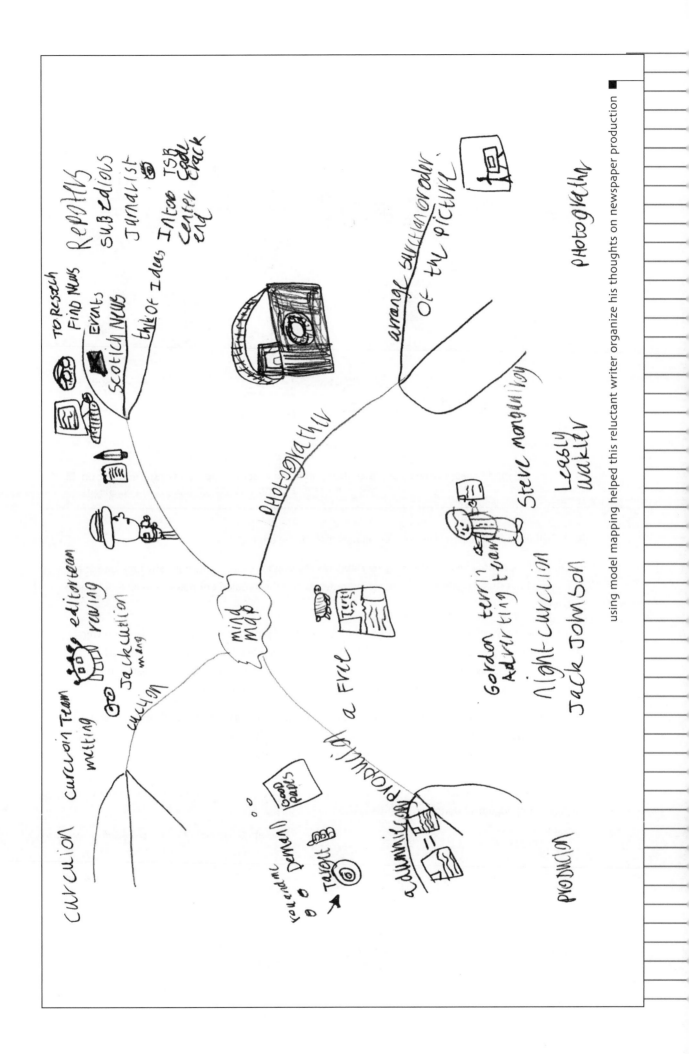

using model mapping helped this reluctant writer organize his thoughts on newspaper production

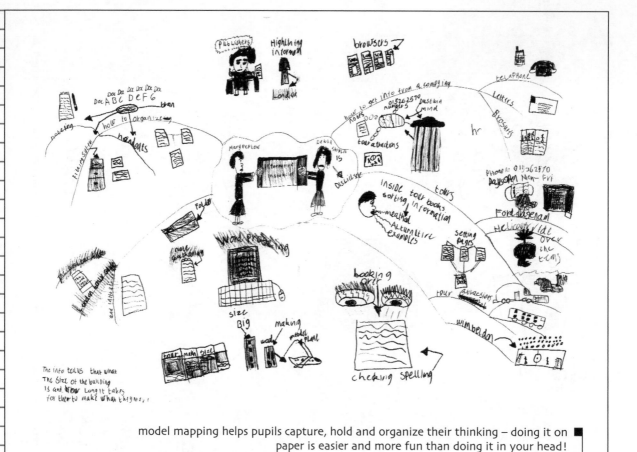

model mapping helps pupils capture, hold and organize their thinking – doing it on ■
paper is easier and more fun than doing it in your head!

■ 2. Gathering information from sources such as texts or the internet

During SEN tutorial times I often watched students revising for exams. This normally took one of two forms: either students simply read or re-read notes or else they copied out notes from textbooks onto paper.

The case study on page 95 describes how I introduced mapping to Laura, a 15-year-old who went on to produce model maps of her notes (see biology map on page 96). For these she worked between textbooks, jotters and a mapping program. Revision maps can also be re-created in exams to serve as the basis for essay writing and Laura used them in this way too.

I teach students to use mapping programs, which can run behind the internet and students Alt/Tab between the two when gathering information. This is extremely useful as it means students have a record of the main subject areas analysed during the data gathering process. This again is a more active form of learning because it requires the students to make selection decisions – something that can be omitted or limited if they are simply copying and pasting chunks of internet text into a word-processing document during an internet session.

Gerry Dolan, SENCO, Dingwall Academy, Scotland

Appendix

Case study

Coppins Green Primary School

Coppins Green Primary School is a very large primary school with over nine hundred pupils ranging from our Nursery to Year 6. We are part of the Clacton and Harwich Action Zone in north-east Essex and have an intake of children with complex social and learning needs.

We are a forward-looking school, constantly reaching out for better ways to do things… so when a few of us had the opportunity to attend a model mapping course led by Oliver Caviglioli, we jumped at it. We quickly realized that we had a powerful tool within our grasp. In fact, on a personal level, I found model mapping so powerful that it really altered the way I worked and gave me an immediate way of focusing on the subject in hand and organizing myself far more efficiently. I find it a quick way in to note taking, planning complex pieces of work such as action plans and a speedy and comprehensive way to take and distribute minutes of meetings. Oh that I had learnt how to do this years ago!

I first introduced mapping skills to my Year 4 class. The students instantly loved it and we worked together to build up our skills – making our own rules for helping us to map well and gradually changing the way we did things by classifying more carefully. I knew the students really had a grasp of what they were doing when, planning a class assembly together, I asked them how we could explain mapping to the rest of the school. They suggested demonstrating it by putting out a huge range of toys and classifying them while drawing a model map of how they were doing it. We'd never used a map that way before!

So, taking the bull by the horns, we made the decision to train our whole staff (both teaching staff and learning support assistants) in model mapping, this time led by Ian Harris. This was a really important decision because having all staff trained to a high level was really supportive to both teachers and students.

At the time of writing this case study we have been using model mapping at Coppins Green for only six months – but the impact has been remarkable and we are delighted at the enthusiasm shown by staff and students. All members of our staff are developing imaginative ways of using mapping across the primary age and ability range, although we all realize that we have a long way to go. In many of our classrooms model mapping is a tool that students now enjoy, feel secure in using and can utilize for a range of different purposes to organize their work. We even use model mapping to minute formal meetings, which saves a mountain of paper!

Following the initial input, we gave staff the brief to incorporate model mapping into their teaching, but gave them the flexibility to use mapping as they felt confident doing. The initial bias has been in the field of literacy across the school, from Reception, where stories shared are mapped, to Year 6, where children use mapping as a frame on which to plan a range of fiction and non-fiction texts for their own writing. Using mapping at the planning stage for writing is, I feel, a really positive development as it tends to free up the students to think of plot or development and really get that sorted. Certainly in the upper school classrooms, modelling of planning and shared planning takes place far more consistently because we are able to use mapping as a vehicle for teacher delivery. At the writing stage the students have said that the map makes them able to concentrate on how they are writing, rather than what they are writing; and of course the written script is now never the same as the plan! Opportunities to plan with or to share maps with talk partners have had a positive impact on speaking and listening in a structure that supports the development of collaborative work and gives a context that is easily managed to develop social skills.

We are at the start of a long but worthwhile journey and now need to extend the range of areas in which we use mapping skills.

On the following pages are some examples of the maps that have been produced by pupils at Coppins Green Primary School, from Reception to Year 6.

Case study by Gillian Last, Assistant Headteacher, Coppins Green Primary School, Clacton-on-Sea, Essex

Reception

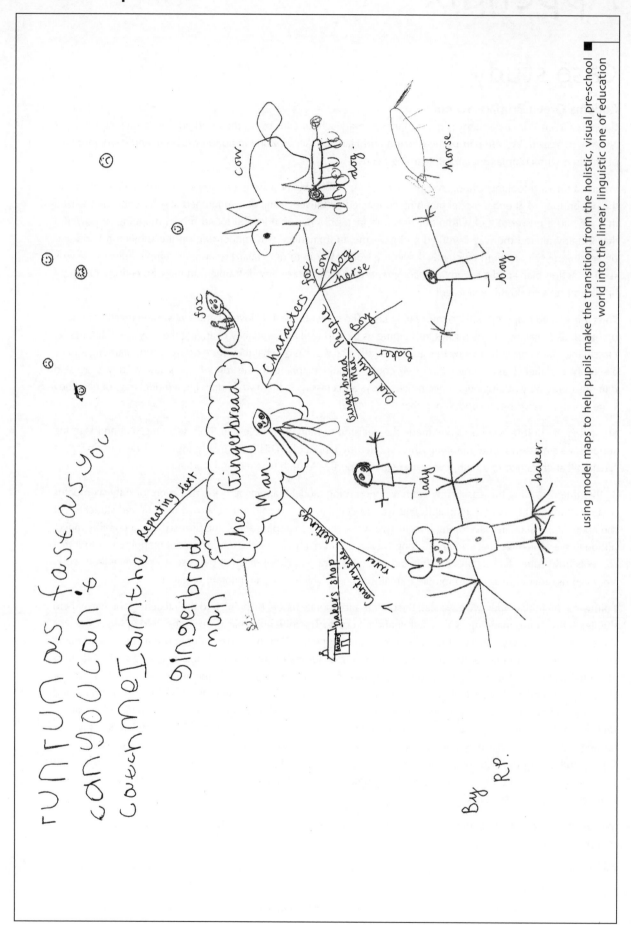

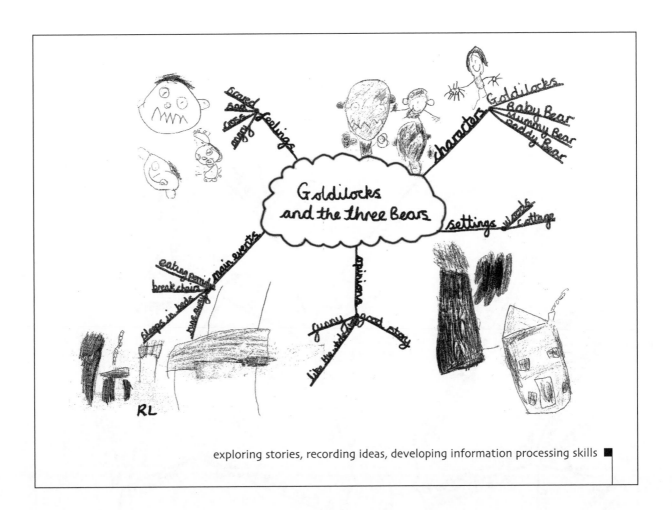

exploring stories, recording ideas, developing information processing skills ■

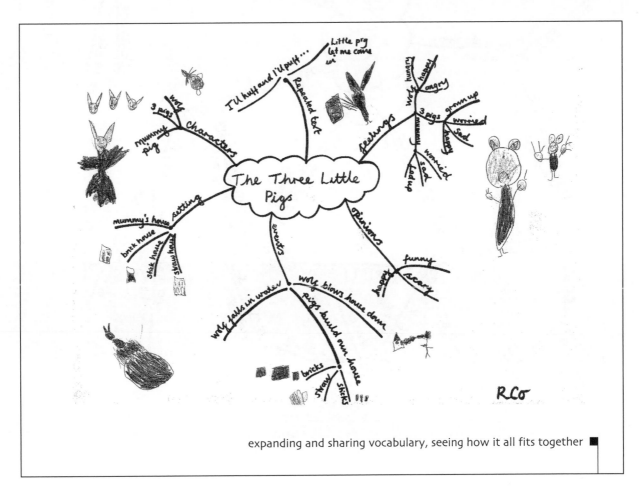

expanding and sharing vocabulary, seeing how it all fits together ■

Year 1

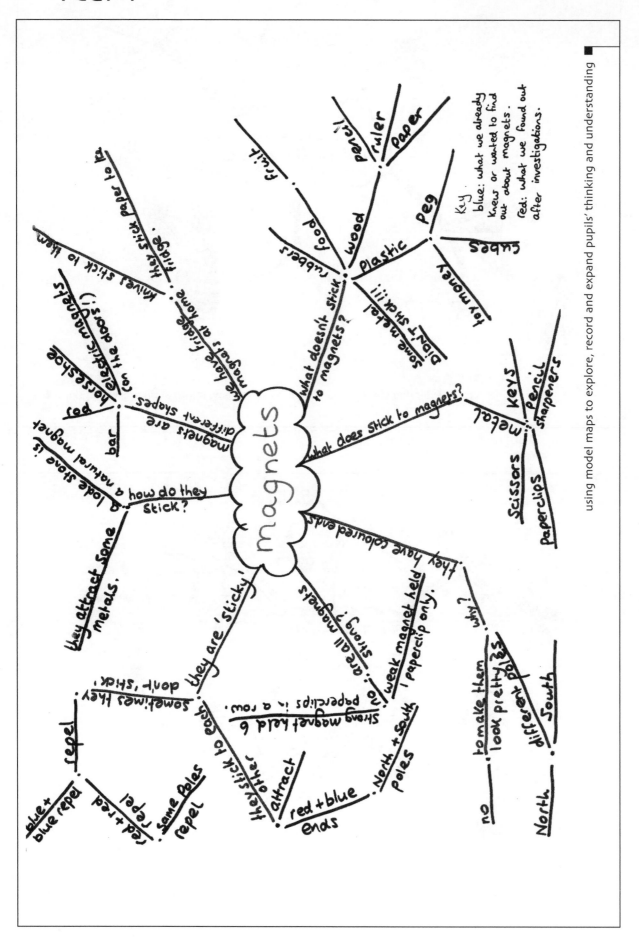

Key:
blue: what we already knew or wanted to find out about magnets.
red: what we found out after investigations.

magnets

what doesn't stick to magnets?
- paper
- pencil
- ruler
- fruit
- wood
- rubbers
- Peg
- Plastic
- cubes
- toy money
- some metal, Didn't stick!!!

what does stick to magnets?
- metal
- Keys
- Pencil sharpeners
- Scissors
- Paperclips

magnets are different shapes
- they stick paper to them
- knives stick to them
- we have fridge magnets at home (on the fridge)
- electric magnets (?)
- horseshoe
- bar
- rod

how do they stick?
- a lode stone is a natural magnet
- they attract some metals.

they are 'sticky'
- are all magnets strong?
  - no: weak magnet held 1 paperclip only.
  - strong magnet held 6 paperclips in a row.
- they have coloured ends
  - why?
    - to make them look pretty?
    - no
  - North + South
  - different poles
    - North
    - South
  - North + South Poles
  - red + blue ends

sometimes they don't stick.
- they stick to each other
  - attract
  - repel
    - blue + blue repel
    - red + red repel
    - Same Poles repel

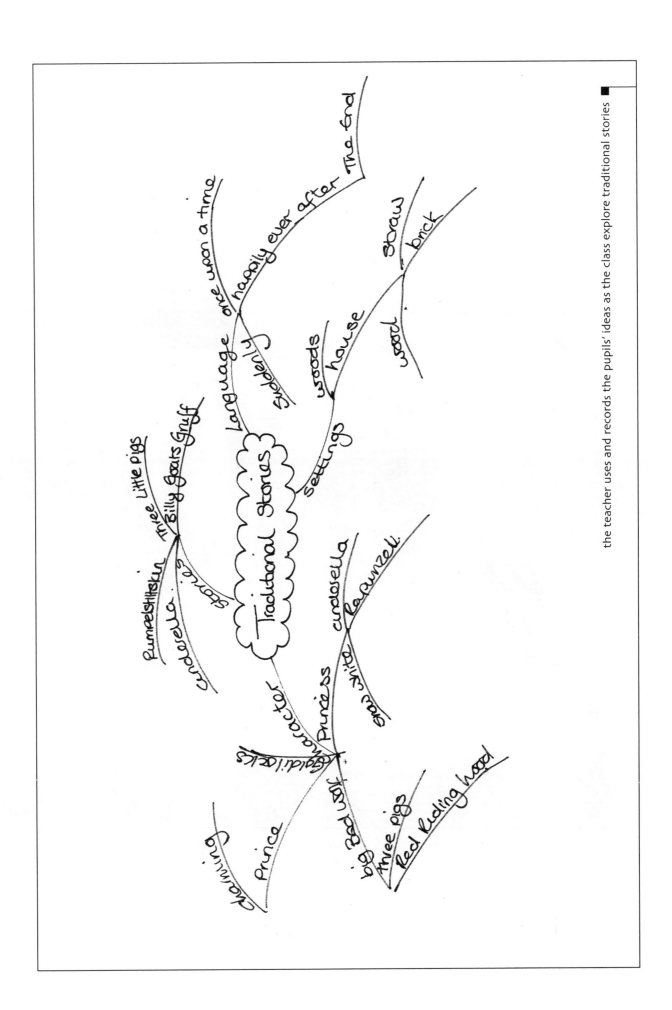

Traditional Stories

once upon a time
happily ever after
The End
Language
Suddenly
woods
house
straw
brick
wood
settings
Three Little Pigs
Billy Goats Gruff
Rumpelstiltskin
Cinderella
stories
Cinderella
Rapunzel
Snow White
character
Princess
Goldilocks
Charming
Prince
big Bad Wolf
Three pigs
Red Riding hood

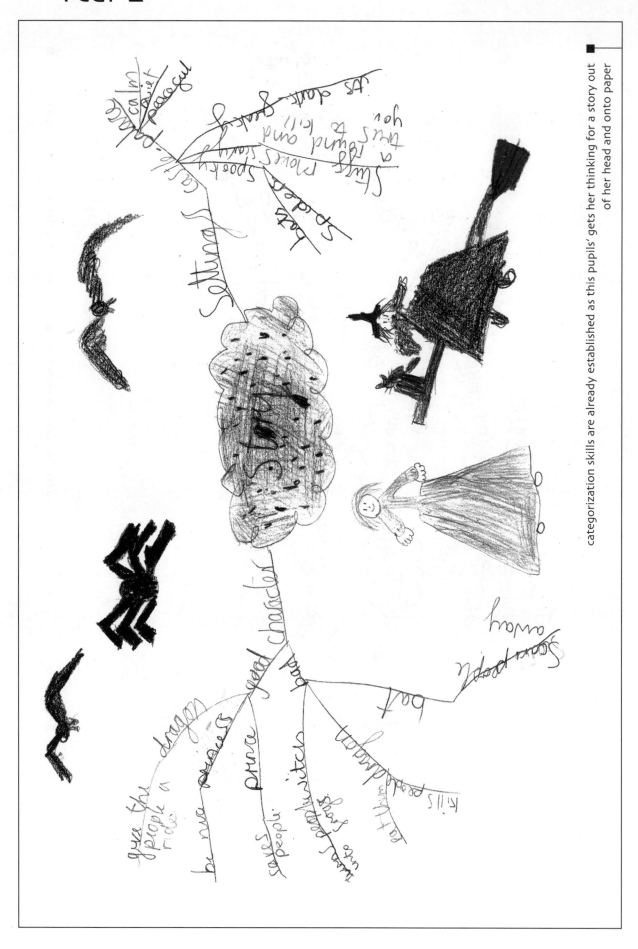

categorization skills are already established as this pupils' gets her thinking for a story out of her head and onto paper

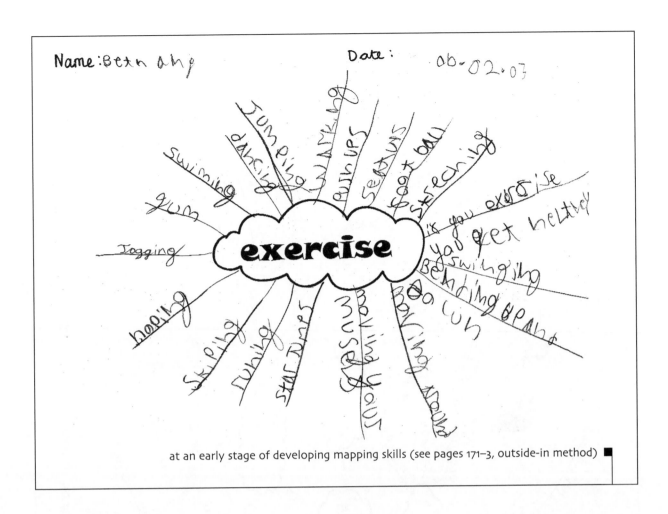

Name: Beth ahp   Date: 06·02·03

at an early stage of developing mapping skills (see pages 171–3, outside-in method) ∎

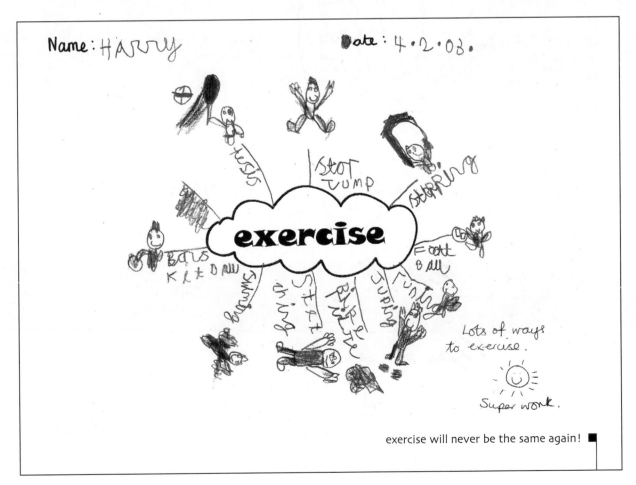

Name: HARRY   Date: 4·2·03.

Lots of ways
to exercise.

Super work.

exercise will never be the same again! ∎

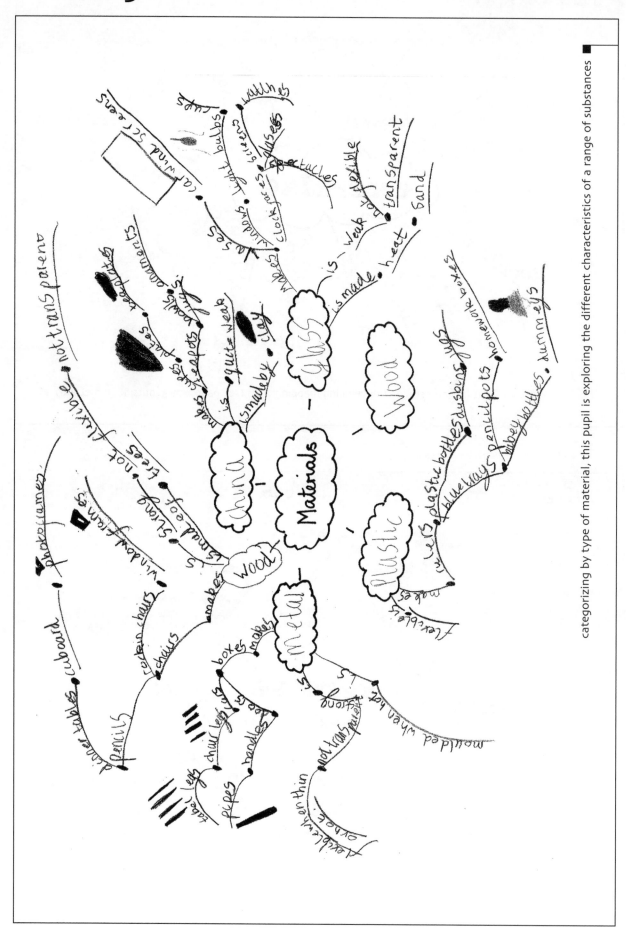

categorizing by type of material, this pupil is exploring the different characteristics of a range of substances

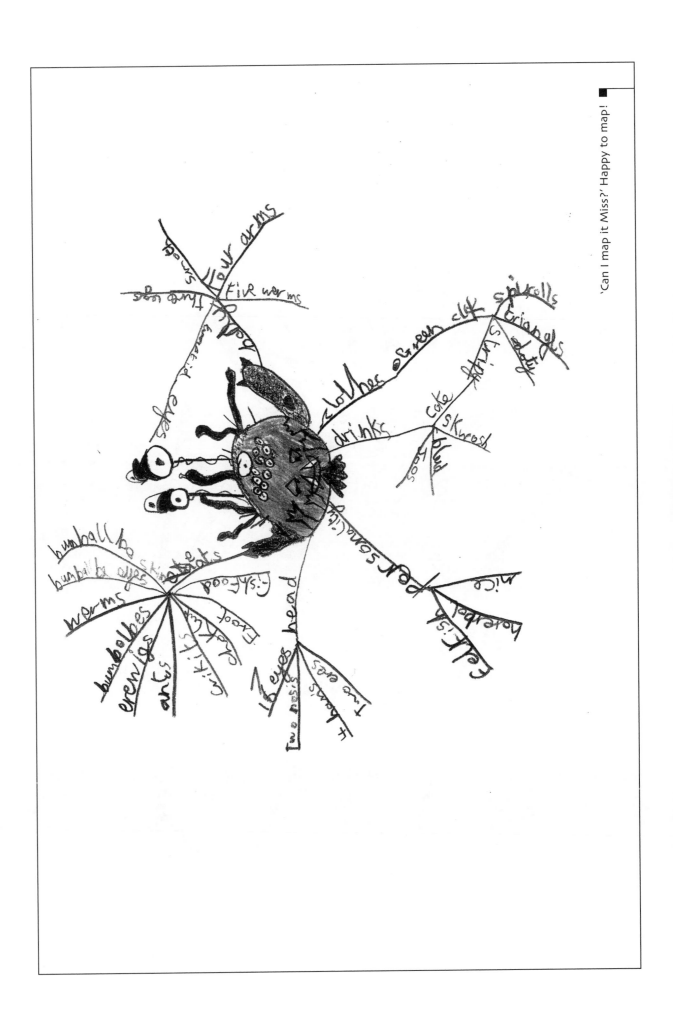

'Can I map it Miss?' Happy to map!

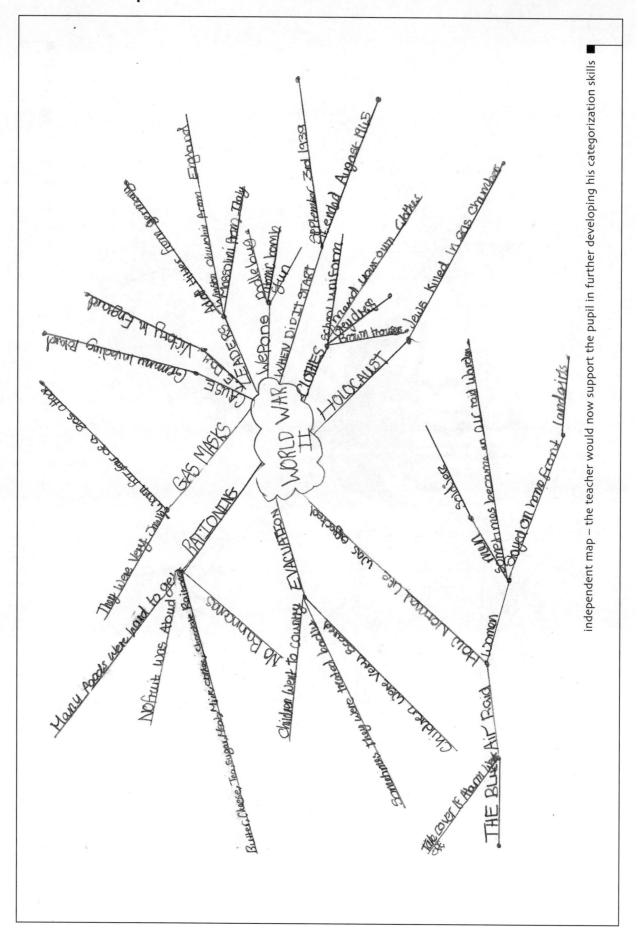

independent map – the teacher would now support the pupil in further developing his categorization skills

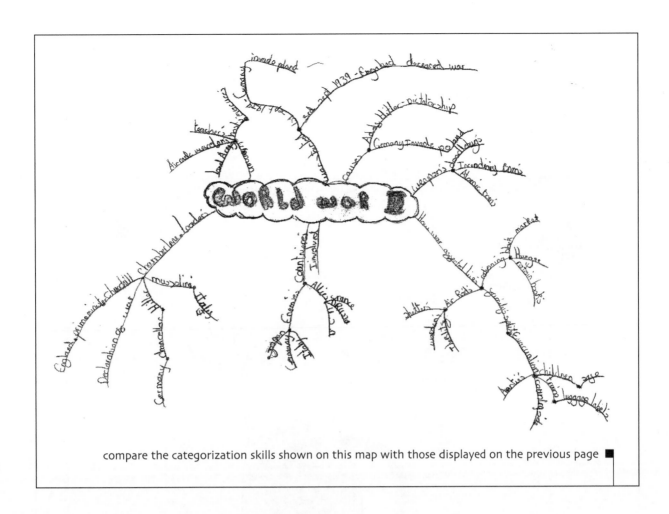

compare the categorization skills shown on this map with those displayed on the previous page ■

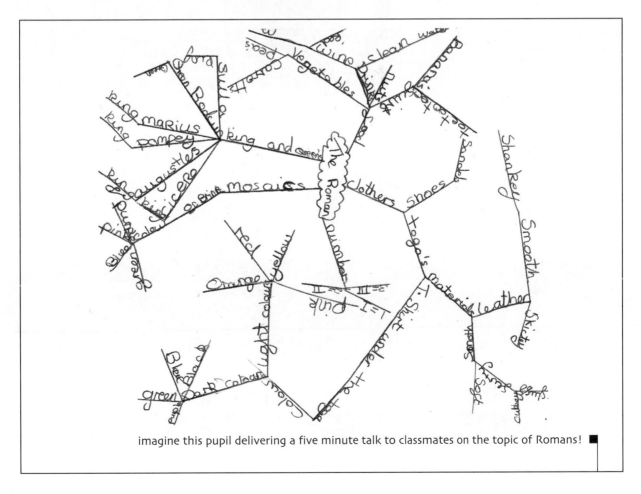

imagine this pupil delivering a five minute talk to classmates on the topic of Romans! ■

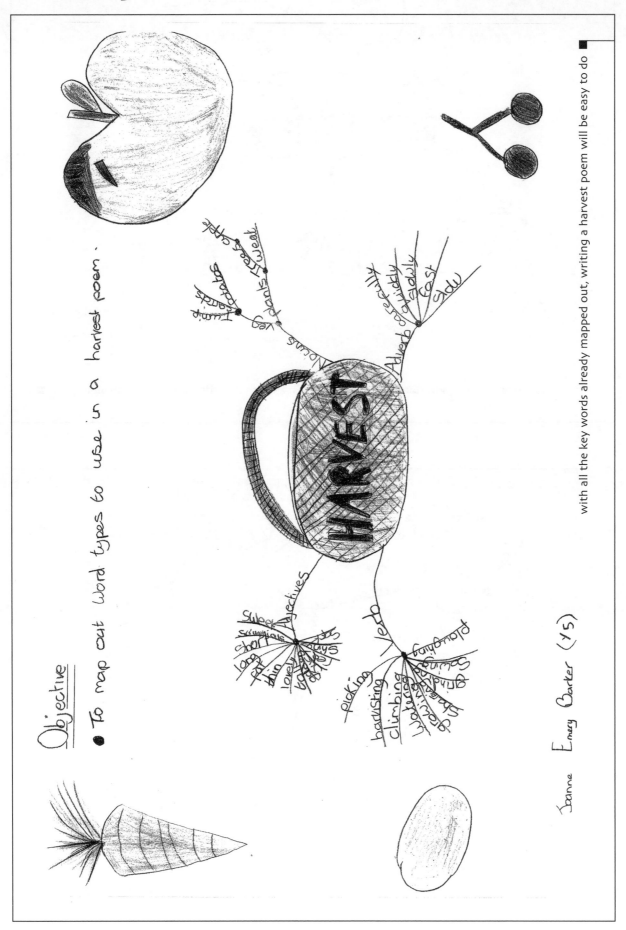

Objective

• To map out word types to use in a harvest poem.

HARVEST

Nouns — fruit, vegetables, bag, plants, sweet, harvester

Adverb — carefully, quickly, slowly, fast, slow

Adjectives — sweet, scrumptious, short, long, fat, thin, lovely, tasty, juicy

Verb — picking, harvesting, climbing, watering, growing, planting, ploughing

with all the key words already mapped out, writing a harvest poem will be easy to do ■

Joanne Emery Baxter (Y5)

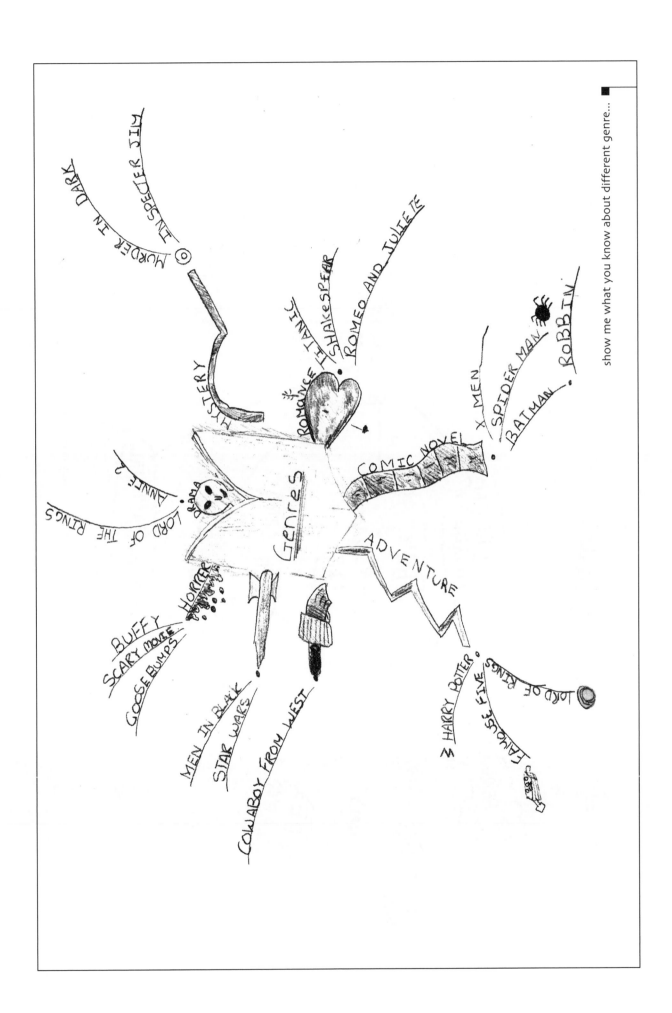

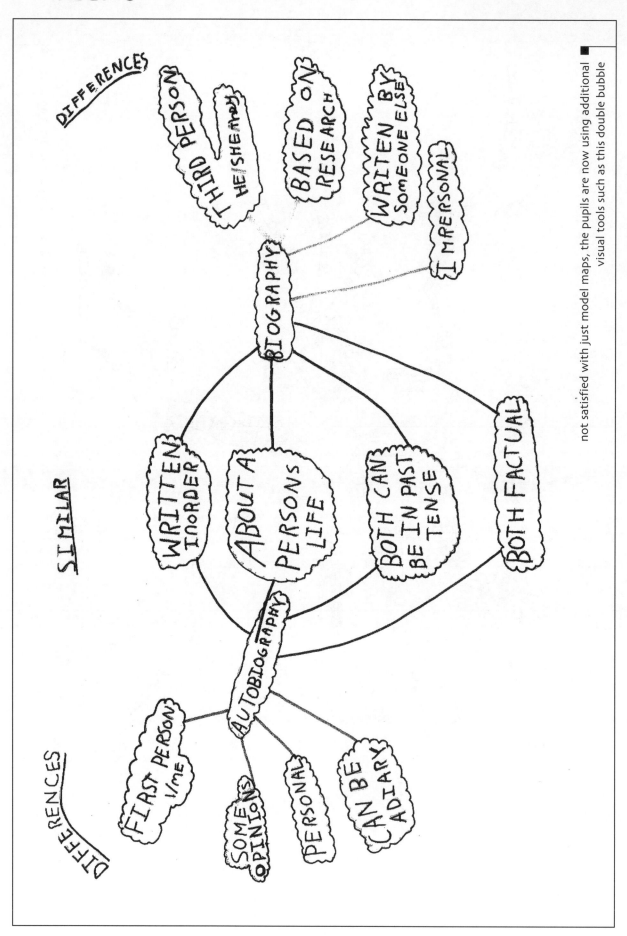

not satisfied with just model maps, the pupils are now using additional visual tools such as this double bubble

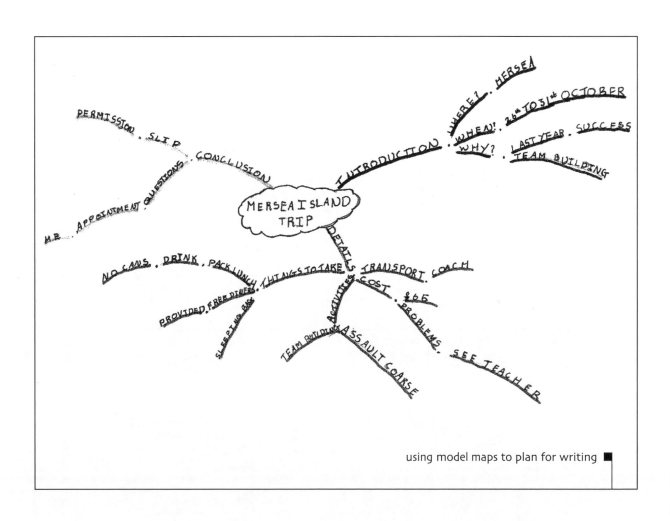

using model maps to plan for writing ■

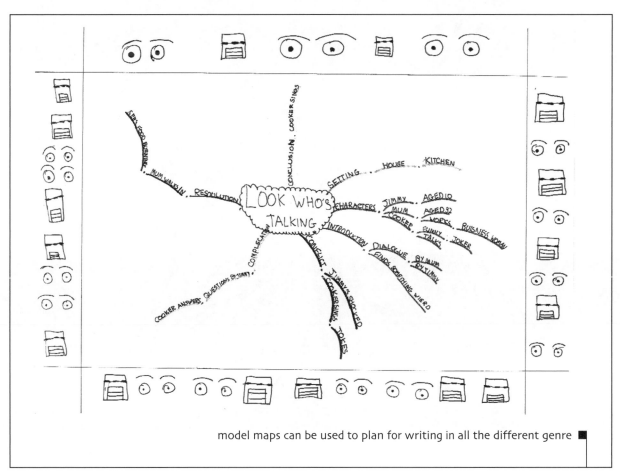

model maps can be used to plan for writing in all the different genre ■

Teacher planning

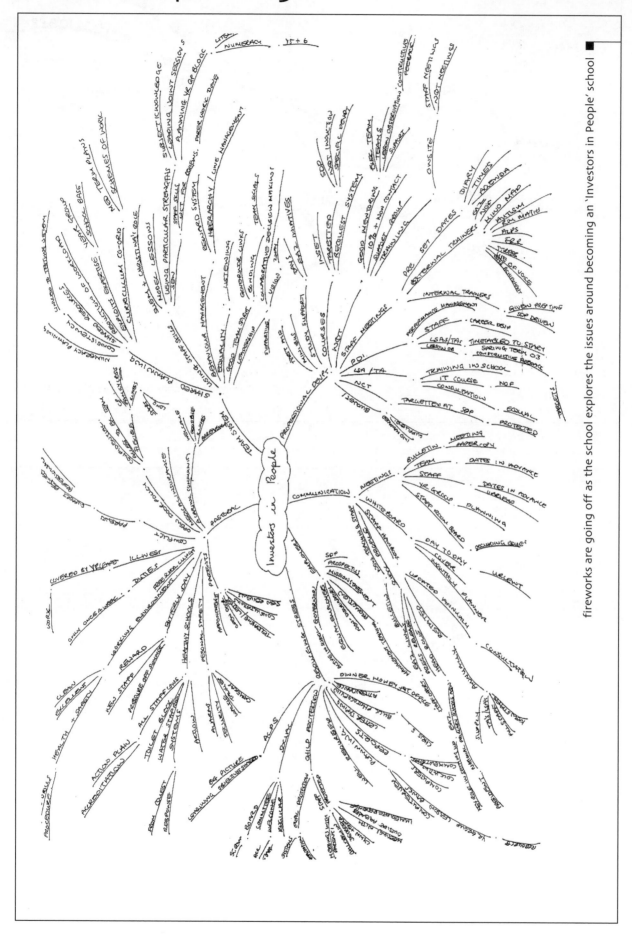

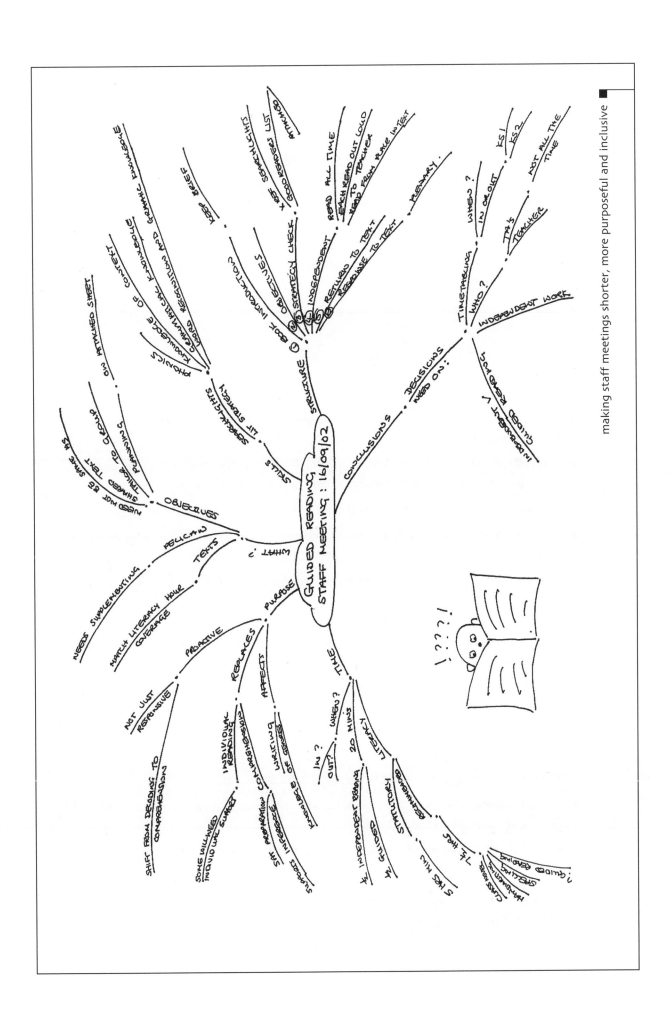

making staff meetings shorter, more purposeful and inclusive

References

■ Ainscow. M. (1994) *Special Needs in the Classroom: A Teacher Education Guide*, Jessica Kingsley, London

■ Andrews, F. and Andrews, G. (1996) *Clear English*, Bloomsbury, London

■ Argyris, C. (1982) *Reasoning, Learning and Action: Individual and Organisational*, Jossey-Bass, San Francisco

■ Ausubel, D. P. (1968) *Educational Psychology: A Cognitive View* 1st edition. (Extract on page 79 reprinted by permission of Wadsworth, a division of Thomson Learning, www.thomsonrights.com, fax: 800 730-2215)

■ Baddeley, A. (1994) *Your Memory – a User's Guide*, Prion Books, London. (Extracts on pages 66 and 93.)

■ Barker, P. and Van Schank, P. (2000) 'Icons in the Mind', in Yazdani, M. and Barker, P. (eds) (2000) *Iconic Communication*, Intellect Books, Bristol, www.intellectbooks.com. (Extract on page 59.)

■ Barley, S. D. (1971) *A New Look at the Loom of Visual Literacy*, Eastman Kodak Company, Rochester, quoted in Moore, D. M. and Dwyer, F. M. (1994) *Visual Literacy*, Educational Technology Publications, Englewood, California

■ Bartlett, F. C. (1968) 'Adventurous Thinking', in Watson, P. C. and Johnson-Laird P.N. (eds) *Thinking and Reasoning*, Penguin, London

■ Bigge, M. L and Shermiss, S. S. (1999) *Learning Theories for Teachers*, Allyn and Bacon, Boston, MA. (Extracts on pages 57 and 60 copyright ©1999 by Pearson Education.)

■ Boak, G. and Thompson, D. (1998) *Mental Models for Managers,* Century, London

■ Bowers, S. (2001) 'Modern visions and the old school of thought', *Guardian Education*, 29 February 2001

■ Braden, R. A. (1983) 'Visualizing the Verbal and Verbalizing the Visual', in Braden, R. A. and Walker, A. W. (eds) (1983) *Seeing Ourselves: Visualizing in a Social Context*, International Visual Literacy Association, Blacksbury, VA

■ Britton, J. (1982) 'Shaping at the Point of Utterance' in Pradl, G. M. (ed) *Prospect and Retrospect: Selected Essays of James Britton*, Boynton Cook, New Jersey

■ Britton, J. (1993) *Language and Learning: The Importance of Speech in Children's Development*, 2nd Edition. Published in the USA by Heinemann, a division of Reed Elsevier, Inc., Portsmouth, NH. Published in the UK by Penguin Books Ltd. (Extract on page 37 copyright © 1993 by James Britton.)

■ Brophy, J. (1998) *Motivating Students to Learn*, McGraw-Hill, New York

■ Brown, G. and Wragg, E. C. (1993) *Questioning*, Routledge, London

■ Bruner, J. S. (1968) 'The Course of Cognitive Growth', in Watson, P. C. and Johnson-Laird P.N. (eds) *Thinking and Reasoning*, Penguin, London

■ Bruner, J. S. (1971) *Towards a Theory of Instruction*, Harvard University Press. (Extract on page 153.)

■ Bruner, J. S. (1988) quoted in Healy, J. M. (1999) *Endangered Minds,* Touchstone, New York

■ Bukowitz, W. R. and Williams, R. L. (1999) *The Knowledge Management Fieldbook*, Pearson Education. (Extract on page 85.)

■ Burgess, C. and coworkers (1973) *Understanding Children's Writing*, Penguin, London

■ Caine, R. N. and Caine, G. (1991) *Making Connections: Teaching and the Human Brain*, Addison-Wesley, Menlo Park, California

■ Carter, R., Martin, J., Mayblin, B. and Munday, M. (1984) *Systems, Management and Change*, Harper and Row, London

■ Caviglioli, O. (2001) Personal notes on financial planning

■ Caviglioli, O. and Harris, I. (2000) *MapWise*, Network Educational Press, Stafford

■ Caviglioli, O., Harris, I. and Tinall, B. (2002) *Thinking Skills & Eye Q*, Network Educational Press, Stafford.

■ Clarke, T. and Clegg, S. (2000) *Changing Paradigms*, HarperCollins Publishers Ltd, ©2000, T. Clarke and S. Clegg. (Extract on page 59.)

■ Claxton, G. (1990) *Teaching to Learn*, Cassell, London. (Extract on page 73.)

■ Claxton, G. (1997) *Hare Brain, Tortoise Mind*, Fourth Estate, London

■ Claxton, G. (1999) *Wise Up*, Bloomsbury, London

■ Cooper, P. and McIntyre, D. (1993) 'Commonality in teachers' and pupils' perceptions of effective classroom learning', *British Journal of Educational Psychology*, No 63

■ Costa, A. L. (1996) 'Introduction' in Hyerle, D. (1996) *Visual Tools for Constructing Knowledge*, Association for Supervision and Curriculum Development, Virginia

■ Coughlan, S. (2000) 'Book of the Week' (a review of *Barrington Atlas of the Greek and Roman World*), *Times Educational Supplement*, 2.10.2000

■ Counsell, C. (2000) 'Why Was Becket Murdered?', *Teaching Thinking*, Issue 1, Summer 2000

■ Craig, M. (2000) *Thinking Visually*, Continuum, London

■ Crystal, D. (1995) *The Cambridge Encyclopedia of the English Language*, Cambridge University Press, Cambridge

■ Csikszentmihalyi, M. (1990) *Flow: The Psychology of Optimal Experience*, Harper and Row, New York

■ Czerniawska, F. (1997) *Corporate Speak*, Macmillan, Basingstoke

■ Davitt, J. (1990) personal communication

■ De Bono, E. (1987) *Letters to Thinkers*, Penguin, London

■ De Bono, E. (1992) *Serious Creativity*, HarperBusiness, New York

■ De Bono, E. (1996) in McAlhone, B. and Stewart, D., *A Smile in the Mind*, Phaidon Press Ltd. (Extract on page 160 taken from the text by Edward De Bono in the introduction © 1996 Phaidon Press Ltd (ISBN: 0-7148-3812, £22.95. www.phaidon.com))

■ Desforges, C. and Lings, P. (1998) 'Teaching Knowledge Application: Advances in Theoretical Conceptions and their Professional Implications', *British Journal of Educational Studies*, ISSN 0007–1005, Vol 46, December 1998

■ Dillon, J. T. (1988) *Questioning and Teaching: A Manual of Practice*, Croom Helm, London

■ Dweck, C. S., Chin, C. and Hong, Y. (1995) 'Implicit theories and their role in judgements and reactions: A world from two perspectives', *Psychological Inquiry*, 6, 267–285

■ Eastwood, C. (2000) 'WordImage', *British Journal of Special Education*, Vol 27, No 4, December 2000

■ Edmiston, A. (2000) 'A term in the life', *Teaching Thinking*, Issue 2, Autumn 2000

- Elhelou, M-W. A. (1997) 'The Use of Concept Mapping in Learning Science Subjects by Arab Students', *Educational Research*, Vol 39, No 3, winter 1997

- Eysenck, M. W. (ed) (1994) *The Blackwell Dictionary of Cognitive Psychology*, Blackwell, Oxford. (Extracts on pages 35 and 65.)

- Feuerstein, R., Rand, Y., Hoffman, M. and Miller, R. (1980) *Instrumental Enrichment*, University Park Press, Baltimore, USA

- Fisher, R. (1992) 'Questions for Thinking', *Multi-Mind*, Summer 1992

- Fisher, R. (1995) *Teaching Children to Learn*, Nelson Thornes. (Extract on page 45 reproduced with the permission of Nelson Thornes, ISBN: 0-7487-2091-X.)

- Flory, J. (1978) *Visual Literacy: A Vital Skill in the Process of Rhetorical Criticism*, Southern Speech Communication Association, Atlanta, GA

- Foley, J. (1998) *The Guinness Encyclopedia of Signs and Symbols*, Guinness Publishing, Enfield

- Funes, M. and Johnson, N. (1998) *Honing Your Knowledge Skills*, Butterworth-Heinemann, Oxford

- Gaarder, J. (1996) *Hello? Is Anybody There?*, Orion Children's Books, London

- Galloway, D., Rogers, C., Armstrong, D. and Leo, E. (1998) *Motivating The Hard To Teach*, Longman, London

- Gardner, H. (1983) *Frames of Mind*, Fontana, London

- Gauvain, M. (1998) 'Thinking in Niches – Sociocultural Influences on Cognitive Development', *Human Development*, 38, 25–45

- Getner, D. and Stevens, A. L. (1983) *Mental Models*, Lawrence Erlbaum, New Jersey

- Gilster, P. (1997) *Digital Literacy*, J. Wiley and Sons, Chichester

- Gipps, C. V. (1994) *Beyond Testing – Towards a Theory of Educational Assessment*. Falmer, London. (Extract on page 71.)

- Goleman, D. (1985) *Vital Lies, Simple Truths*, Bloomsbury, London

- Gopnik, A., Meltzoff, A. and Kuhl, P. (1999) *How Babies Think*, Weidenfeld & Nicolson, London

- Greenfield, S. (2000) *The Private Life of the Brain*, Penguin, London

- Halé, J. (1998) *From Concepts to Capabilities*, J. Wiley, London

- Hamer, D. and Copeland, P. (1998) *Living with our Genes*, Macmillan, London, UK. (Extracts on page 86.)

- Harding, D. E. (1998) appendix 'On Diagrams, and Some Aspects of Symbolism' in Harding, D. E. (1998) *The Hierarchy of Heaven and Earth*, The Sholland Trust, London

- Harding, D. E. (1998) *The Hierarchy of Heaven and Earth*, The Sholland Trust, London

- Hargreaves, D. H. (1999) 'The Knowledge-Creating School', *British Journal of Educational Studies*, ISSN 0007–1005, Vol 47, No 2, June 2000. (Extract on page 16.)

- Healy, J. M. (1999) *Endangered Minds*, Simon & Schuster. (Extract on page 16 reprinted by permission of Simon & Schuster Adult Publishing Group. Copyright © 1990 by Jane M. Healy)

- Hodgson, T. and Tait, F. (2000) *Crashing into the present: facilitating decision through fast scenario thinking*, www.metabridge.com

- Hoffman, D. (1998) *Visual Intelligence*, Norton, New York

- Holt, J. (1983) *How Children Learn*, Penguin, London

■ Hortin, J. (1980) 'Symbol Systems and Mental Skills Research: Their Emphasis and Future', in *Media Adult Learning*, 2, (2), 3–6

■ Hyerle, D. (1996) *Visual Tools for Constructing Knowledge*, Association for Supervision and Curriculum Development, Virginia. (Extract on page 105.)

■ Hyerle, D. (2000) *A Field Guide to Using Visual Tools*, Association for Supervision and Curriculum Development, Virginia

■ Jeffries, M. (2000) quoted in Constantine, A., 'Let's Think Laterally', *Times Educational Supplement*, 2, June 2000

■ Jensen, E. (2000) *Brain-Based Learning*, Brain Store Inc., San Diego, CA

■ Johansson, J. K. and Nonaka, I. (1996) *Relentless – The Japanese Way Of Marketing*, Butterworth-Heinemann, Oxford

■ Joyce, B., Calhoun, E. and Hopkins, D. (2000) *Models of Learning – Tools for Teaching*, OU Press. Extracts on pages 15 and 87 reproduced by permission of McGraw-Hill Education

■ Kelly, G. (1955) *The Psychology of Personal Constructs*, Norton, New York

■ Kinchin, I. M., Hay, D. B. and Adams, A. (2000) 'How a Qualitative Approach to Concept Map Analysis Can be Used to Aid Learning by Illustrating Patterns of Conceptual Development', *Educational Research*, Vol 42, No 1, spring 2000

■ Kitchin R. and Freundschuh, S. (eds) (2000) *Cognitive Mapping*, Routledge, London. (Extract on page 59.)

■ Lake, M. (1990) 'Unfold Your Arms and Start Talking', *Special Children*, June/July 1990

■ Lake, M. (1994) 'Narrative, Pictures and Imagination', in *Centre for Thinking Skills Information Pack*, Vol 3, No 2

■ Lake, M. (2000) 'Improving Concentration and Memory Skills' in *Teaching Thinking*, Issue 1, Spring 2000

■ Lakoff, G. and Johnson, M. (1980) *Metaphors We Live By*, University of Chicago Press, Chicago

■ Lawless, C., Smee, P. and O'Shea, T. (1998) 'Using Concept Sorting and Concept Mapping in Business and Public Administration, and in Education: An Overview', *Educational Research*, Vol 40, No 2, Summer 1998

■ LeDoux, J. (1996) *The Emotional Brain: The Mysterious Underpinnings of Emotional Life*, Simon & Schuster, New York

■ Light, P., Sheldon, S. and Woodhead, M. (1991) *Learning to Think*, Routledge, London

■ Lissack, M. and Roos, J. (1999) *The Next Common Sense*, Nicholas Brealey, London. (Extract on page 83.)

■ Lloyd, R. (2000) 'Understanding Learning', in Kitchen, R. and Freundschuh, S. (eds) *Cognitive Mapping*, Routledge, London

■ Manguel, A. (1996) *A History of Reading*, HarperCollins, London

■ Marzano, R. J., Pickering, D. J. and Pollock, J. E. (2001) *Classroom Instruction That Works*, Association for Supervision and Curriculum Development, Virginia

■ Mason, M. (2001) 'Mind your Language' in *Teaching Thinking*, Spring 2001, Issue 3, published by Questions Publishing, Birmingham. (Extract on page 35.)

■ McAleese, R. (1998) *A Theoretical View of Concept Mapping*, website www.icbl.hw.ac.uk

■ McBer, H. (2000) *A Model of Teacher Effectiveness*, report to the Department for Education and Employment, London

■ McCabe, D. (1999) *The Concept Mapping Workshop*, www.CncptMapp.Wkshp

■ McCaskey, M. B. (1991) 'Mapping: creating, maintaining, and relinquishing conceptual frameworks', in Henry, J. (ed) *Creative Management*, Sage, London

■ McGuiness, C. (1999) *From Thinking Skills to Thinking Classrooms: A Review and Evaluation of Approaches for Developing Pupils' Thinking*, DfEE, London. (Extract on page 53.)

■ McKenzie, M. (1996) 'Grazing the Net, From Now On', *The Educational Technology Journal*, 5, 5, January/February 1996

■ McKim, R. H. M. (1972) *Experience in Visual Thinking*, Brookes College, California

■ McPeck, J. E. (1990) *Teaching Critical Thinking*, Routledge Inc. (Extract on page 51 copyright ©1990 by J. E. McPeck. Reproduced by permission of Routledge, Inc., part of The Taylor & Francis Group.)

■ Meier D. (2000) *The Accelerated Learning Handbook*, McGraw-Hill, New York. (Extract on page 29.)

■ Minto, B. (1995) *The Pyramid Principle*, Pitman, London. (Extract on page 37.)

■ Moll, L. C. and Whitmore, K. F. (1998) 'Vygotsky in Classroom Practice', in Moll, L. C. and Whitmore, K. F. (eds) (1998) *Learning Relationships in the Classroom*, Routledge, London

■ Moore, D. M. and Dwyer, F. M. (1994) *Visual Literacy*, Educational Technology Publications, Englewood Cliffs. (Extracts on pages 45 and 47.)

■ Murris, K. (1992) *Teaching Philosophy with Picture Books*, Infonet Publications, London

■ Nonaka, I. and Takeuchi, H. (1995) *The Knowledge Creating Company*, Oxford University Press, Oxford

■ Novak, J. D. (1993) 'Human constructivism: a unification of psychological and epistemological phenomena in meaning making', *International Journal of Personal Constructive Psychology*, 6, 167–93

■ Novak, J. D. (1998) *Learning, Creating and Using Knowledge*, Lawrence Erlbaum Associates, Publishers, New Jersey. (Extracts on pages 65 and 99.)

■ Novak, J. D. and Gowin, D. B. (1984) *Learning How to Learn*, Cambridge University Press. (Extract on page 29.)

■ Nutbrown, C. (1999) *Threads of Thinking*, Paul Chapman, London

■ O'Connor, J. and McDermott, I. (1997) *The Art of Systems Thinking*, Thorsons, London

■ Ornstein, R. and Ehrlich, P. (1991) *New World, New Mind*, Paladin, London

■ Paine, N. (2000) in Walker, D. 'A Prophet in Open Learning', *TES Online*, 13 October 2000

■ Palmer, S. (2000) 'Can't Write, Won't Write?', *Times Educational Supplement, Curriculum Special (Science and Technology)*, Spring 2000

■ Parks, S. and Black, H. (1992) *Organising Thinking*, Critical Thinking Books and Software, Pacific Grove, California

■ Peacock, A. (2000) 'What is Visual Literacy?', *Times Educational Supplement, Curriculum Special (Science and Technology)*, Spring 2000

■ Petterson, R. (1989) *Visuals for information: research practice*. Educational Technology Publications, Englewood Cliffs, NJ

■ Piaget, J. (1960) *Language and Thought of the Child*, Routledge, London

- Pinker, S. (1997) *How the Mind Works*, Penguin, London

- Pinker, S. (1999) *Words and Rules*, Weidenfeld & Nicolson. (Extract on page 150.)

- Pollard, A. (1999) 'Towards a New Perspective on Children's Learning', *Education*, October 1999

- Postman, N. (1990) *Teaching as a Conserving Activity*, Delacorte, New York

- Postman, N. (1992) *Technopoly*, Knopf, New York

- Poyner, N. (1996) *Typography Now Two*, Booth-Clibborn, London

- Pumfrey, P. and Stamboltizis, A. (2000) 'Reading Across Genres: A Review of Literature', *Support for Learning*, Vol 15, No 2

- Riding, R. and Rayner, S. (1998) *Cognitive Styles and Learning Strategies*, David Fulton, London

- Robinson, K. (2001) *Out of our minds,* Capstone, Oxford

- Roszak, T. (1986) *The Cult of Information*, Pantheon, New York

- Saljo, R. (1998) 'Thinking With and Through Artefacts', in Faulkner, D., Littleton, K. and Woodhead, M. (eds) (1998) *Learning Relationships in the Classroom*, Routledge, London

- Senge P. M. (1990) *The Fifth Discipline*, Hutchinson. (Extract on page 23 reproduced by permission of The Random House Group Limited.)

- Senge, P., Ross, R., Smith, B., Roberts, C. and Kleiner, A. (1994) *The Fifth Discipline Fieldbook*, Nicholas Brealey, London

- Sharron, H. (1987) *Changing Children's Minds*, Souvenir Press, London

- Sharron, H. (1999) 'Teaching Thinking Skills – Changing the Role of Teachers', *Professional Development Today*, Autumn term

- Sherwood, D. (1998) *Unlock Your Mind*, Gower, Aldershot. (Extracts on pages 23 and 115 reproduced by permission of Gower Publishing Ltd.)

- Siler, T. (1996) *Think Like A Genius*, Bantam, New York

- Smith, A., (2001) *The Brain's Behind It*, Network Educational Press Ltd. (Extracts on pages 71 and 77.)

- Smith, F. (1990) *Writing and the Writer*, Heinemann, Oxford. (Extracts on pages 25 and 31.)

- Smith, F. (1992) *To Think,* Routledge, London

- Smitsman, A. W. (2000) 'Slumbering Talents: Where Do They Reside?' in Lieshout, F. M. V. and Heymans, P. G. (eds) (2000) *Developing Talent Across the Lifespan*, Psychology Press, Hove

- Stewart, T. A. (1998) *Intellectual Capital*, Nicholas Brealey Publishing, London

- Stigler, J. W. (1984) 'Mental Abacus: the Effect of Abacus Training on Chinese Children's Mental Calculations', *Cognitive Psychology*, 16, 145–176

- Stigler, J. W., Chalip, L. and Miller, K. F. (1986) 'Consequences of Skill: The Case of Abacus Training in Taiwan', *American Journal of Education*, 94, 447–479

- Sylwester, R. (1995) *A Celebration of Neurones*, Association for Supervision and Curriculum Development, Virginia

- Trent, S. C., Pernell Junior, E., Mungai, A. and Chimedza, R. (1998) 'Using Concept Maps to Measure Conceptual Change in Preservice Teachers Enrolled in a Multicultural Education/Special Education Course', *Remedial and Special Education*, Vol 19, No 1, January/February 1998

- Tufte, E. (1990) *Envisioning Information,* Graphics Press, Connecticut

- Tulving, E. (1983) *Elements of Episodic Memory*, Oxford Univeristy Press, Oxford

- Uttal, D. and Tan, L. S. (2000) 'Cognitive Mapping in Childhood', in *Cognitive Mapping* Kitchin, R and Freundschuh, S.

- Van Nagel, C., Reese, M. & Siudzinski, R. (1985) *Mega Teaching and Learning*, Metamorphous Press, ISBN:1-503-228-4972. (Extract on page 25 printed with permission from Metamorphous Press, PO Box 10616, Portland, OR 97296. USA.)

- Vygotsky, L. S. (1962) *Thought and Language*, MIT Press, Cambridge, MA

- Wandersee, J. H. (1990) 'Concept Mapping and the Cartography of Cognition', *Journal of Research in Science Teaching*, 27, 10

- Watson, J. (2000) 'Constructive Instruction and Learning Difficulties', *Support for Learning*, Vol 15, No 3

- Wells, G. (1986) *The Meaning Makers*, Hodder and Stoughton, London

- Wenger, W. (1980) *The Einstein Factor*, Prima, California

- Wheton, D., Cameron, K. and Woods, M. (1996) *Effective Problem Solving*, HarperCollins, London

- Winston, R. (1998) *The Human Body*, BBC video

- Wittgenstein, L. (1953) *Philosophical Investigations*, Oxford University Press, Oxford

- Woditsch, G. A. (1991) *The Thinking Teacher's Guide to Thinking Skills,* Lawrence Erlbaum Associates, New Jersey

- Wurman, R. S. (1991) *Information Anxiety*, Pan, London. (Extracts on pages 83 and 152.)

- Zelazny, G. (1996) *Say it with Charts*, McGraw-Hill, New York

Index

accelerated learning *see* learning

ADHD 138

agendas 128

Allen, Woody (1935–), actor and director

models 23

analytic 46

Animal Farm, model map 58

animals, model map 63

Asperger syndrome 136, 137, 152

assessment, model map 104

Ausubel, D. P., learner's knowledge 5, 79

autism 31–2, 152 (see also Asperger syndrome)

autobiographies, class exercise 153

Baddeley, A.

chess 66

knowledge 93

Barker, P. and P. van Shank,

knowledge frameworks 59

behavioural models *see* learning models

BFG, model map 6–8, 9

Big Picture 9, 32, 70

displays 121

mapping 71, 73–4

Bigge, M. L. and S. S. Shermiss

understanding 57, 60

Birley Community College

life and death, model map 72

Year 8, model map 32

bodies, model map 61

Britton, James, language hierarchies 37

Bruner, J. S., thought 155

Bukowitz, W. R. and R. L. Williams

tacit knowledge 85

Caribbean, case study 80

case studies *see* name of school

categorization 10, 35, 37, 150, 153

exercises 154, 155–9, 161, 162–6

organization 179

Caviglioli, Lyn, teacher, displays 121

Caviglioli, Oliver, memory 63

central executive (brain), 65

central label (maps) 177

chocolate, model map 84

circle time 18

clip art 178

clusters-to-maps method 173–5

cognitive psychology 25

cognitive subsumption 59–60

cognitive understanding (*see also* thought)

knowledge 57

maps 5

monitoring 108

processes 16

colour, in maps 177–8

communication 135

teachers' meetings 127

communities, model map displays 125

computers 179

connections 77, 79–80

model map 76

constructivism 16, 25

Coppins Green Primary School, Essex

model maps 192–207

training in mapping 191

Cropley, A. J.

creative thinking 68

cultural festivals, model map displays 124

curriculum

mapping 71

model maps 172–3

Danley Middle School, Maidstone, history mapping 95

de Bono, Edward (1933–), psychologist

roundabouts, on maps 178

visualization 160

deductive thinking 171–3

Delaware Primary School 144

model maps 24, 27

teacher's planning 100–102

design, maps 177–9

developing maps 176

development planning 114, 115, 117, 118

Dingwall Academy, Scotland 153

mental maps

exam revision 95, 190

literacy skills 40, 41

displays 121–5

model map 102

Dolan, Gerry, teacher

note-taking 190

DOM (Dump it, Organize it, Map it) 80, 100 (*see also* clusters-to-maps method)

Egypt, model map 81

English literature, model maps 88

environment, model map 167

exercises, maps 179

Eysenck, M. W.

hierarchies 35

facts, knowledge 57, 60

farming, model map 58

farming enquiry skills, model map 49

feedback

assessment 107–8

meetings 128

teachers and learners 17–18

Title from Network Educational Press

THE SCHOOL EFFECTIVENESS SERIES

Book 1: *Accelerated Learning in the Classroom* by Alistair Smith
ISBN: 1-85539-034-5

Book 2: *Effective Learning Activities* by Chris Dickinson
ISBN: 1-85539-035-3

Book 3: *Effective Heads of Department* by Phil Jones and Nick Sparks
ISBN: 1-85539-036-1

Book 4: *Lessons are for Learning* by Mike Hughes
ISBN: 1-85539-038-8

Book 5: *Effective Learning in Science* by Paul Denley and Keith Bishop
ISBN: 1-85539-039-6

Book 6: *Raising Boys' Achievement* by Jon Pickering
ISBN: 1-85539-040-X

Book 7: *Effective Provision for Able and Talented Children* by Barry Teare
ISBN: 1-85539-041-8

Book 8: *Effective Careers Education and Guidance* by Andrew Edwards and Anthony Barnes
ISBN: 1-85539-045-0

Book 9: *Best behaviour and Best behaviour FIRST AID* by Peter Relf, Rod Hirst, Jan Richardson and Georgina Youdell
ISBN: 1-85539-046-9

Best behaviour FIRST AID
ISBN: 1-85539-047-7 (pack of 5 booklets)

Book 10: *The Effective School Governor* by David Marriott
ISBN 1-85539-042-6 (including audio tape)

Book 11: *Improving Personal Effectiveness for Managers in Schools* by James Johnson
ISBN 1-85539-049-3

Book 12: *Making Pupil Data Powerful* by Maggie Pringle and Tony Cobb
ISBN 1-85539-052-3

Book 13: *Closing the Learning Gap* by Mike Hughes
ISBN 1-85539-051-5

Book 14: *Getting Started* by Henry Leibling
ISBN 1-85539-054-X

Book 15: *Leading the Learning School* by Colin Weatherley
ISBN 1-85539-070-1

Book 16: *Adventures in Learning* by Mike Tilling
ISBN 1-85539-073-6

Book 17: *Strategies for Closing the Learning Gap* by Mike Hughes and Andy Vass
ISBN 1-85539-075-2

Book 18: *Classroom Management* by Phillip Waterhouse and Chris Dickinson
ISBN 1-85539-079-5

Book 19: *Effective Teachers* by Tony Swainston
ISBN 1-85539-125-2

Book 20: *Transforming Teaching and Learning* by Colin Weatherley, Bruce Bonney, John Kerr and Jo Morrison
ISBN 1-85539-080-9

Book 21: *Effective Teachers in Primary Schools* by Tony Swainston
ISBN 1-85539-153-8

ACCELERATED LEARNING SERIES

General Editor: **Alistair Smith**

Accelerated Learning in Practice by Alistair Smith
ISBN 1-85539-048-5

The ALPS Approach: Accelerated Learning in Primary Schools
by Alistair Smith and Nicola Call
ISBN 1-85539-056-6

MapWise by Oliver Caviglioli and Ian Harris
ISBN 1-85539-059-0

The ALPS Approach Resource Book by Alistair Smith and Nicola Call
ISBN 1-85539-078-7

Creating an Accelerated Learning School by Mark Lovatt and Derek Wise
ISBN 1-85539-074-4

ALPS StoryMaker by Stephen Bowkett
ISBN 1-85539-076-0

Thinking for Learning by Mel Rockett and Simon Percival
ISBN 1-85539-096-5

Reaching out to all learners by Cheshire LEA
ISBN 1-85539-143-0

Leading Learning by Alistair Smith
ISBN 1-85539-089-2

Bright Sparks by Alistair Smith
ISBN 1-85539-088-4

Move It by Alistair Smith
ISBN 1-85539-123-6

More Bright Sparks by Alistair Smith
ISBN 1-85539-148-1

EDUCATION PERSONNEL MANAGEMENT SERIES

Education Personnel Management handbooks help headteachers, senior managers and governors to manage a broad range of personnel issues.

The Well Teacher – management strategies for beating stress, promoting staff health and reducing absence by Maureen Cooper
ISBN 1-85539-058-2

Managing Challenging People – dealing with staff conduct by Bev Curtis and
Maureen Cooper
ISBN 1-85539-057-4

Managing Poor Performance – handling staff capability issues
by Bev Curtis and Maureen Cooper
ISBN 1-85539-062-0

*Managing Allegations Against Staff – personnel and child protection issues
in schools* by Maureen Cooper and Bev Curtis
ISBN 1-85539-072-8

Managing Recruitment and Selection – appointing the best staff
by Maureen Cooper and Bev Curtis
ISBN 1-85539-077-9

Managing Redundancies – dealing with reduction and reorganisation of staff
by Maureen Cooper and Bev Curtis
ISBN 1-85539-082-5

Managing Pay in Schools – performance management and pay in schools
by Bev Curtis
ISBN 1-85539-087-6

VISIONS OF EDUCATION SERIES

The Power of Diversity by Barbara Prashnig
ISBN 1-86953-386-0

The Unfinished Revolution by John Abbott and Terry Ryan
ISBN 1-85539-064-7

The Learning Revolution by Jeannette Vos and Gordon Dryden
ISBN 1-85539-085-X

Wise Up by Guy Claxton
ISBN 1-85539-099-X

ABLE AND TALENTED CHILDREN COLLECTION

Effective Resources for Able and Talented Children by Barry Teare
ISBN 1-85539-050-7

More Effective Resources for Able and Talented Children by Barry Teare
ISBN 1-85539-063-9

Challenging Resources for Able and Talented Children by Barry Teare
ISBN 1-85539-122-8

MODEL LEARNING

Thinking Skills & Eye Q by Oliver Caviglioli, Ian Harris and Bill Tindall
ISBN 1-85539-091-4

Think it–Map it! by Oliver Caviglioli and Ian Harris
ISBN 1-85539-139-2

OTHER TITLES FROM NEP

The Thinking Child by Nicola Call with Sally Featherstone
ISBN 1-85539-121-X

StoryMaker Catch Pack by Stephen Bowkett
ISBN 1-85539-109-0

Becoming Emotionally Intelligent by Catherine Corrie
ISBN 1-85539-069-8

That's Science! by Tim Harding
ISBN 1-85539-170-8

The Brain's Behind It by Alistair Smith
ISBN 1-85539-083-3

Help Your Child To Succeed by Bill Lucas and Alistair Smith
ISBN 1-85539-111-2

Tweak to Transform by Mike Hughes
ISBN 1-85539-140-6

Brain Friendly Revision by UFA National Team
ISBN 1-85539-127-9

Numeracy Activities Key Stage 2 by Afzal Ahmed and Honor Williams
ISBN 1-85539-102-3

Numeracy Activities Key Stage 3 by Afzal Ahmed, Honor Williams and George Wickham
ISBN 1-85539-103-1

Teaching Pupils How to Learn by Bill Lucas, Toby Greany, Jill Rodd and Ray Wicks
ISBN 1-85539-098-1

Creating a Learning to Learn School by Toby Greany and Jill Rodd
ISBN 1-85539-186-4

Basics for School Governors by Joan Sallis
ISBN 1-85539-012-4

Imagine That... by Stephen Bowkett
ISBN 1-85539-043-4

Self-Intelligence by Stephen Bowkett
ISBN 1-85539-055-8

Class Talk by Rosemary Sage
ISBN 1-85539-061-2

Lend Me Your Ears by Rosemary Sage
ISBN 1-85539-137-6

**For more information and ordering details, please consult our website
www.networkpress.co.uk**

About the authors

Ian Harris

Ian has 13 years' teaching experience across the age and ability range. He spent two years as a deputy head and three years as a Special Needs Co-ordinator. Ian now spends the majority of his time travelling around the UK and Europe leading training courses based on his books. The rest of the time Ian spends at home with Lorraine in Brentwood, Essex.

Oliver Caviglioli

Oliver has been a headteacher for nine years. In 1981 he was asked to do a presentation on Accelerated Learning techniques such as model mapping to Her Majesty's Inspectorate. After two decades we find that the ideas are at last catching on. Oliver lives with his family in Basildon in Essex as part-time head, part-time author and trainer and full-time husband and dad.

Together

Ian and Oliver are passionate about learning. They have researched and directly experienced a wide range of training in the areas of personal development, psychology and thinking skills. They are trained in the use of deep tissue body therapy and, perhaps more relevant, in a number of thinking skills programs. *Think it – Map it!* is their third book published by Network Educational Press. In 1999 they set up Model Learning, an educational training company that specializes in providing high quality INSET to schools and LEAs.

To contact the authors or to arrange INSET:

email	theoffice@modellearning.com
telephone	01277 202812
fax	01277 200019
write to	PO Box 5346 Brentwood CM14 5RW

For further information on courses, testimonials, or forthcoming conferences you can visit their website at www.modellearning.com.